D0482014

# The One and the Many

# Arthur Mann

# The One and the Many
## Reflections on the American Identity

The University of Chicago Press

*Chicago and London*

The University of Chicago Press, Chicago 60637
The University of Chicago Press, Ltd., London

© 1979 by The University of Chicago
All rights reserved. Published 1979
Printed in the United States of America
83  82  81  80  79      7  6  5  4  3  2  1

*Library of Congress Cataloging in Publication Data*

Mann, Arthur.
    The one and the many.

    Bibliography p.
    Includes index.
    1.  Minorities—United States.   2.   National
characteristics, American.   I.   Title.
E184.AIM28        301.45′1′0973        78–27849
ISBN 0–226–50337–2

ARTHUR MANN is the Preston and Sterling
Morton Professor of American History at the
University of Chicago. He is the author of *Yankee
Reformers in the Urban Age*; *LaGuardia, A Fighter
against His Times, 1882–1933*; and *LaGuardia Comes
to Power: 1933*, all published by the University of
Chicago Press.

*To my Students,*
*past, present, future,*
*with gratitude*

# Contents

# Preface

Americans spring from a multitude of stocks, yet share a common nationality. This study examines the character of that nationality and its relationship, over the past two centuries, to the variety of ethnic affiliations that have flourished in the United States.

The subject has been one of my major interests since I began teaching and writing American history in the 1940s, and the day was bound to come when I would try to set my thoughts to paper. But the following attempt—and it is meant to be an essay, rather than a definitive history, about an enormously elusive aspect of the American experience—started out differently from the form it finally took. A prefatory word is therefore especially in order on the making of the book.

In 1967 I was invited to join a research project on black history funded by a federal agency at the University of Chicago. My role was to prepare a monograph on the multiethnic character of northern cities to which southern blacks had been moving in large numbers since World War II. All the project's studies were to be not only scholarly but also helpful to government in devising a workable strategy to secure legitimate rights for blacks.

Unaccustomed to writing for policy makers, I was uneasy about that thrust of my assignment. Every historian knows how hard it is to get the past straight when one explores it for its own sake. The difficulties multiply when the historian is called upon to relate the past to solve an urgent social problem. Unlike the physical or natural sciences, the discipline of history claims no branch of applied research.

I eventually downed my misgivings because I thought there was a need to point out that the civil rights movement, no longer confined to the South, was mistakenly assuming that northern and southern whites were alike. Their histories were different. In 1920 the overwhelming majority of schoolchildren in northern cities had been, in contrast to those of the predominantly Anglo-Saxon South, the children of immigrants from almost everywhere. Their heterogeneous kind, grown to adulthood in the 1960s, were the hosts whom southern blacks encountered in their move north. We now take the nature of that encounter for granted, but policy makers ten years ago seldom did.

No sooner did I start the research than the white-ethnic revival got under way. Here, too, because of my previous writings on the history of group life in America, I was asked to put my knowledge to public use. Before long I found myself addressing white ethnics and their allies in the foundations and government, but much else besides my audience had changed. America was becoming increasingly fragmented, a process of which the ethnic revival was both a symptom and a contributing factor.

With such thoughts I made three lecture trips abroad, beginning in 1970, under the auspices of the United States Information Agency. Wherever I spoke—Venezuela, Portugal, Germany, Yugoslavia, Romania, Israel, Fiji, Australia, New Zealand, Indonesia, Malaysia, Singapore—my hosts expressed a particular interest in the multiethnic character of the United States. Like many another American overseas before and since, I discovered that what I had taken for granted at home had to be thought through and spelled out for foreigners. They became a third audience for the reflections I was trying to put together on the American population mix.

Events moved so quickly after the late 1960s that, in writing about them, I had difficulty in keeping my tenses straight. What was past? What was present? What was the ongoing past into the present? Historians were not alone, of course, in trying to get a handle on the tumultuous changes of those years.

More important, the rush of events overtook the purpose of my original assignment. The presidential elections of 1968 and 1972, as well as other charged signals, demonstrated that the urban North was very multiethnic indeed. Not only was it unnecessary to document the obvious; there was now a need to confront the distorted claims that the white-ethnic revival was making in the name of a new pluralism. But to do so effectively seemed an impossible challenge when America was in upheaval.

Perhaps even now we lack the perspective to see the late 1960s and early 1970s in large historical context. Yet the passionate divisiveness has ebbed, at the same time that many of the issues remain of prime importance. One of them, as my hosts abroad often reminded me, is how the world's oldest ethnically pluralist democracy approached the universal problem of reconciling unity and diversity: the problem of the One and the Many.

Therein lies the theme of the belatedly born essay in your hands. It is not written for specialists seeking a lot of new information, although I hope that even they find a few surprises in the account. I address myself to a matter of interest to Americans in general, namely, the connection between ethnic identities on the one hand and the national identity on the other.

But to grasp the connection one first has to know the character of the two identities in time and over time. There is a history to tell. My own is not organized like most accounts of the past, and I therefore feel obliged to let readers know beforehand the structure of the argument.

It opens with a view of America's coming unstuck a decade ago. Although adults need no reminder of the experience, a new college generation dimly understand what went on. Besides addressing them, the first chapter should make clear to all readers my angle of vision. I was trained to believe that historians have the charge of painting the picture whole. It is not for me to say whether the book you are about to read succeeds in that task, but it is appropriate at this point to own up to caring for this country. Accordingly, I respect the fragile ties that hold together the bewildering variety of groups that make up America.

Hence the thrust of chapter 2, which reviews the white-ethnic revival. My purpose is not to deny the constructive uses of ethnicity but to correct the excesses of ethnic ideologues. Contrary to their assertions, ethnicity was known to be important before its "rediscovery"; it means different things to different people; and it hooks into a common nationality in which Americans of diverse antecedents have a vital stake.

The rest of the book develops those themes. Chapter 3 recalls how the Revolutionary generation formulated a peculiarly ideological nationality for the then newest nation-state in the world. Stressing the rights of a democratic citizenship, the eighteenth-century legacy set the terms for the next two hundred years, as chapter 4 shows, by which the host people admitted tens of millions of immigrants to their own patrimony. The tensions between American nationality and ethnic identity are the subject of the next two chapters, which survey the history of three theories: the melting pot, Anglo-Saxon supremacy, and cultural pluralism. Not only important for when they originated seventy-five and more years ago, those theories still define the boundaries of present thinking about the One and the Many. But if the last two chapters are valid, experience is a better guide than theory for comprehending the distinctive looseness of America's pluralism. Throughout, the essay compares where relevant this country's experience with that of other countries, on the premise that fully to know ourselves we have to look outside ourselves.

It is good to have this opportunity to acknowledge my debts. Rayman L. Solomon helped with the research in an early stage and Wiliam J. Poole, Jr., in a later; Mary Anne Kasavich typed the final draft; René de la Pedraja and Leslie G. Fenton checked footnotes and related items. I am grateful to one and all, as well as to Saul Bellow, John Hope Franklin, Andrew M. Greeley, Myron A. Marty, and Aristide R. Zolberg for their suggestions and criticisms.

Without the encouragement of four persons to hang in when confusion and despair set in, I would have laid down the burden of this essay a long time ago. They are Oscar Handlin, Peter d'A. Jones, Martin E. Marty, and my wife Sylvia B. Mann. Would that the outcome justified their faith in me to make a contribution to the public philosophy. Needless to say, the author assumes sole responsibility for the shortcomings in the pages that follow.

# 1     The Ungluing of America

In 1970 a popular news magazine asked six prominent historians to comment on the ailing American spirit. There was as little agreement among them as among the population as a whole. Arthur Schlesinger, Jr., took the position that "the turmoil, the confusion, even the violence may well be the birth pangs of a new epoch in the history of man." At the other extreme, Richard Hofstadter declared: "If I get around to writing a general history of the recent past, I'm going to call the chapter on the '60s 'The Age of Rubbish.' "[1]

The radically divergent views of the two Pulitzer Prize scholars reflected a major breakdown in American unity. Not that this continent-sized "nation of many nations," as Walt Whitman described the United States in the last century, had ever been of a single piece. Nor was the crisis deriving from the 1960s the first in American history. Yet the times were nonetheless critical, if for no other reason than the pervading feeling that things were coming apart.

Middle-aged men and women felt especially disturbed. They remembered a more cohesive time, the immediate decades before Vietnam, when their country seemed to be history's darling and a model for much of the world. The United States was not only wealthy and powerful; it was free, and its multiethnic people were held together by shared values they believed worth sharing. Abroad as well as at home, it was said that the second half of the twentieth century was destined to be the American century.

The mood shattered on the upheavals that began in the late 1960s, and by the next decade the scattered bits and pieces looked like remains from a distant past. In 1973 Theodore

White put the matter this way: "For several years the sense had been growing in me that nothing any longer was the same, no rules held, the world we knew was coming to an end." Similarly, after lamenting the decline of America's faith in itself and the erosion of "our sense of peoplehood," Daniel P. Moynihan asked: "And so what is left if so much is gone?"[2]

Few advanced nations escaped a similarly corrosive temper that was eating into the United States. "Yesterday's authority is gone," said France's Raymond Aron, "and today's authority doesn't exist yet." As for the Third World countries, their sudden surge broke apart the post–World War II structure of international relations. In 1974 André Malraux remarked that mankind was "between civilizations—the colonial one and a decolonized one—which we do not really know yet, but only sense." He could have added that, after Vietnam, much of the decolonized world rejected America's democratic model.[3]

Clearly, an era passed between the mid-1960s and the mid-1970s, not just for Americans but also for most other peoples. The shape of the emerging age was blurred, for change followed change with such velocity that it was next to impossible to distinguish between forces of transient and lasting significance. But the fracturing of the American spirit was immediately apparent. Not only consequential in itself, it set the stage for the white-ethnic revival.

## From Celebration to Distrust

It is hard to think of a people less prepared than the Americans for the late 1960s. The dominant view before then looked upon the ungluing of society as something that happened only to other countries. America was exempt because of the supposition that its unique history had made its society forever durable. The Revolution was a permanent revolution—more, the sole modern revolution not to have betrayed the hopes of its people; and the Constitution was the world's oldest written one in use. More generally, prevailing opinion considered the United States an unrivaled going concern, preeminent in getting things done.

There were problems, of course, but there was also confidence in American know-how to convert them into opportunities. When Hollywood's Dore Schary called the United States a happy-ending country, he summed up a common view among TV commentators, editorial writers, politicians, scholars, generals, clergymen, civil rights and business leaders, and other shapers of the American consciousness. The idea that some problems might be insoluble was foreign to the national spirit. They would yield, as they had in the past, to ingenuity, will, good-will, money, and concerted effort.

Were the Russians first in launching their *Sputnik*? Never mind. Our New Frontier government and scientists and engineers and astronauts would still beat the Soviet Union to the moon. Were there poor people in the land? The Great Society, through generously funded legislative programs, would set things right. Were black Americans segregated as inferiors? Martin Luther King, Jr., had a dream that soon they, too, would be part of the American dream. The audience he addressed at the Washington Monument, estimated to be the largest civil rights rally in history, shared his hope. That was in the summer of 1963.

When later in the decade trouble piled on trouble, young dissenters thought the postwar optimism strange and even absurd. Too much was then made of the generation gap; differences existed within generations as well as among them. All the same, a divide opened in the 1960s between many middle-aged persons and many college students coming of age. One side had faith in America because of the good it had done; the other distrusted it for failing to live up to professed ideals. Different eras breed different ways of looking at things.

Optimism stems from pride of achievement, and it is customary for people who have lived long enough to have a sense of time to measure achievements against a base point in the past. To Americans of that sort before the mid-60s, the base point was the worldwide crisis that began with the crash of 1929 and extended through the cold war. The United States survived that era; more, in the opinion of tens of millions of people the world over, the United States coped brilliantly.

It came through the economic collapse of the 1930s, which toppled many a country, with democratic institutions intact and even enhanced. In the 1940s it led the way in defeating a hideous tyranny in a war that practically everyone who believed in civilization supported as necessary. In the 1950s, for reasons not only of self-interest but also because of a concern for freedom outside its own borders, the United States saved western Europe from falling to another totalitarian aggressor.

The victories over the Great Depression, Fascism, and Stalinism carried over into the 1960s as vivid memories to Americans over forty. Seldom has it fallen to one age group to be part of such a succession of large national accomplishments. They meant very little if anything to young people, on the other hand, whose formative public experiences began with the bitterness of Vietnam and continued through the squalor of Watergate. Small wonder that parents and children disagreed about what the real America was.

But when the 1960s began there was no generation gap of the kind that later developed. Public opinion polls reported that most Americans, of all ages, took personal pride in their extraordinarily successful country. The United States was the premier democracy and acknowledged leader of the free world. The American standard of living was unrivaled. Nowhere else did close to half the college-age youth go to college. And people the globe around admired American technology, science, and scholarship, American literature, architecture, painting, music, and movies.

The race problem dampened the mood of national celebration, but not altogether, because encouraging steps had been taken and were being taken to solve it. Through presidential order in the 1940s, momentous Supreme Court decisions in the 1950s, and legislative programs in the first half of the 1960s, the federal government undermined the legal foundations of segregation. In the opinion of the nation's foremost southern historian, C. Vann Woodward, nothing less than a New Reconstruction was in the making.[4]

Concurrently, the American-born sons and daughters of "the new immigrants"—a term coined at the end of the last century for allegedly inferior types from southern and eastern Europe— were entering the middle class in significant numbers. Their climb from the slums prompted Samuel Lubell to remark, in the 1950s, that the upward mobility of the frontier had reappeared on "the tenement trail" to the suburbs. Not only were the immigrants' adult children materially better off than the parents had been; they and their own children encountered much less prejudice. By the 1960s even anti-Semitism had declined to a point where Jewish communal leaders acknowledged that it no longer seriously stood in the way of making one's way into American life.[5]

The easing of former group tensions culminated in two highly publicized events. In 1960 the White House doors opened to the first Catholic President. Five years later Congress repealed the national-origins quotas in the immigration laws, which, since the 1920s, had discriminated against the new immigrants and in favor of Protestant "Nordics" from western and northern Europe. Both events were accompanied by struggle, but the latter added pleasure to the outcome. A southern President signed the new immigration bill in the Statue of Liberty, and stated that America belonged to all the immigrant groups that had peopled it and believed in it.

By then it had been common for some time to refer to the United States as a pluralist society. The history of American immigration, long a neglected field, entered the cultural mainstream after World War II; so did the ethnic novel and studies of the ethnic basis of class, religion, and politics in American life. Those cultural changes took place before the black revolution and white-ethnic revival of the late 1960s and early 1970s. Like John F. Kennedy's election and the new immigration laws, they reinvigorated the idea that being an American also meant being a member of one ancestral group or another.[6]

We touch here on a major issue in the American experience. Logically as well as historically it comes down to this: the

United States has stood for both ethnic diversity and national unity, but they are opposite terms and therefore have to be reconciled if each is to have its due. The big question is: How? Insofar as public policy for persecuted minorities is concerned, two alternatives are available to draw them into the larger community. One would protect their equal rights by making it illegal to discriminate against anyone for reasons of race, color, religion, or national origin. The other would grant special privileges to minorities in compensation for past deprivations. Until the advent of the black revolution and women's liberation, the policy after World War II favored the first alternative.

The objective was not the equal achievement of groups, but equal opportunity for individuals. Therein lay the thrust of the law to proscribe unfair employment and housing practices; to delegitimize Jim Crow; to forbid quotas not only with respect to immigration but also in admissions to college and the professions. Later on such measures would be criticized as negative, as merely defining what was impermissible. The fact is, they were designed to enforce an unambiguously affirmative principle; namely, that individual Americans of no matter what descent or faith must all be treated the same.[7]

Stated in another way, the doctrine of equal treatment safeguarded the right to be different. It resulted not only in admitting more individuals to the benefits of American life but also in strengthening the pluralist cause. This last, as expressed by such widely read writers as John Kennedy and Oscar Handlin, praised ethnic diversity for making the country more open and colorful and interesting and human than it would otherwise be if everyone were culturally just like everyone else. At the same time, pluralists emphasized, as the later ethnic revival would not, that the country's various ancestral groups had many things in common as Americans. In brief, the postwar generation believed in—as they phrased it—unity amidst diversity.

The regard for unity accounts for the popularity of the word consensus. Critics deplored it, along with "continuity," but in vain. In politics there was a bipartisan accord to contain Communism abroad; and after President Dwight Eisenhower reconciled his party to past Democratic domestic policies, there was bipartisan support for maintaining a welfare and regulatory state. Even John Kennedy, who campaigned in 1960 to get America moving again, shared the political consensuses of the day. No one could doubt his anti-Communist position. As for the "central domestic issues of our time," he said in an address at Yale University, they "relate not to basic clashes in philosophy or ideology but to ways and means of reaching common goals."[8]

That statement appealed to many intellectuals, for their own thinking had been moving along similar lines for around a decade and a half. One line rejected ideological politics as destructive, and another as unnecessary. They were destructive in that they fostered irrationality, oversimplifications, paranoia, extremism, and divisiveness. They were unnecessary because Americans already had a worthy ideology in the principles that had given birth to the Republic. The political task was to achieve those given ends through the equally given democratic process.[9]

But every free society is subject to debate, and America was no exception between the end of the Second World War and the mid-1960s. Dominant opinion placed the highest value on pride in country, unity amidst diversity, toleration and moderation, consensus and continuity, and a pragmatic political style that stayed within the bounds of the nation's vital center. Of the groups that challenged those beliefs, the extreme left and extreme right deserve special attention.

The old left of the 1930s, consisting of Communists, fellow travelers, Socialists, Trotskyists, and independent Marxists, passed from the American scene in the 1950s. Many factors contributed to the demise, ranging from personal exhaustion to second thoughts about the nature of man, society, and history. Additionally, Communists and their dupes were subject to government repression, internal disputes, and a campaign by liberals to free their trade unions, veteran groups, and political associations of Stalinist influence. Above all and beyond everything else, Russia's postwar aggressions and Khrushchev's reve-

lations of Stalin's horrors extinguished lingering illusions not
only about the Soviet Union but about utopian expectations
in general.

Concurrently, the virtues of a capitalist democracy took on
a new appeal. In a *Partisan Review* symposium of 1952, former
left intellectuals declared that they no longer felt alienated
from the United States. On the contrary, they identified with
their country's cold war policies against the Soviet Union, stating that Stalinism was as deadly a totalitarian threat as Hitler-
ism had been. Equally to the point, they embraced America's
postwar social system, with all its imperfections, as a more
sensible alternative than the perfectionist ideologies that had
attracted them during the Great Depression.

As Daniel Bell later put it, America's prodigal children of
the thirties came home. Many of them rose during the pros-
perous fifties and sixties to prominent positions in the universities, publishing, and journalism. Like Max Lerner, to cite a
random example, they wrote with affection about America's
affluence, pluralism, free institutions, democratic values, and
unique history. There were conspicuous exceptions to the
mood of reconciliation, notably the readers and writers of
*Dissent* magazine, and ex-Marxists who veered sharply to the
right. But until a new alienated left took charge in the mid-
1960s, the main drift of the left in the postwar interregnum
was toward the center.[10]

As for the much larger right, it was not absorbed but overcome. That is how most Americans remembered, in 1960, the
McCarthyite fever of 1950–54. It was awful while it raged,
causing some people to fear that the United States might suc-
cumb to a right-wing dictatorship. But Senator McCarthy went
too far in his irresponsible investigation of Communist threats
to internal security, and in 1954 his senatorial colleagues
turned on him. The Wisconsin demagogue then dropped from
public sight, and died a broken figure in 1957.

Seven years later a new right, allied to McCarthyite elements, captured the Republican presidential nomination for
Senator Barry Goldwater. Although more genial and less ex-

treme than the ultras among his followers, Goldwater accepted the nomination with a defiant defense of extremism. Millions of moderate Republican voters repudiated him, with the result that his Democratic opponent received the largest popular majority in the history of the presidency up to then. In 1964, as in 1954, the center held.

And then, suddenly, things turned upside down. Three assassinations made a mockery of the world's oldest written constitution. Policemen assigned to anti-riot duty themselves rioted in the streets. Blacks demanded separation. Intellectuals extolled unreason over reason. Affluent children turned against affluence. Professors and students savaged their own campuses. Shortly before the 1960s closed, with tens of millions of TV viewers watching, the nation's oldest political party nominated a President in a setting that called to mind the antics of a banana republic.

As the turmoil mounted, the country soured. Time and again after the mid-sixties the media described the American people as unhappy, confused, adrift, distrustful, and divided. The rancorous temper permeated all levels of society, and among large numbers of intellectuals there was a revival of the recently disowned cult of alienation. By the end of the 1960s— by historic time only a day after yesterday's national confidence—America seemed unable to do anything right.

What went wrong? Even now, removed by several years from the passion and partisanship of events, the historian is hard put to answer the question. To millions of persons at the time, though, Vietnam seemed to be the major unstabilizing force. It was, but it also acted in concert with other forces. What is also worth remembering, over half a decade passed before America's involvement in the distant jungles of Southeast Asia exploded as a divisive issue.

There was no significant public controversy in 1960 when President Eisenhower replaced American civilian with military advisers in South Vietnam; or in 1963 when the Kennedy administration increased United States personnel to 17,000; or in the summer of 1964 when President Johnson ordered the first American air strikes against the Hanoi regime; or as late as the beginning of 1967 when United States troops in Vietnam passed the 400,000 mark.

The more the initial buildups increased, the more a sizable public assumed the necessity to contain international Communism. Hardly anyone then foresaw that the actual fighting would be bloody, expensive, and drawn out, or that it would result in driving a wedge into the American people. Even fewer persons thought the unthinkable, namely, that America could lose the war to a tiny foe. By such calculations, many a later dove was a hawk in the first seven years of Vietnam.

Those calculations turned out to be massive miscalculations after the Tet Offensive of January-February 1968. The Vietnam controversy then broke with full force, although it had been mounting in fierceness since the previous summer. Hawks and doves could not have confronted each other in more charged circumstances. The country was torn by ghetto violence, the black power movement, student radicalism, the counter-culture, urban crime, and a rising backlash. In the spring, assassins claimed the lives of Martin Luther King, Jr., and Robert Kennedy. America's multiple troubles intensified the divisive dispute over Vietnam, just as Vietnam magnified their impact on the raw national psyche.

The discord continued into the next decade, releasing along the way additional discontents as expressed in the formation of the Chicano, Native American, white-ethnic, women's, and gay liberation movements. Meanwhile, the economy both slowed down and overheated, to the bafflement of public officials who knew well enough how to cope with unemployment or inflation but not with both at the same time. The "rules of economics are not working quite the way they used to," the chairman of the Federal Reserve Board ruefully announced in the summer of 1971.[11]

Much else no longer worked right. The regulatory state needed regulating; the bipartisan foreign policy against Communism was breaking up; the welfare state was a mess. Despite a heartening increase of educated young blacks in the middle class, there remained a depressingly large black underclass, and the central cores of many big cities were still decaying. Even men and women who once thought themselves liberals came to wonder, after close to a decade of Kennedy-Johnson reforms, if any governmental remedies could succeed against the entangled urban pathologies of poverty, broken families, illiteracy, drugs, juvenile delinquency, adult crime, and racism black as well as white.[12]

Other liberals stayed loyal to the reform faith, but the national malaise had developed into something more fundamental than differences of opinion over social action. Its most revealing index was the breakdown of the consensus that America was a going concern. Upwards of 60 percent of the people, according to public opinion surveys in the late 1960s and early 1970s, lost confidence in the country's financial, industrial, military, scientific, educational, and governmental institutions and the men who ran them. Because of this last, in 1972 the vice-president of Louis Harris Associates characterized the American crisis as "a total crisis of leadership."[13]

In the same year Dr. Gallup reported that 12 percent of the population was thinking of emigrating to another country. Few actually did so, yet Gallup's findings were nevertheless symptomatic of a deeply troubled society. The United States had been the chief immigrant-receiving country in the world, and here were some twenty million Americans saying they were in the mood to reverse the process. But fully to appreciate the separatism that entered American life we must look elsewhere.

## Militancy, Backlash, Constitutional Emergency

The more the sense of wholeness dissolved after the mid-1960s, the more people split off into angry, contentious, vindictive factions. By 1970 the fragmentation had proceeded so rapidly that a French visitor, Jean-François Revel, thought America had broken into dissatisfied "nations."[14] But it was more customary to call such groups militant—militant blacks, militant students, militant women, militant Chicanos, militant

Indians, militant homosexuals, militant welfare mothers, militant hippies (Yippies), or whatever the case was.

The term was apt. Militants struck bellicose poses, made unconditional demands, and staged massed confrontations. Some of them resorted to guns, explosives, and fire. All of them asserted that America was the land and the home of victims and victimizers, and that they were the victims, but not for long. Disdaining debate and compromise, the conventions of orderly change in civilized politics, militants behaved as if they were on a battlefield.

Sympathetic observers explained that there was much to assault: poverty, racism, the war in Vietnam, limited opportunities for women, the repression of homosexuals. True enough. But it was also understandable that other observers should have objected to the corollary that militants embodied the tradition of American criticism and reform at its finest. Some of their ends smacked of authoritarianism, their methods were often undemocratic, and for the most part they despised the majority of their countrymen. Above all, militants were not critical of America's defects, they were against America itself, charging it with being the purest possible concentration of evil.

But what such spiritual outsiders said and did affected the consciousness of all Americans. For it was no longer the case, as once it had been well into this century, for militants to air special grievances and make special demands only through special publications of their own. They were also able, after the middle of the 1960s, to spread their message in the established media.

Ralph Waldo Emerson, who lived during America's first age of reform, wrote that "there are always two parties"—of "the Establishment and the Movement." The line that separated them blurred as the 1960s moved into the 1970s, so that it was sometimes hard to tell the difference between the New York *Times* and the *Village Voice*. It is still a matter of speculation why the cultural establishment adopted the posture of what Lionel Trilling called the adversary culture. But the result is a matter of record. A steady flow of news about the victimization, or alleged victimization, of this or that group, together with other bad news, magnified the public awareness of the centrifugal forces in American life.[15]

When the quadrennial contest for the presidency opened in 1968, it was unclear which of the many aspirants would ride the nation's troubles into power. We now know, of course, that it was Richard Milhous Nixon. He had seemed to be finished in 1962 after his defeat for the California governorship, but in the next few years the forces tearing at the American fabric pumped new life into his political career. By 1968 they also tore the Democratic party apart, and Nixon won the election with a mere 43.4 percent of the popular vote (to Hubert Humphrey's 42.7 percent and George Wallace's 13.5 percent).

Four years later he was swept back into office by the greatest landslide in the history of the presidency. How did Nixon do it? No more than in the past was he a widely loved leader; and never before had he united a large and varied electorate. A loner by temperament and a divider in style, Nixon had previously touched base in a political minority; and even they were less likely to feel warmly toward him as a human being than to respect his abilities as their tough, shrewd, tenacious, slashing, partisan infighter. Yet there he was in 1972, the choice of every state in the Union save the home state of the slain Kennedy brothers.

Nixon's greatest asset was the man who ran against him. George McGovern made just about every mistake in the book, but two related aspects of his campaign turned out to be fatal. First, he owed his nomination to a minority faction in the Democratic party: peace leaders, proponents of a "new politics," and self-called spokespersons for youth, women, blacks, the Spanish-surnamed, and the poor. Second, he called upon his countrymen to purge themselves of racism and poverty and sexism at home and of Nazi-like aggression and genocide abroad. In both instances McGovern misjudged the majority's mood. Instead of sharing his sense of guilt for the sins he ascribed to America, they made him the target for a rage that had been building up since the late 1960s against militants.

Every election touches and arouses the emotions, but the response to McGovern's candidacy was unusually visceral. You felt with him or against him, depending on how you felt about the reform ferments that began in the 1960s and spilled into the 1970s. Were they the signs of a more democratic epoch in the making, or were they the expressions of an age of trash? When the votes were counted in 1972, there could be no doubt about the country's answer.

In an exultant post-election analysis in *Commentary*, which for years had been condemning the upheavals of the 1960s, Norman Podhoretz, quoting Elizabeth Hardwick, wrote that the "disgust" for McGovern's candidacy stemmed from a disgust " 'for show-off students, for runaways, for attacks on the family and the system, for obscenity, for pot, for prisoner-pity, for dropping out, for tuning in, for radical chic, for storefront lawyers, for folk singers, for muggings, for addicts, for well-to-do Wasps grogged on charity binges.' "[16]

The anti-McGovern backlash swung across party lines. Indeed, without a huge defection of normally Democratic voters, Nixon could not have carried every state except Massachusetts. Many defectors were Wallace Democrats, but McGovern's candidacy also repelled Democrats who had supported the New Deal, the Fair Deal, the New Frontier, and the Great Society. Some of the latter voted for Nixon, whom they had disliked for years, or did not vote at all, knowing that by withholding their usual preference for a Democratic presidential candidate they were guaranteeing McGovern's defeat.

They felt as displaced as Wallace Democrats in the McGovern Democracy, although for different reasons. The old liberal coalition, dating from the Great Depression, had consisted of organized labor, big-city machines, and ethnic groups of every sort. Those elements were underrepresented at the 1972 National Democratic Convention, whose delegates reflected the newly instituted quotas of representation based on age, sex, color, and economic deprivation. More galling still, the convention unseated some of the delegates of the old liberal coalition, most notably the Chicago contingent led by

Mayor Richard Daley, and replaced them with leaders of McGovern's new liberal coalition.

Once again the response was visceral. Does the McGovern faction "know what it does to the American voter," exploded an FDR-JFK Democrat, "to be told that Bella Abzug, Shirley MacLaine, Jesse Jackson, Bill Singer, Walter Fauntleroy [*sic*], Robert Drinan, Abbie Hoffman, Jerry Rubin, and the Minnesota and New York representatives of gay liberation belonged on the floor of the Democratic convention while Richard Daley did not"? And why were Americans of Polish, Italian, and other European origins left out of the McGovern quotas?[17]

What further bothered old liberal Democrats was that the McGovern movement was essentially an alliance between the educated "elite" and the underclass of poor nonwhite minorities. That limited partnership left out the large majority of the American people. Here is how Stewart Alsop put it to Anthony Lewis, an exponent of the new politics:

> Consider the results of your kind of liberalism. The old liberalism identified itself with the interests of ordinary people. . . . Your kind of liberalism excludes such people as rigidly as old Joe Pew's "real Republicanism" excluded them. One result was last November's liberal disaster, which saw an unloved president, burdened with a snowy scandal, score a historic landslide. . . . The reason was that a great many ordinary Americans perceived your kind of liberalism as against them and worse, against the United States.[18]

The lopsided presidential return in 1972 was, clearly, less a landslide for Nixon than a landslide against McGovern. Only McGovern's true believers were surprised. As early as 1968 it was apparent that the electorate would turn against a candidate even remotely identified with the disorders of the left. Four years later the connection was anything but remote; as a member of the Democratic Platform Committee said, "There won't be any riots in Miami because the people who rioted in Chicago are on the Platform Committee—they outnumber us by three or four to one."[19] Millions of Americans who viewed the Democratic Convention on TV came to the same conclusion.

McGovern was the Goldwater of the left, but the 1972 election differed from that of 1964 in a profound respect: the center did not hold. It was said that race was not an issue in the campaign,[20] but that claim hardly squared with the evidence of Nixon's receiving most of the Wallace vote. What is even more telling, the revulsion for the McGovern movement was so strong that it moved normally liberal Democrats to the right. Nixon was not, nor had he ever been, a man of the center.

Scarcely had the McGovern movement been routed than the hope withered that an allegedy new Nixon would bind up the nation's wounds. The final withdrawal of United States troops from Vietnam quieted the American pulse but did not give the people a lift or bring them together again. Then came Watergate, and public outrage shifted against Nixon and his surprised clique of true believers. One kind of divisiveness replaced another. Twenty-one months after humiliating George McGovern, Richard Nixon resigned from the White House in disgrace.

His exit resolved a constitutional crisis. The House was on the point of impeaching the President for, among other things, the obstruction of justice. That was a criminal offense, and the evidence was so damning that the Senate seemed certain to remove him from office. Nixon escaped the indignity by resigning, but the country did not mind. It willingly let go a leader who had forfeited the right to lead and who, in the final month of his tenure, was so emotionally disturbed that he was incapable of attending to the nation's business.[21]

Watergate had a reassuring fallout. Nixon's abuse of power betrayed a historic faith in the presidency, and the reaction to that breach testified to America's strengths. Not only was the lawless chief executive brought down by democracy's self-correcting processes; the public proved that it had the resilience to absorb the unprecedented shock of a President ingloriously driven from office.

But as the Bicentennial year neared, it was premature to conclude that Watergate had purged, at long last, the ailing national spirit. On the contrary, the sense persisted that things were still not right with America. The multiple problems of the inner cities remained a source of major anxiety. No bonds of political unity had replaced the eroded postwar consensuses. Not since Eisenhower in the 1950s had anyone occupied the White House for two full terms. The uneasiness included private concerns, for an ongoing cultural revolution was upsetting traditional notions of sex, marriage, and the family.

The turbulence of the recent past receded but was not easily to be forgotten. In an interview in the summer of 1976, Alistair Cooke was asked if Watergate and Vietnam still affected the country's mood. They did indeed, answered Cooke, because they were still remembered for the traumas they had caused. Perhaps the worst of America's bad times is over, Cooke concluded; but perhaps, too, "the present comparative calm is . . . the dead eye of the hurricane and the next time it will be worse."[22]

## *National Identity Crisis*

Of the cleavages to emerge in the 1960s, none was potentially more threatening to the wholeness of this nation of many nations than the ethnic cleavage. The surge of black consciousness led to an intensification of self-awareness on the part of Chicanos, Puerto Ricans, American Indians, and ancestral groups of European origin. These last, called white ethnics, generated their own centrifugal force.

American opinion was as unprepared for the white-ethnic revival as it was for the other movements of the sixties. Indeed, until the end of the decade, nobody used the term white ethnics. Its inventors believed that it was certain to be around for some time to come. For, as Father Andrew M. Greeley, director of the Center for the Study of American Pluralism, put it in 1970 before a congressional committee:

> One of the most extraordinary events of our time has been the resurgence of tribalism in a supposedly secularized and technocratic world. Science and economic rationaliza-

tion had been expected to reduce, if not eliminate, man's attachment to ancient ties of common ancestry, common land and common faith, but suddenly ties of race, nationality, and religion seem to have taken on new importance.[23]

The year before, at a widely publicized "consultation on ethnicity" in Chicago, a participant exclaimed: "If it's 'in' to be Black these days, it's also 'in' to be Polish!" Variations on this theme were expressed by Italian, Ukrainian, Jewish, Irish, Greek, and still other participants. But blacks were less a target of resentment than "liberal elites" who allegedly set public policy and molded public opinion at the expense of America's "backbone." "They talk about the black problem, they talk about Cesar Chavez, they talk about peace," a participant complained of liberals—"but why don't they ever talk about ethnics?"[24]

Those words should have given warning to the emerging McGovern movement, but the new politics dismissed them as the rhetoric of northern big-city rednecks. In retrospect we can see that the white-ethnic revival was part of the multi-crisis that mushroomed in the late sixties. It fed into, and was fed by, the divisiveness issuing from war, prejudice, poverty, welfare, violence, crime, pornography, pollution, the counter culture, the breakdown of authority, inflation, and everything else that called into question the legitimacy of American society.

Revival leaders saw in the new ethnic fragmentation the beginnings of a "new pluralism." "Ethnics are trying to find out who they are," said the Reverend Paul J. Asciolla in 1971. America as a whole, Father Asciolla further observed, was passing through a "national identity crisis."[25] No one could quarrel with that diagnosis, or with the corollary that the American people needed desperately to know what kind of people they were, had been, and ought to be. The big question was how the ethnic revival proposed to resolve the national identity crisis.

# 2  Ethnicity Revived and Politicized

Contemporaries spoke of the ethnic revival in the singular, but the movement actually consisted of two parts. One was a reassertion of group identity among the descendants of what had been called the new immigrants; the other was a rediscovery of ethnicity by the media, government, the foundations, and academia. Each part fed the other. The first provided the second with a cause, and the second supported the first with prestige, money, publicity, and sympathy.

Typically, in a speech in 1967, Robert C. Wood, Undersecretary of Housing and Urban Development, described "the average white ethnic male" as deeply troubled. He struggled to support a family as a blue- or white-collar worker on between one and two hundred dollars a week; worried about being laid off; suffered from rising taxes, inflation, and debt; dreaded the black ghetto next to or expanding toward his neighborhood; feared sending his children to college when professors and students seemed to have gone mad; and considered himself maligned, neglected, and politically powerless. Like other aggrieved groups, the undersecretary warned, white-ethnic workers felt alienated.[1]

The speech was a preview of things very soon to come but went largely unnoticed at the time. The agenda of social concern then centered elsewhere. It offered a Peace Corps and a Job Corps and Vista to the young, and civil rights legislation and Model City programs and other measures to blacks. As for white-ethnic workingmen, Daniel Patrick Moynihan observed, they had "little to show from either the New Frontier or the Great Society."[2]

19

At the beginning of the 1970s two events in high places signified that the pendulum was swinging to compensate for the neglect of the previous decade.

In 1971 the Ford Foundation awarded research grants to six institutions* to inquire into "the problems of white working-class American communities." The purpose, announced President McGeorge Bundy, was "to widen our understanding of the continuing role of ethnicity in American life." To allay the fears of blacks that they might be abandoned for other disadvantaged groups, Mr. Bundy promised to honor his foundation's earlier commitment to their quest for social justice. But Americans of various European origins, he pointed out, also needed help and sympathy.[3]

The next year President Richard Nixon signed the Ethnic Heritage Studies Programs Act. Introduced by Congressman Roman Pucinski of Chicago and Senator Richard Schweiker of Pennsylvania, it aimed to provide a curriculum for schoolchildren "to learn about the nature of their own cultural heritage, and to study the contributions of the cultural heritages of other ethnic groups to the Nation."[4] We shall later look at the Schweiker-Pucinski bill in detail. Here it is enough to say that, like the Ford Foundation, the federal government legitimized the white-ethnic revival.

Intellectually, the revival began as a protest against the Kerner Report (1968)† for depicting America as two nations: white over black. Spokesmen for the revival accepted the description as true for only the South. The law of that section, upheld by the Supreme Court for more than a half-century,

---

*The recipients were the Center for Urban Affairs sponsored by the United States Catholic Conference; the American Jewish Committee; the National Opinion Research Center of the University of Chicago; the Research Foundation of the City University of New York; the Center for Policy Study, Ann Arbor; and the University of Michigan.

†The official title is *Report of the Advisory Commission on Civil Disorders*. Commissioned by President Lyndon B. Johnson in 1967, after four summers of riots in black ghettos, the volume was popularly known by the name of the commission's chairman, Governor Otto Kerner of Illinois.

had not only segregated the races but raised one above the other. Equally important, because few immigrants settled in the South after the eighteenth century, the region's blacks lived amidst a largely homogeneous white population.

Neither aspect of the southern experience, contended white-ethnic leaders, characterized their own northern cities. Legal segregation did not exist there, and heavy immigration had made the white North heterogeneous. Blacks therefore encountered a variety of white communities, here or there—depending on the city or any given part of it—predominantly Italian, Irish, Jewish, Polish, Greek, Hungarian, almost across the ancestral spectrum. Contrary to the Kerner Report, in short, the urban North contained not two but many nations.

The Ford Foundation and the federal government responded by affirming that ethnic pluralism was a condition of American life. But tens of millions of persons, living in or near cosmopolitan towns and cities, had taken the condition for granted long before the revival. The same was true of historians and novelists and political scientists and pollsters whose stock in trade consisted of rendering the American people in their many variations. Why was it said therefore, a decade after John Kennedy's campaign for the presidency, that ethnicity had been rediscovered?

## The Problem Is the Subject

When a society is hurting, the collective memory tends to become both grossly amnesiac and highly selective. In the late 1960s enrollments fell in traditional college history courses, and many high schools dropped the discipline altogether from the required curriculum. Conversely, there was a surge of historical interest in blacks, the Spanish-surnamed, American Indians, women, cities, and violence. In troubled times the problem is the subject, and the message is rediscovery.

The media are crucial for delivering the message. White ethnics discovered this as the sixties moved into the seventies. It was news when the Jewish Defense League sprang up in New York City to "protect Jewish lives"; when the residents of a Hungarian-Slovakian neighborhood in Cleveland took police training at Case Western Reserve University in order to patrol their own streets at night; when Tony Imperiale formed an Italo-American vigilante committee in Newark; when toughs of Slavic background attacked black neighborhoods in Pittsburgh; when Irish South Boston's Louise Day Hicks, the foe of busing, came close to being elected mayor of her city.

Newspapers and magazines, followed soon after by the book, TV, and movie industries, turned the searchlight on urban neighborhoods previously ignored. The terms for the allegedly typical resident of such communities varied—Joe, Archie Bunker, Hardhat, plain fellow, middle American, lower-middle-class worker, blue-collar American, whitetowner. Behind the euphemism or pejorative stood Robert Wood's average white-ethnic male. The media described him as cheerless, troubled, disaffected, powerless, angry, leaderless, and bigoted.

"Naturally, there's bitter feeling on the part of white ethnics toward Negroes," the *Wall Street Journal* quoted John Pankuch, president of the National Slovak Society, in 1969. The society had its headquarters in Pittsburgh, a workingman's town of blacks and still self-conscious Germans, Hungarians, Italians, and Slavs of various backgrounds. "There are more white poor than black, and very little has dribbled down to the white poor," President Pankuch complained. "But perhaps if the ethnics begin to speak as one voice, maybe somebody will pay attention to us as well as to them." Toward that end the National Confederation of American Ethnic Groups, which claimed a membership of close to twenty million persons in sixty-seven societies, announced a drive to win white ethnics a share of federal aid.[5]

All this was bad news because it meant that the civil rights movement, no longer confined to the South, was running into a northern backlash. To George Wallace, on the other hand, the tidings were very glad indeed. In his 1968 campaign for the presidency outside his own section, the Alabama governor spoke, typically, in a Ukrainian church located in polyglot, racially troubled Gary, Indiana. There and in similar northern cities the southern demagogue worked on the resentments that seethed among white-ethnic workers and their families. Although much less successful with such voters on election day than in the primaries and polls, Wallace cut into their normally Democratic return.

So did the Republican Nixon, and in 1969 Kevin Phillips, a White House aide, proposed that the administration exploit white-ethnic hostilities in order to enlarge an "emerging Republican majority." To Phillips the 1968 returns were as much a preview of future American politics as the 1928 election had been for its time. Al Smith then appealed to more white-ethnic voters than any other previous Democratic presidential candidate; and the political realignment that Smith initiated Franklin D. Roosevelt completed.[6] Nixon recalled that historic turning point after he entered the White House and laid plans not only for his own reelection but also for an era of Republican hegemony.

After the presidential contest and the publication the next year of Kevin Phillips's manual on the blessings of bigotry, one would have expected liberal Democratic leaders to protect their electoral base. White ethnics had formerly been called labor and minority groups, and together with blacks had constituted the most important elements in the northern coalition for close to forty years. But local issues strained the relationship in many cities.

The New York City teachers strike of 1968, which pitted a largely Jewish trade union against advocates of black-community control, split liberal opinion. In the city's mayoral campaign the following year, it was considered funny to ask what kind of linoleum the Democratic candidate, Mario Proccacino, would install on the living-room floor of Gracie Mansion. A coalition of chic whites and the black underclass had no need of white-ethnic slobs. That lofty attitude was to carry into the McGovern movement.[7]

But before then old-line liberals moved to restore traditional alliances. They proposed building bridges between non-affluent blacks and non-affluent white ethnics. The task required, in the words of Bertram H. Gold, executive vice-president of the American Jewish Committee, "a deep understanding of the needs, fears, and life styles" of white-ethnic groups. Otherwise, such groups "can only be condemned; with it, they can be worked with, in very new ways."[8] That kind of thinking led, in the next few years, to the Ford Foundation grants of 1971 and the Ethnic Heritage Studies Programs Act of 1972.

White ethnics had been around for a long time in American history, but opinion makers and policy makers and lawmakers took notice of them only after they saw them as a problem. The same was true of blacks, Puerto Ricans, Mexican Americans, and women. They, too, were rediscovered, because they, too, were perceived as a problem. The various claimant groups suffered from many injustices whose rectification was overdue. But did the problem—in this case, white ethnics—have a solution for what ailed America?

Their proposed way out was a new pluralism. Although the concept dated from Horace Kallen's writings of more than fifty years earlier, the revival's leaders showed no familiarity with that philosopher's considerable body of work. Perhaps that was why they christened their position new. Or was it because Americans habitually attach the adjective to their programmatic slogans? Examples that come immediately to mind are the first Roosevelt's New Nationalism and the second Roosevelt's New Deal, Woodrow Wilson's New Freedom and John Kennedy's New Frontier. In the 1950s a movement arose with the contradictory cry for a New Conservatism.

Yet the new pluralists were clear in stating what they wanted. The rank and file, lower-middle-class whites who lived in cities close to blacks, hoped to preserve and improve their neighborhoods. The leaders, for the most part Catholic and Jewish intellectuals, were mainly interested in replacing the metaphor of the melting pot with that of an ethnic mosaic. To trace the evolution of those two goals, the one material and the other cultural, we have to return to the closing years of the 1960s.


## *America Is a Sizzling Cauldron*

The prime mover of the new pluralist movement was the American Jewish Committee. One of the six Ford Foundation grantees, it was the first old-line liberal organization to warn that an explosive situation was building up in northern cities between blacks and white ethnics. Inasmuch as that situation involved Jews, as New York City's teachers strike dramatized, the American Jewish Committee responded to the urban crisis out of self-interest. Equally to the point, having long equated the political right with anti-Semitism, the committee feared George Wallace's rising popularity. "Mainstream America groups must help the ethnics organize," wrote an AJC official in 1968, "lest they fall into the hands of right-wing extremists."[9]

But by the 1960s the American Jewish Committee had outgrown its original purpose, dating from its founding in 1906, of defending only Jewish rights. It operated on the principle that no minority was safe unless all were. A historic ally of blacks in their quest for justice, the AJC had also played an important role in the repeal of the racist quotas of the immigration laws. Linked since World War II with the interconnected worlds of the universities, publishing, the foundations, and government, the American Jewish Committee ranked as the country's most influential voluntary association in the promotion of intergroup harmony.

The essential step for "depolarizing" relations between the races outside the South, thought the committee, required the nation to hear from and about white ethnics. Accordingly, in 1968 it set up the National Consultation on Ethnic America, with an advisory board of prominent non-Jews as well as Jews.

Taking place amidst much publicity at Fordham University, the first consultation drew around 150 social workers, scholars, clergymen, trade union leaders, and representatives of ethnic neighborhoods and institutions. The format was repeated elsewhere over the next two-and-a-half years, so that when the American Jewish Committee received a Ford grant in 1971 it claimed, correctly, that its consultations had "stimulated interest, concern, and action" in more than a dozen cities across the land.[10]

Meanwhile, as "an action follow-up" to the consultations, the committee had founded the National Project on Ethnic America in 1969. Also consisting of non-Jews as well as Jews, the project was charged with the responsibility of devising means to improve the delivery of public services to neglected neighborhoods. Experimental programs were initiated in Baltimore, Philadelphia, Newark, and New York City, but less as ends in themselves than to attract attention. Like the consultation, the project's ultimate purpose, in Director Irving M. Levine's words, was "to sensitize mainstream mass media and organizational leadership" to the existence of the white-ethnic working class and its discontents.[11]

From the outset of its depolarization activities, the American Jewish Committee declared that it was necessary to move from "epithets to analysis." And here it turned to the universities for help, particularly but not exclusively to sociologists. The result was a number of position papers—on the multiethnic texture of northern cities and on such sources of white-ethnic unhappiness as economic insecurity, rapid social change, frustration, and obsolete institutions.

Private opinions at the consultations differed over the question of whether white ethnics were racists, but practically everyone agreed that the Kerner Report was trying to overcome racism in the wrong way. "A strategy which constantly rubs the nose of the white ethnic group into the ground and keeps saying, 'You're guilty, you're guilty, you're guilty, you're guilty,' " the AJC's Murray Friedman warned, may "ultimately be a no-win strategy."[12] Further, it was unfair as well as unwise to blame white ethnics for slavery and Jim Crow in the South.

Most of their immigrant ancestors arrived in America after slavery was abolished, and settled with few exceptions in the North.

The sensible tactic was to give white ethnics an opportunity to say why *they* felt persecuted. They so expressed themselves. At the Philadelphia Consultation of 1969, Barbara Mikulski, a Polish-American social worker, said:

> I'd like to tell you why we are troubled. First, we are tired of being politically courted and then legally extorted. Second, we are sick and tired of institutions, both public and private, not being responsive or responsible to the people they were instituted to serve. Third, we feel powerless in our dealings with these monoliths. Fourth, we do not like being blamed for all the problems of black America. Fifth, and perhaps the key, we anguish at all of the class prejudice that is forced upon us.

What is more, Miss Mikulski complained, "No one listens to us and our problems, no one cares about us or appreciates the contribution we have made to American life." Angered by the epithets of bigot and backlasher, Miss Mikulski pointed out that white ethnics knew what it was like to be black: "Those who remain blue-collar workers are the field hands and we who move up into the white-collar positions are the house niggers with all of the brain-washing that it implies." But blacks were competitors for jobs and housing, Miss Mikulski continued, and in both instances "we feel threatened by black people." She asked outsiders to understand how hard it was for white ethnics to make way for blacks; the "only place we feel any sense of identity, community, or control is that little home we prize."

Nevertheless, as she defined the term, Miss Mikulski denied that she and her kind were racists. "Ethnic Americans do not feel that black people are inferior," Miss Mikulski summed up the case, "but regard them as territorial aggressors on their residential and employment turfs."[13]

The American Jewish Committee files were filled with such statements. More to the point, the consultations were publicized wherever they were held, not just in the local press, radio, and TV, but in magazines and newspapers that reached a national audience. Proud of winning a hearing for white-ethnic America, a committee official declared: "Opinion-molding forces throughout the country have expressed eager interest in our findings and analysis."[14]

Besides "sensitizing" the media, the American Jewish Committee succeeded in its other goal; namely, to involve "organizational leadership" in the ethnic revival.

One of the sponsors of the Fordham Consultation was the American Council for Nationalities Services. Later it became part of the National Project on Ethnic America. Founded earlier in the century when the immigrant problem was the great "racial" question in the North, the council had had some fifty years of experience in helping the foreign-born adjust to America. With agencies in thirty-six major cities, it knew at first hand the discontent that led to racial polarization. In 1969 the council's executive director, J. Frank Dearness, warned: "Lower-income white ethnics have problems that must be resolved, and if we don't resolve their problems, then all black progress will be lost because they'll turn to a Wallace or somebody like that."[15]

The American Jewish Committee won trade union support for its program. Local labor leaders attended consultations in New York City, Chicago, St. Louis, Providence, Detroit, and still other cities. Brendan Sexton of the United Auto Workers sat on the advisory committee to the National Project on Ethnic America. In 1970 the United Steelworkers of America's newspaper summed up the AJC's influence in these words:

> Ethnic power should have no more ominous attachment to it than black power. For implementation really means that each utilizes the cultural heritage and bonds within each to achieve the priorities that have been lost: together they can change the political values which have placed supersonic transports ahead of desperately needed better city school systems, missiles ahead of financial help for cities which are

virtually bankrupt. In short, both groups have the potential strength and capacity to save our urban civilization if they can find a way to work together.[16]

Of the organizations that responded to the depolarization program initiated by the AJC, none was more strategically placed than the Catholic church. Most white-ethnic working-class families belonged to that church. When the first consultation took place at Fordham, its sponsors included the National Catholic Conference for Interracial Justice and the Social Action Department of the United States Catholic Conference (formerly called the National Conference of Catholic Bishops). And when the advisory committee to the National Project on Ethnic America was formed, many Catholics were placed on it. The most influential was Andrew M. Greeley, a Chicago sociologist and priest. His *Why Can't They Be Like Us?* (1969) was the American Jewish Committee's opening statement on the survival of ethnicity in American life.

In 1970 Catholics held the first of their own deliberations. Convened in Washington, D.C., by the Urban Task Force of the United States Catholic Conference, it included participants from previous AJC consultations. One of them, Barbara Mikulski, began her talk in these words: "America is not a melting pot. It is a sizzling cauldron for the ethnic American . . . who is sick of being stereotyped as a racist and dullard by phony white liberals, pseudo black militants and patronizing bureaucrats." Miss Mikulski concluded on a neo-populist note:

> Unfortunately, because of old prejudices and new fears, anger is generated against other minority groups rather than those who have power. What is needed is an alliance of white and black, white collar, blue collar and no collar based on mutual need, interdependence and respect, an alliance to develop the strategy for a new kind of community organization and political participation.[17]

A few months later, in their Labor Day Statement, the United States Catholic bishops observed: "It is obvious that if there is to be a resolution of the racial crisis which currently grips our society, a critical role will be played by white ethnic working class communities." Like the AJC, the bishops warned against making white ethnics "a scapegoat for this racial crisis," and urged "considering how to assist the people in those communities which are situated on the racial frontier."[18]

The co-author of the bishops' statement, Monsignor Geno C. Baroni, was on the advisory committee to the American Jewish Committee's National Project on Ethnic America. Like other advisers, he had been deeply involved in the civil rights movement until events forced him to reconsider traditional tactics to achieve racial justice. In his own words,

> The end of the 1960's was the end of an era, both for the country and for me personally. I was in Washington for the black revolution, and I saw things change so much. Blacks became so much more aggressive. At the same time, blacks became increasingly resentful of whites who tried to work with them, and rightly so. I believe the black community should do its own thing. Of course, when blacks tell me this, I have to smile. I tell them "our thing" in Italian is "cosa nostra."

Also by the end of the 1960s, Monsignor Baroni continued, "I became sensitive to where the resistance to the black revolution was." It came from white ethnics in communities like Acosta, Pennsylvania, where the monsignor, an immigrant miner's son, had grown up. "This was my side of the street," Geno Baroni mused, "and I had left it for Washington."

In returning home Baroni saw the need for a new approach to group life in America. More specifically,

> We have to go beyond the old civil rights struggles. Here in Washington I had gotten used to thinking black. Liberals and blacks have been screaming "bigot" and "racist" and "pig" for so long that, politically, someone like Spiro Agnew was bound to come along and talk about pseudo-intellectuals. The working class can be exploited in a regressive way, and Agnew has the touch. Working people see themselves on a collision course with blacks. Many are in stable communities that are starting to fall apart. They

provide buffer zones between poor blacks and middle-class whites.

Like Miss Mikulski, Baroni expressed hopes for an alliance of all have-nots:

> I feel there is an untapped energy in the working class that could eventually lead to coalitions with the blacks. The value system of the working class has a positive side: self-help and self-determination. Blacks use different language and different words, but they don't want handouts either. I believe that as the ethnic groups become more and more self-confident, they will recognize that they have a lot in common with the blacks. Maybe they will start telling Spiro Agnew, "What you're saying about pseudo-intellectuals is fine, but what are you doing for me?"[19]

Monsignor Baroni's Catholic-sponsored Center for Urban Ethnic Affairs, together with the American Jewish Committee and Father Andrew Greeley's National Opinion Research Center of the University of Chicago, received the bulk of the Ford Foundation's 1971 grant. The alliance of those voluntary associations testified to the AJC's skill as a broker in intergroup relations. Protestant money had made common cause with Catholic and Jewish leaders to promote a new pluralism. Nor was the ecumenicism merely religious. Some blacks joined the movement whose professed goals embraced black and white interests alike. The advisory committee to the National Project on Ethnic America included a representative each from the National Council of Negro Women, the A. Philip Randolph Institute, and the National Urban League.

Despite the presence of the last-named groups, in 1970 the Reverend Robert C. Chapman, a black director for racial justice of the National Council of the Churches of Christ in the U.S.A., accused the United States Catholic Conference and the American Jewish Committee of "banding together . . . in a conscious and concerted effort to buttress and fortify the mistakenly sagging morale of the 'America-Love-It-Or-Leave-It' crowd of near fascists."[20]

The cauldron was still sizzling.

## New Pluralism, Old Dualism

Chapman's outburst was just the sort of name-calling the revival's leaders deplored as self-defeating. They asked the clergyman to understand that white ethnics wanted much the same things as blacks: economic well-being, control over their own communities, the enjoyment of urban amenities, and a sense of belonging and of self-esteem. That being the case, the two groups ought to be able to work together in the pursuit of common interests.

The argument was reasonable and sincere, but it also raised questions about whether the new pluralism was really pluralist. In placing blacks in one box and white ethnics in another, revival leaders contradicted their assertion that northern cities were a mosaic of a lot of different ancestral groups. Worse still, when Barbara Mikulski said that white ethnics, regardless of specific origin, saw blacks as territorial aggressors, she confirmed the Kerner Commission's Report that whites, no matter what kind or where, closed ranks against blacks.

Precisely that condition, of course, led the American Jewish Committee to launch a depolarization movement. Bertram Gold remarked in 1968 that only after understanding the causes of confrontation could one remove them through constructive programs. Toward that end the revival's leaders eventually proposed that non-affluent whites and blacks coalesce in their respective cities for better jobs, housing, police protection, sanitation, mass transit, playgrounds, schools, and the like.

The projected coalitions never got beyond the drawing board, but even if they had, the new pluralists' dilemma would have remained. Their suggested political remedies were accompanied by the promise, time and again, that the benefits would accrue to white ethnics on the one hand and to blacks on the other. That was not the language of pluralism, which means not two but many groups.

The difficulty was not semantic but sociological and historical. When the civil rights movement jumped over the Mason-Dixon line in the mid-1960s, there were numerous cities in which white-ethnic groups had lived, if not quite together, at least harmoniously in the same neighborhoods. Mayor Richard Daley's Bridgeport, for example, was predominantly Irish, Polish, and Lithuanian. It was also Catholic, but the residents no more cared to share their residential turf with black Catholics than with black Baptists.

Bridgeport was special only in regard to its ethnic mix. Other northern urban communities might be heavily Irish and German, or Jewish and Italian, or Norwegian, Syrian, and Irish, or Czech, Polish, and Lithuanian, or Slovakian and Hungarian. In Philadephia's Kensington, with a population of around 100,000, the mosaic comprised Irish, Hungarian, Italian, Polish, Ukrainian, German, Jewish, and other whites. Whatever the distribution, white ethnics were as unwilling as Bridgeporters to live with blacks.

It was natural, new pluralists contended, for people to gather with their own kind. It was, but in the American context, what did one mean by one's kind? The answer was clear enough in solidly Polish Hamtramck; just outside Detroit, it wanted to preserve itself against non-Poles of every sort.[21] But if the Irish and Lithuanians and Poles could share Bridgeport, then in the name of pluralism blacks should have had a chance to be part of the residential mix, too.

At no time did the new pluralists come out in favor of coloring the ethnic mosaic through open housing. On the contrary, they emphasized the benefits, not only for the people involved but for society as a whole, of maintaining the old neighborhoods and the ties they fostered in families, friends, local organizations, and churches. No one could fault that ideal, but it was also understandable that blacks should have been suspicious of the proposition that they were, in fact, an acceptable group among many in the pluralist North.

None of this is meant to suggest that the descendants of slaves are just another immigrant group, and it serves no useful purpose for scholars to say they are. But if Americans of African origin are unique, it does not follow that Americans of European origin are all alike. Were they so the concept of pluralism would be meaningless. Therefore, whatever they said to the contrary, the new pluralists acted in terms of the old dualism. They tried not to, but when it came to neighborhoods and jobs, particularly neighborhoods, white ethnics were unable to free themselves from the worry that brought their movement into being; namely, the large black presence in northern cities.

Blacks also shaped the cultural side to the revival. "I think those of us in the ethnic bag can learn from the blacks about the importance of cultural identity," Monsignor Geno Baroni said in 1970. "We are beginning to celebrate our differences instead of insisting that everybody has to be the same."[22]

## Goodbye to the Melting Pot

At the end of his engagingly written *Why Can't They Be Like Us?* Andrew Greeley tells the following anecdote.

He was standing before a church in the west of Ireland, camera in hand, thinking he had tracked down the church where his grandfather had been baptized. The parish priest immediately took him for an American and inquired if he was looking for a copy of his grandfather's baptismal record. Father Greeley, who had come to photograph the church, said that he hadn't thought of the idea.

"Do a lot of people come seeking such records?" he asked the parish priest.

"Indeed they do," was the answer. "Indeed they do."

The reply confirmed Father Greeley's certainty about the durability of the ethnic group, which he defined as a collectivity of people who share an actual or imagined descent. More than that, Father Greeley believed that "presumed common origin . . . seems to touch on something basic and primordial in the human psyche." The Irish priest to whom he was speaking did not express himself in those terms, but he agreed with his Chicago visitor that American ethnics were in search of themselves.

"Those poor people," he said, "they've been in the States now for three generations and they come seeking roots; they want to know who they are; they want to know all about their past and their ancestors. The poor people, I feel so sorry for them. Well," he concluded, "the least we can do is to be of some help to them. That's why I had all their baptismal records put on microfilm. It makes it a lot easier for people to find their roots."[23]

Greeley's story was true to Hansen's law. It is an "almost universal phenomenon," wrote Marcus L. Hansen in 1938, "that what the son wishes to forget the grandson wishes to remember." Accordingly, whenever a sizable third generation appears in an immigrant group, as instanced by the Scotch-Irish in the 1880s and 1890s and the Germans in the decade before World War I, there occurs a "renaissance" of pride in "heritage—the heritage of blood." The phenomenon was expressing itself in the 1930s among Swedish-Americans, to whom Hansen addressed his remarks; and he predicted, accurately, that other groups would repeat it in the future.[24]

But more was involved in the 1960s than Hansen's law of third-generation filiopiety, and here it is instructive to compare the white-ethnic revival with the Anglo-Saxon revival of 1890–1920. The most genealogically minded Americans were then the descendants of the colonial stock. Fearful of being displaced by an increasing number of non–Anglo-Saxon immigrants, they invoked a heroic Anglo-American past to bolster group pride. Among other things, they tracked down ancestors who had fought in the War of 1812 or the Revolution, or who had founded Jamestown or Plymouth, or who had crossed the Channel with William the Conqueror in the Norman Conquest of England. Behind such efforts lay a great deal of anxiety about to whom America would eventually belong, but the oldest stock never doubted their superiority to the newest groups. In a nation fed by many nations, they regarded themselves as the real Americans.[25]

To the extent that the host people of the 1960s felt threatened by the newcomers of *their* day, the white-ethnic revival resembled the Anglo-Saxon revival of a half-century and more earlier. But there the likeness ended. The 1960s movement sprang, in many instances, from feelings of inferiority. Not only complaining that they had been left behind in the race for the economic and political prizes of America, white ethnics cried out that they had been stripped of their respective cultural identities.

Among the revival's spokesmen, Monsignor Geno Baroni best summarized the sense of that double deprivation and the relation of the one to the other. "In our eagerness to 'make it,' " he remarked, "we cut ourselves off from our roots too fast." But the damage was reparable. "Now we are discovering that we aren't all making it," Baroni continued, "and we are learning just how important those roots are."[26]

It was implicit in the monsignor's remarks that he and his fellows were at least partly responsible for their plight, but most other spokesmen for the revival were much less self-incriminatory in fixing the blame. Anglo-Saxons were blamed, liberals were blamed, establishments were blamed, intellectuals were blamed, elites were blamed—almost always it was because of "others" that white ethnics had lost their respective cultural moorings. Above all, the accusing finger pointed at a concept—the melting pot.

The intensity of the melting pot's denunciation was an index to the powerlessness that white ethnics felt. In assaulting a symbol they regarded as someone else's making, they took out their rage against a power structure that allegedly had betrayed them. At one Catholic conference, for example, the Italo-American caucus inveighed against the melting pot as "a myth which has been perpetuated by the elite-dominated American educational system to commit cultural genocide on our people."[27]

In his illuminating *Whitetown, U.S.A.*, Peter Binzen, a Philadelphia newspaperman who served as an adviser to the National Project on Ethnic America, noted that rank-and-file ethnics were often surer of what they were against than what they were for. With regard to things cultural, however, their leaders knew what they wanted. When the Italo-American caucus condemned the melting pot, it also demanded that the national Bicentennial celebration in 1976 be "a celebration of pluralism in America."

To celebrate is one thing, and to implement another. What did pluralism mean to the revival? And how did its advocates propose to achieve it?

In 1970 Congressman Roman C. Pucinski of Chicago, a Democrat, introduced a bill to fund the creation of Ethnic Heritage Studies Centers. Leaders of the ethnic revival, together with an array of scholars and school administrators, testified in favor of the bill. Its purpose was twofold—to give every American child an opportunity to study his own ethnic group and to appreciate the heterogeneity of American society. Toward those ends the centers, to be scattered throughout the country, would design curricula, disseminate them, and train teachers in their use.

As chairman of the General Subcommittee of the House Committee on Education and Labor, Mr. Pucinski set the tone of the hearings on his bill. On the opening day he objected to the tendency "to homogenize 200 million human beings into a single monolith, instead of recognizing that America is a magnificent mosaic, made up of many cultures." The following week, in an exchange with a Japanese-American authority about the inadequacy of schoolbooks, the congressman wondered "if there was a conspiracy to deny the heterogeneous aspect of our existence." Later that same day he declared: "I find the whole doctrine of the melting pot frankly very repugnant. I don't want to be melted down to a monolith."[28]

In those words the congressman, who represented Chicago's mixed but heavily Polish-American northwest side, summed up the essence of the 363 pages of hearings. Dozens of witnesses joined him in rejecting the melting pot as a model for America as it is, was, and ought to be. That pernicious metaphor was destroying the sense of self in old and young alike, and was therefore responsible for the fragmentation of America. Only pluralism could restore America's wholeness, for only by respecting one's self could one respect others.

But the supporters of the Pucinski bill seldom expressed interest in others. They wanted government funds to underwrite the study of their own ethnic group, and the Pucinski bill promised them just that. Filiopietistic, they had in mind a curriculum that would celebrate their own kind and make their own young feel proud. Their separatist approach was identical to, because it was influenced by, the black-studies movement.

The bill failed the first time around, and a new tack was taken. Warning that if unamended the Pucinski measure could Balkanize the United States, the American Jewish Committee and the American Council for Nationalities Services urged the comparative study of ethnic groups, so that students could appreciate the similarities as well as the differences of America's ethnic groups. Senator Richard Schweiker of Pennsylvania, a Republican, wrote that approach into his bill, and both houses passed it just before the 1972 presidential sweepstakes got underway. The timing could not have been better for Richard Nixon, who put his signature to a law that promised to benefit his campaign for reelection.

The new pluralists were jubilant in winning official recognition for their cultural objectives, but their victory turned out to be a good deal less substantial than they originally thought. For one thing, the 1972 act provided only "seed money" for pilot programs, and those programs have yet to transform the nation's school curricula. For another, the "craving for historical identity" was not so much "a people's movement," Gunnar Myrdal wrote in 1974, as the articulation of "a few well established intellectuals, professors, writers—mostly, I gather, of a third generation."[29]

Myrdal could have been thinking of Italo-American leaders who played a conspicuous role in the white-ethnic revival. In 1969 the recently formed American Italian Historical Association had a conference on the Italian-American novel. Contrary to a widespread misconception, many such novels had been written—forty-five, to be exact, since the 1920s; and some of them, particularly by Pietro Di Donato, Rocco Fumento, and John Fante, brilliantly recaptured the Italian experience in America. Yet few Italo-Americans, the conferees were sad to say, read their own novelists, let alone bought their works.[30]

Or consider the case of the Polish-Americans, whose leaders were also prominent in the revival. St. Mary's College, located since 1909 at Orchard Lake, Michigan, shared a campus with a prep school and seminary for Polish-Americans. The educational complex was a model for institutions of higher learning that Italo-American leaders were demanding for their kind. It taught the ancestral language and history, supported research in those areas, and in the 1960s brought representatives to the campus from a dozen and more different ethnic groups for conferences on pluralism.[31]

But except for the training of priests, the Orchard Lake Schools exerted a minimal influence on the cultural life of the masses of Polish-Americans. When young people of that background attended college they went in largest number to other institutions. St. Mary's College, with an enrollment in the 1960s of between 100 and 125, attracted considerably fewer Polish-American students than Michigan's public institutions. On the lower levels, in New England high schools heavily attended by Polish-Americans, the Polish language was dropped as an elective in the 1960s for want of student (and parental) interest.

No more than the Poles and Italians did the mass of rank-and-file Irish Americans show signs of being swept into a cultural renaissance. Apart from some, the Irish had lost so much of their heritage, Andrew Greeley wrote, that they were unable to take advantage of the fashion that it was "in" to be ethnic. An accomplished raconteur as well as an astute sociologist, Greeley told of a visit to a Catholic girls' college. The president of the campus Irish club, Peggy, was bright and enthusiastic but couldn't identify Eire's counties, the Sinn Fein, or the Easter Rebellion. When asked who Eamon de Valera was, she replied: "Isn't he the Jewish man that is the Lord Mayor of Dublin?" Peggy later married an American boy with a German name.[32]

The Jews were special, for their self-consciousness was affected not only by the ethnic vogue, but by the additional and coincidental impact of two Israeli-Arab wars. There was an enthusiastic response to Irving Howe's best-selling *World of*

*Our Fathers* (1976), an affectionate history of Eastern European Jews in the United States. Yet, as the author pointed out in his perceptive conclusion, the intensification of group identity did not result, among many people, in a commitment to serious Jewish education.

Gunnar Myrdal was right: the movement for cultural distinctiveness was limited to a minority of intellectuals. Their major constituencies did not reside in the respective ethnic communities for which they claimed to speak, but in foundations, publishing houses, universities, the mass media, and ultimately the government. One wonders if the revival's intellectuals appreciated the irony of such support. It emanated from the top, consisting of establishment types whom the new pluralists ritualistically flayed as elitists.

Meanwhile, popular interest in the ethnic past was reflected in large and enthusiastic audiences for *The Emigrants, Fiddler on the Roof,* and *The Godfather.* All three movies generated a universal appeal, so that one did not have to be Swedish to be moved by the first, or Jewish by the second, or Italian by the third. As for the Jews and Italians and Swedes, viewing one's kind on the screen produced a real or feigned pleasure of recognition—but of a world that had vanished with the immigrant forebears and that practically no one cared to resurrect.

The cultural side of the revival was mostly a matter of nostalgia. Rank-and-file ethnics expressed strongest consciousness of kind when they perceived their interests to be at stake with regard to jobs, housing, neighborhoods, police protection, balanced political tickets, control over schools, busing, and the like. Those concerns were of a different order from the yearning for historical identity that was supposed to be gratified by the Ethnic Heritage Studies Programs Act of 1972. Small wonder that veteran scholars of ethnic affairs regarded its passage as a hollow victory.

Besides lacking a popular following for their cultural objectives, the new pluralists were criticized by old pluralists for exaggerating America's pluralism. A month after the American Jewish Committee's consultation took place in Chicago in 1969, the Midwest branch of B'nai B'rith's Anti-Defamation League, the Chicago Urban League, and Loyola University

held a rival conference on ethnicity to coincide with Loyola
University's 100th anniversary. The speakers were unanimous
in rejecting the new pluralism for being as mythical as the
melting-pot concept it wanted to succeed.

"We have neither complete assimilation nor pluralism," said
Thomas F. Pettigrew, professor of social psychology at Harvard. He warned against substituting one extreme for another to
account for the subtle and complex American population mix.
As a rejoinder to Father Greeley's parish-priest story in the
west of Ireland, Professor Pettigrew told a story of his own.

> I, too, "returned" with my immigrant mother to "the old
> country"—Scotland. And we went to Inverness to check on
> our roots and even found the Fraser homeplace still in-
> habited by Frasers. But I do not need the heartfelt sympathy
> of the Irish parish priest. For I learned how different I
> really was from my Scots relatives, whom I liked very much.
> In short, though proud to be of Scottish origin, what I
> really found was that my roots are in America, that I am
> disgustingly American. Perhaps, the best way to dispel the
> myth of complete pluralism would be to have Americans,
> black and white, of all religions and nationality groups,
> return to their supposed "homelands" and learn the same
> thing.[33]

How a Pettigrew or a Greeley saw himself in the sum of
things was a private matter, just as it was for countless others
who defined for themselves their own ethnic identities. But because Pettigrew was far from special in having weaker primordial ties than revival thinking allowed, he directed public attention to where the new pluralism had gone wrong. It was
more fixed and closed, less fluid, less many-sided, and less
hospitable to differences than the country's actual pluralism.

## A Distorted View

The white-ethnic revival was the product of a seriously
divisive moment in history. Like previous revivals in America
and elsewhere, secular as well as religious, the 1960s–1970s

movement rested on the belief that the only way out for a troubled people lay in the return to a precious but languishing heritage. Congressman Pucinski summed up both the mood and the message in these urgent words: "The spirit of ethnicity, now lying dormant in our national soul, begs for reawakening in a time of fundamental national need."[34]

But instead of bringing the American people together again, the revival added to the fragmentation and discord from which it emerged. Like the dissidents against whom they often railed—black militants, radical students, hippies, welfare mothers, peace leaders, homosexuals, women's libbers, and the like—white ethnics bristled with the resentments of self-proclaimed victims. The late 1960s and early 1970s encouraged plaintiveness. For one thing, the people who received the most attention were the people who claimed they were the most mistreated. For another, even under the Nixon administration, there was a predisposition to redress grievances through government.

The grievances existed before the revival legitimized them. Two years prior to the formation of the National Consultation on Ethnic America, a Bostonian summed up the material complaints of fellow ethnics as follows:

> This is a slum . . . but it's a white slum, so no one cares about it. There's no glamour in white slums, only Negro ones. The suburban housewives and the Ivy League students, they've gone poor-crazy, but only for the colored poor. They've been pushing us around all these years before the Negroes started coming up from the South, and now they have someone to do it for them. They do a good job, too, the Negroes do. They act as if they own the world, just like their friends out there in the suburbs. It's contagious, you see. The ministers and the students come on Saturdays to tutor the Negro kids and take them to the park. They drive right by this neighborhood without blinking an eye. We have overcrowded schools. We have rotten buildings that should have been torn down years ago. We have lousy parks that aren't half the size they should be. A lot of people here have jobs that barely give them enough to get by; and the others, I'll tell you, are on relief or unemployment checks or veterans' checks, or something. We have our

delinquents and our drop-outs—the works. Who cares
though? Who has ever cared about this neighborhood?[35]

Revival leaders believed they were serving the common good
in bringing such hurts into the open. Out of public hearing
and public sight, they would fester and grow nastier. Additionally, justice required that the official agenda of social concern make room for white-ethnic concerns. Nothing less than
that, it was emphasized, could defuse the explosive tensions
on the racial frontiers of the North's major cities.

The motives were worthy, but the sociology was faulty. If
one knew only the literature of the revival, one would conclude
that the whole of ethnic America was contained in communities like South Boston, Kensington, Gage Park, and Hamtramck. That profile left out millions of families who lived in
pleasant small towns, comfortable suburbs, and stable neighborhoods on the outer rims of big cities. They were left out
because, although ethnics, they were not a problem.

Stated differently, the revival confused white ethnicity with
a beleaguered class. As late as the mid-1970s, despite a great
deal of evidence to the contrary, Michael Novak persisted in
equating white ethnics with big-city workers who lived in fear
of neighboring blacks. Many such people existed, but it was a
mistake to imply that all ethnics—or even a majority of them
—were people of that sort. Without meaning to, revival leaders
like Novak contributed to the stereotype of the white ethnic as
racist hardhat.[36]

With respect to things cultural, the revival's intellectuals
exaggerated to the point of hyperbole. Unmasking conspiracies
where none existed, they denounced the melting pot as a genocidal plot. Mistaking Columbus Day and Steuben Day Parades
for deep stirrings, they deceived themselves into believing there
was mass support for ethnic studies programs. Swayed by the
high-flown rhetoric of the black studies movement, they failed
to see that the courses resulting from that movement were
academically shoddy and poorly attended, and that many
would soon be phased out.

There were other excesses. A literature about the "rage" of
being ethnic reduced the entire experience of those groups in

America to ordeals and defeats. There was also a malicious baiting of WASPs, accompanied by extravagant tributes to PIGS, the curiously affectionate acronym of one revival author for America's defiantly "unmeltable" Poles, Italians, Greeks, Slavs. Such a view of the United States differed from that of past Anglo-Saxon supremacists only in the designation of which groups were desirable and undesirable. It was a bigoted view.[37]

As the "fever of ethnicity" (Robert Alter's phrase) rose, critics of the revival increased. They included, as one might expect, universalists and leftists. The one protested that human beings are fundamentally alike whatever their antecedents, and the other that ethnic differences are insignificant in comparison to class divisions. Neither argument was effective, because both ignored an American—more, a worldwide—reality: the reality of ethnic feelings.

A third group of critics consisted of Oscar Handlin, Nathan Glazer, Daniel Patrick Moynihan, John Higham, and other old pluralists of the postwar generation. Having established the study of ancestral groups as an academic discipline before the subject's rediscovery, they did not have to be reminded of the persistence of ethnicity in American life. Also, they sympathized with white ethnics living on racial frontiers; indeed, some of them helped the revival in its initial phase. Before long, however, they found fault with its growing petulance, rancor, divisiveness, and distortions.

What disturbed them most was the portrayal of American society as merely a collection of different and competing ethnic groups. The rendering was not only factually incorrect; it was also and more dangerously an invitation to the "tribalization" of the United States. Like all oversimplifiers, the new pluralists chose to see only what they cared to see. Ignoring the nation's common heritage, they failed to grasp that America's uniqueness was not so much diversity per se—there were other ethnically pluralist countries—but how America achieved unity in that diversity.[38]

Some scholarly good, however, came out of the revival. Thanks to the monographs prepared at Andrew Greeley's Center for the Study of American Pluralism, we know more than we used to about the continuity, through the generations, of

certain ancestral characteristics and values. That line of research is still going forward and is of a high order. So is the
Center's journal, *Ethnicity*, launched in 1974 with the backing
of reputable historians and sociologists who, like Greeley, had
been working in the field before it became trendy.

This last point is worth emphasizing. The study of ethnicity
had taken hold in the academy before the revival, but expanded
as a result of it. Many new scholars entered the field, college
course offerings increased, and the foundations enlarged the
number of research grants. Ethnic studies were "in." Yet very
few writers who were entirely a product of the revival did any
distinguished work. The same was true, parenthetically, of the
black and Chicano and native American studies movements.

Andrew Greeley, however central to the white-ethnic revival
in his popular writings, was also exceptional to it in his scholarly publications. No Johnny-come-lately to the sociology of
ethno-religious groups, he deplored the revival's excesses and
distortions. Although an activist, his views were informed by
hard data. Sensitive to what was going on, he understood that
the cultural thrust to the revival struck its most responsive
chord, not in ethnics, but in establishment officials who thought
ethnicity a good thing for other people. More plainly, Greeley
saw things whole.[39]

Such was not the case, alas, of the revival in general. To
the degree that it helped to make differences safe, it strengthened a major democratic tenet. Yet the revival neglected to
show how the persistence of ethnic differences can lead to a
sense of national wholeness. It fell down in that task because
it failed to transcend the crisis from which it derived.

More specifically, in its literature and consultations and
conferences, the revival gave the impression that the most important bond among Americans was the fact that they sprang
from different ancestors. That message hardly reassured a
confused and divided people. Questionable logic aside, it mis-
read the past, to which the new pluralists often alluded but
which they seldom took the trouble to examine. And it is to
the past we now turn, with particular reference to how the
Americans, over two centuries, defined their collective identity
among the world's peoples.

# 3    A Special Kind of
Identity

Now that their nation-state is one of the oldest
in the world, Americans ought to be both unassertive and
unself-conscious about the national character. The tendency
to talk about identity, among countries as well as individuals,
is usually a condition of being young. Yet no American trait
since the War of Independence has been more enduring than
that of articulating America's uniqueness.

In this as in many other instances, Alexis de Tocqueville, the
brilliant young French visitor of the 1830s, helps us to understand ourselves in the context of comparative history. He observed that Americans were not tied together by an "instinctive
patriotism," like the peoples of Europe, but by a "patriotism
of reflection." The one bond was given and historic; the other
was expressed and ideological. Wherever he traveled in the
United States, Tocqueville explained (and complained),
Americans would tell him that they constituted the world's
only democratic nationality.[1]

Innumerable foreign travelers and foreign scholars subsequently testified to the continuing validity of Tocqueville's insight. In the 1920s Lord Bryce noted that Canada was as
much a democracy as America, yet unlike the Americans the
Canadians did not make their attachment to democracy "a
self-assertive, obtrusive, gesticulative part of the national consciousness." A quarter-century later, in his monumental study
of the Negro problem, Gunnar Myrdal attributed to Americans
a "peculiar brand of nationalism": namely, a quasi-religious
devotion to democratic values, which the Swedish social scientist called "The American Creed."[2]

46

All this makes the national identity sound abstract, but Americans *have been abstract*, time and again, in saying what kind of people they are and ought to be. When they proclaimed their independence from England, they linked themselves to a philosophy of universal rights. Four score and seven years later, amidst the fratricidal bloodletting of the 1860s, they renewed the covenant of "a new nation, conceived in Liberty, and dedicated to the proposition that all men are created equal." During the Great Depression of the 1930s, they reaffirmed their "rendezvous with destiny." In the more recent past, they have assembled committees and conferences and commissions to formulate the American goals, the American mission, the American purpose, the American style, the American civil religion, the American idea—in short, to articulate what it meant to be an American.

Tocqueville and Bryce and Myrdal were right—the self-assertive patriotism of reflection is a peculiar brand of nationalism. It locked the American people into a two-centuries-long dialogue with themselves about the meaning and implementation of their distinguishing idea. The history of the United States has therefore been a history, in large measure, of continuing self-examination, with periods of self-adulation mixed with bouts of self-criticism and even self-flagellation, and of recurring appeals for self-renewal.

Communist countries also define themselves ideologically, but America differs from them in at least two respects. For one thing, unlike China, Poland, Bulgaria, or other Marxian polities with a relatively homogeneous population, American nationality has nothing to do with an earlier folk identity. It is purely ideological. For another, the United States is from 140 to 175 years older than the Communist nation-states. As a result, the Americans have been self-conscious for a much longer time about their distinctive creed.

The key to the process is the Revolutionary generation, which initiated the national dialogue and established the foundations of the American identity.

## Who Were Our Romulus and Remus?

To the founders of the Republic, the American Revolution was a transforming experience. It brought about a separation from the parent country, the creation of a unique and independent polity, and a conviction among Americans that they were a special breed of men. Looking back on those radical changes, Thomas Jefferson, just elected President of the United States, exclaimed: "We can no longer say there is nothing new under the sun. For this whole chapter in the history of man is new."[3]

Jefferson was typical of his contemporaries. No more than he did they foresee in the 1760s that the quarrel with England over taxes would end a quarter-century later with the drafting and the adoption of the Constitution. The result was an extraordinarily self-conscious nationalism. "Before the establishment of the American States," Jefferson wrote in 1801, "nothing was known to history but the man of the old world."[4]

The words are clear, but the meaning behind them is puzzling. The Revolutionary generation founded a nation-state without the then traditional prerequisites for nationhood. Americans did not occupy a territory "naturally" their own. They did not look back on a long history whose beginnings shaded off into legend. They did not share an ancient folklore in the oral or written tradition. They did not belong to the same church. Above all, the Americans did not descend from a common stock.[5]

Alexis de Tocqueville had such considerations in mind when he remarked that the United States lacked the roots of an instinctive patriotism. "Picture to yourself . . . if you can, a society," he wrote to a European friend, unlike any society in the Old World. The Americans were not held together by such emotional ties as ancient memories, ancient habits, ancient prejudices, ancient heroes, an ancient dynasty, an ancient faith, or ancient attachments to place. And picture, too, Tocqueville added, "a society formed from all the nations of the world."[6]

The assumption that eighteenth-century America was ethnically homogeneous is false. The English were, of course, the largest stock. They were also the most influential, and it would be hard to overstate the importance, then or now, of the English language, of English law, of English religious ideas, and of English political ideals and institutions. All the same, the English were not—nor were they destined to be—the parent stock of the American people as a whole.

Since this is a statistical matter, statistics are in order. Of the 3,929,000 inhabitants enumerated in the first census of 1790, the English and their descendants constituted just under half the population. The next largest group—from Africa— accounted for close to 20 percent. Almost a third or so consisted of persons of Scotch-Irish, German, Scottish, French, Irish, Swiss, Spanish, Dutch, and still other origins.[7]

The same stocks were represented in the 250,000 inhabitants of the British colonies in 1700, and it would therefore seem that the population had been pluralist as early as the seventeenth century. It was not, because of a lopsided proportion of groups to each other. Except for scattered ethnic pockets (eighteen different languages were spoken in seventeenth-century New York City), the British settlements in 1700, stretching in a thin, broken line along the Atlantic seaboard, were almost wholly English in birth or derivation.

Things changed in the decades after the Treaty of Utrecht of 1713. With France and Britain no longer at war in the New World, a huge migration set in from Europe. Concurrently, an extraordinary increase took place in the importation of African slaves. Even the best colonial statistics are extrapolations from a variety of sources, but it is safe to say that, between 1700 and 1775, at least two and a half times as many people came to America as the 250,000 who had lived there in 1700. More significantly still, although the English were among the newcomers, they were outnumbered by the combined arrivals from Ireland, Germany, Scotland, Wales, France, Switzerland, and Africa. By the time of the Revolution, "the English homogeneity of the colonies had been decisively broken."[8]

But the resulting heterogeneity varied from one part of the colonies to another. New England's population, relatively unaffected by the eighteenth-century migrations from continental

Europe, non-English Britain, and Africa, remained the most English into the Revolutionary period. The most multiethnic areas were Pennsylvania, the Carolinas, and the 600-mile-long southern backcountry. New York fell between the two extremes, although its principal city was well on the way toward becoming the major symbol of New World cosmopolitanism. With tragic consequences for the future, in the eastern parts of the South a population took shape that was not mixed but dual—English and African.

The inner life of the eighteenth-century mosaic has received much less attention from historians than its geographical contours. Then as now, though, religious pluralism accompanied ethnic pluralism. Immigrant groups transplanted their churches, challenging the religious hegemony that the English had enjoyed in the seventeenth century. By 1775, as a result of the shift in the sources of immigration, the number of non-English houses of worship was equal to those in the Anglican and Congregational denominations.[9]

In 1776 a committee appointed by the Continental Congress proposed that the Great Seal include a symbol for the major lands from which the American people had originated. New Englanders might think that "God . . . made none but New England folks," wrote a Pennsylvanian, but it was common knowledge that a Maryland signer of the Declaration descended from an old Irish family; that most of Pennsylvania's general officers in the War of Independence were foreigners; that three Continental Congress presidents bore French Huguenot names; that a major architect of the Constitution had been born in Scotland; that Hamilton's successor as Secretary of the Treasury had immigrated to America from Switzerland. Even that great Virginian of universal principles, Thomas Jefferson, thought it of some importance to point out, at the beginning of his autobiography, that he was Welsh on his father's side. Despite an English preponderance, the founders were a mixed lot, and knew it.

But not as mixed, it has been argued, as a mere enumeration of different stocks would imply. At the end of the nineteenth century it became the fashion to say, in some circles, that white Americans at the time of the Revolution belonged to branches of a common "Nordic race." By the 1920s that contention provided a rationale for immigration legislation that favored northern European stocks. The laws were repealed in the 1960s, but the idea they embodied is not quite dead. Today even learned men sometimes refer to eighteenth-century white Americans as WASPs, the currently fashionable but pejorative acronym for white Anglo-Saxon Protestants.

The question at hand, however, is not the picture that later generations have had of the Revolutionary generation, but how that generation identified itself. The term Nordic was unknown to Americans in the eighteenth century. Nor did they designate themselves Anglo-Saxons, Anglo-Saxon Protestants, or white Anglo-Saxon Protestants. Those categories of speech also came into use later in American history.

Some founders may have thought in such terms before they were coined. In urging fellow New Yorkers to ratify the Constitution of the United States, John Jay wrote in the *Federalist* (1788): "Providence has been pleased to give this one connected country to one united people—a people descended from the same ancestors."[10] He could have believed this last, but one wonders if he was not carried away by a debator's zeal. Jay's paternal grandfather was a French Huguenot immigrant, and his Knickerbocker mother a Van Cortlandt.

Other leaders of the Revolutionary generation made careful, even invidious distinctions among northern Europeans in America. Alarmed by the huge German influx in Pennsylvania, Benjamin Franklin scorned the newcomers as "the most ignorant Stupid Sort of their own Nation" and warned his fellow English that the Germans "will soon . . . out number us." Charles Lee, equally disturbed by the mixed but heavily Ulsterized back settlements in Virginia, referred contemptuously to that frontier as a "Mac-ocracy" in which the reigning group was "a banditti of low Scotch-Irish whose names usually begin with Mac." Sentiments like Franklin's and Lee's were by no means unusual before the Revolution.[11]

But as independence approached, ethnic diversity was celebrated for making America unique. Of some four hundred pamphlets published in the decade and a half leading up to the Revolution, Tom Paine's *Common Sense* (1776) was the most widely read and the most influential. In it Paine asserted: "Europe, and not England, is the parent country of America." A few years later, in a work also admired, J. Hector St. John de Crèvecoeur, a naturalized New Yorker, gave praise to "that strange mixture of blood, which you will find in no other country." Neither Paine nor Crèvecoeur traced the mixture to a homogenizing genetic source in northern Europe. "This new world hath been the asylum for the persecuted lovers of civil and religious liberty from"—Paine italicized his point—"*every part* of Europe."[12]

It has been said that Paine and Crèvecoeur were unrepresentative. In a generation of sober nation-builders, the argument goes, both men were romantic propagandists. Further, neither was a native American, Paine fell from favor in the 1790s, and Crèvecoeur even earlier when he rejected the patriotic cause and returned to his native France in 1780. Nevertheless, their understanding that white Americans were a "promiscuous breed," not a common northern European folk, meshes with evidence from an unimpeachable source.

The quietly stated observations of David Ramsay, the best contemporary historian of the American Revolution, merit attention. Born in New Jersey in 1749 of Scottish Presbyterian parents, Ramsay settled in Charleston, South Carolina, after being educated at Princeton. He "was far superior to any person we ever graduated at our college," Benjamin Rush said of him. Ramsay was a physician by trade, but like many other learned men of the Enlightenment, he was a jack-of-all-trades. He took part in the affairs of his adopted state, representing South Carolina in the Continental Congress, and was also well known as a writer of biography and history.

In tracing the history of South Carolina, Ramsay called attention to "a medley of different nations" that had peopled the state. He made much of their differences. The Germans, for example, farmers almost to a man, enriched South Carolina's agriculture through "the virtues of industry and economy." The more urbanized and better educated Scots, in contrast, provided the state with a disproportionate number of writers, "physicians, clergymen, lawyers, and schoolmasters."

The question of who joined or opposed the movement for independence and why fascinated Ramsay. The most important variables were income, region, age, and ethnic background. With regard to this last, Ramsay observed that his own Scots tended to be tories; the Scotch-Irish patriots; and the Germans "rather passive than active" supporters of the break with Great Britain. As for the English, the most ardent patriots among them were seldom immigrants or the children of immigrants, Ramsay wrote. They were most often third- and fourth- and fifth- and sixth-generation Americans, in whom time, distance, and New World conditions had eroded the ancestral tie to the parent country.[13]

We shall probably never know with statistical exactitude just how many Americans shared Ramsay's multiethnic view. Place of residence strongly affected perceptions. The founders who most often equated Americans with English origins were New Englanders, whose region was the most homogeneously English in eighteenth-century America. Elsewhere, as is clear from the testimony of New Yorkers, Pennsylvanians, Virginians, and Carolinians, leaders of the Revolutionary generation recognized that their new society had been peopled by a medley of different nations.

All this means that when the Americans founded a nation-state and proclaimed their common peoplehood, they could not claim a common ethnic descent. Their past had denied to them, and to their posterity as well, that kind of nationalizing cement. "For who was our father and our mother?" Herman Melville asked in 1849, after listing the different stocks that had formed the American people and were still forming it. "Or can we point to any Romulus and Remus for our founders?" The New York writer summed up an enduring fact in the American experience when he remarked: "Our ancestry is lost in the universal paternity."

But if that was so, what, then, was American about the Americans?

## An Etymological Note

Melville's answer was something of a non-answer. "Settled by the people of all nations," he wrote, America is "not a nation, so much as a world." According to the then conventional usage of the word nation, Melville was etymologically correct. The word is of Latin origin, deriving from the past participle of the verb *to be born*, and for centuries had meant race—in other words, a human group sprung from the same genetic source. Melville must have had that usage in mind when he declared that the Americans did not form a nation; "for unless we may claim all the world for our sire, like Melchisidec, we are without father or mother."[14]

But even while Melville was writing, experience had been expanding the meaning of nation. Modern dictionaries, reflecting the history of nationalism during the past two centuries, have added to the common-origins definition of nation: "the people of territory united under a single government; country; state." In that respect, Melville was less perceptive of the modern world, which had been emerging in his own country, than his contemporary Walt Whitman. To the poet of democracy, America was "the Nation of many nations."

That phrase has been repeated so often, sometimes in the original but usually in one variant or another of it, that it has become one of the staler platitudes in the national vocabulary. Yet it is well to keep in mind that a platitude is a profundity taken for granted, and that when first expressed some profundities sounded absurd. Whitman's was one of them. To men who represented the conventional wisdom of his day, like Melville, the idea that America could be a nation of many nations was a contradiction in terms.

But the American poet's turn of speech obscured a major historical problem, and for its formulation we must return to Alexis de Tocqueville.

The French visitor, coming from a country where few ethnic differences existed, was immediately struck by the multiple origins of the American people. But that observation was merely the starting point for his inquiry into America's singularity. If America is uniquely multiethnic, he reasoned, it also must be unique in the social alchemy through which it transmuted diversity into unity. What was the "connecting link," asked Tocqueville, in America's variegated population? "How are they welded," he wanted to know, "into one people?"[15]

And so we are back to the puzzle with which we started. Americans established a nation-state, at the end of the eighteenth century, before they constituted a nation as that term was once understood. The source of their nationality has since intrigued students of comparative nationalisms; more important, it was central to what the founders thought their movement was all about. For whatever else the Revolution entailed, it required the leaders to state what kind of people they and their countrymen were. Crèvecoeur summed up the issue in 1782. After commenting on "that strange mixture of blood, which you will find in no other country," he asked: "What then is the American, this new man?"[16]

## The American as Idealized Citizen

The founders' answer was ideological. Crèvecoeur himself, although opposed to independence, described the American as "a new man, who acts upon new principles . . . new ideas . . . new opinions." Revolutionary leaders made the same point in one way or another. In a long and tendentious work published in 1792, Joel Barlow argued that what Americans think is what Americans are. An ideological answer was the only sort possible to the then youngest country in the Western world. The ✳ Americans could not claim an ancestral land, a long history, an old folklore, a common church, or the same progenitors.

Recognizing that their countrymen were not a nation in the then traditional sense, the founders used the word "people" when they referred to Americans in their collectivity. In the Declaration of Independence, Jefferson justified the necessity "for one People to dissolve the Political Bands which have connected them with another." Similarly, the Preamble to the Con-

stitution reads: "WE THE PEOPLE of the United States . . ." A
quarter-century later, in a retrospective look at the origins of
the Revolution, John Adams traced them to "the Minds of the
People."[17]

Is it possible, too, that the eighteenth-century architects of
the United States preferred the word people to nation because
nation was too static in its connotation for their purpose? A
nation was then regarded as the sum, and therefore as the
custodian and the captive, of its parochial past. The people,
in contrast, were unfettered and dynamic, endowed with the
power to choose and to change, to break the crust of custom if
need be and to shape the future. A nation *was* history; the
people *made* history.

Such attributes of will were essential to the Revolutionary
mind. What we think, Joel Barlow said, is what we are—and
dare to become. The people chose, in 1776, "to assume among
the Powers of the Earth . . . [a] separate and equal Station."
Six years later Tom Paine informed a French correspondent:
"We are now really another people."[18] In 1787–88, at still another turning point, the people decided to "form a more perfect
Union," by ordaining and establishing a new constitution.

In addition to will, the people were invested with rights, deriving from God, Nature, or Law. The Declaration stated
that, by right, the American people ought to be independent.
As for the Constitution, it actually contained a *Bill of Rights*.
Together with other sections of the national charter, it defined
and enumerated the rights and privileges and liberties and
immunities that belonged to the people. Their supreme right
was the right of sovereign power.

What, then, was an American? To the eighteenth-century
founders, an American was a bundle of rights, freely chosen.

Fully to document how the national identity came to be expressed in that way would require telling the intellectual history
of the American Revolution from the 1760s through the
1780s. Happily, historians have already shown how the de-
velopments leading up to independence resulted in "a radical
idealization and conceptualization of the previous century and
a half of American experience"; and that the Constitution con-

solidated, through law, the ideological consensus that had evolved in the struggle against England.[19] More plainly, the Americans discovered what kind of people they were by having to say in what kind of society they believed.

The process of self-definition went on for close to thirty years. At critical points in the Revolution there was a need to convince public opinion, at home as well as abroad, of the legitimacy of the movement. The founders were learned men and drew on arguments from varied sources—biblical, classical, legal, Whiggish. Above all, they expressed themselves in the language of the eighteenth-century Enlightenment, proclaiming that the American people had been born free and meant to stay free through institutions of their own making.

Because of that kind of thinking, historians have remarked that, when compared to the French and Russian Revolutions, the American Revolution was "conservative." The insight is valid. The Americans did not start out to overthrow a reactionary regime, as did the French and the Russians, but to hold on to liberties they had long enjoyed in the then freest empire in the world. Indeed, from the beginning of the imperial crisis with the parent country in 1763 until the final rupture thirteen years later, the colonists were confident of devising a formula to safeguard their rights as Englishmen.

But if seen in another light—as the first successful anti-colonial movement in modern history—the American Revolution wrought its own kind of radical transformation. It broke the century-and-a-half-old hyphen in the Anglo-American identity, thereby releasing the full force of American nationalism. Thenceforth the Americans asserted, unambiguously and without qualification, that they constituted a new, distinct, indivisible nationality. Neither America nor the world has been the same since that root change in self-awareness.

Like everyone else who has ever claimed to be liberated from an old identity, the founders equated the past with folly, and themselves and their country with all that was good in the present and likely to be good in the future. The Great Seal of the United States, adopted in 1782, declared that America's independence had inaugurated "a new order of the ages"

(NOVUS ORDO SECLORUM). Even more epoch-making than the war, in the minds of the Revolutionary generation, was the making of the Constitution. One of its principal drafters, James Wilson, exclaimed that nothing like the American compact had been put together in the "six thousand years since the creation of the world."[20]

Had the Revolutionary leaders been ignorant men given to extravagant flights of speech, their rhetoric could be dismissed as the enthusiasm of Yahoos. But they were a learned lot, and also sober, hardheaded, and legal-minded. At a time when few persons went to college, more than half the delegates to the Constitutional Convention were college men. Wilson himself, trained in the classics and a lawyer by profession, attended three Scottish universities. He and his contemporaries prided themselves on their knowledge of history, especially the history of politics and government extending back to ancient times.

No, it was not due to ignorance—on the contrary, it was because they claimed to know the past through careful study—that the founders were certain that the United States was "without example in the world." When Jefferson said that America was "new under the sun," he also said that until the creation of the American Republic "nothing was known to history but the man of the old world." The us-them image contained in those words—the antithesis between the New and the Old Worlds—was fundamental to the national self-image. Americans were what Europeans were not and had never been.[21]

Revolutionary spokesmen were tireless in pointing out why that was so. Unlike Europe, which the founders homogenized into a bundle of evils, America stood for liberty, opportunity, religious toleration, balanced and representative government, equality before the law, and a better tomorrow for everyone. Above all, this side of the Atlantic defied the conventional wisdom that no nation could survive without the historic props of king, aristocracy, and established clergy. A republican people were themselves a sufficient source of authority.

Therein lay the heart of a transformed nationality. "A citizen of the *United States*," wrote David Ramsay in 1789, "means a member of this new nation." Formerly subjects of the British monarch, the Americans changed status through the republic they created. The effect, Ramsay went on to say, was radical to the extreme. "Subjects look up to a master, but citizens are so far equal, that none have hereditary rights superior to others."

The doctrine of citizen-rule legitimized both the War of Independence and the foundations of the American state. It denied the principle, in which even Whigs believed, that the sovereign power resided in the throne. More profoundly, in the name "of reason and philosophy," it rejected the whole hierarchical view of mankind. The "political condition of citizens is more exalted than that of noblemen," explained Ramsay. "Dukes and earls are the creatures of kings, and may be made by them at pleasure: but citizens possess in their own right original sovereignty."[22]

The polarity that the founders saw between America and Europe was reinforced from two sources: an inherited sense of mission and contemporary foreign opinion of the Revolution.

In the previous century of colonization, settlers had also described the New and Old Worlds in terms of opposites. More than that, the Puritans set out for New England with the conviction that God had chosen them to regenerate, by example, Europe's false and dying forms of Christianity. The Reformation-derived sense of mission continued into the 1700s. Jonathan Edwards, who believed that the Second Coming was at hand and would take place on this side of the Atlantic, wrote that God had designated America as "the glorious renovator of the world."

But the eighteenth century was a secularizing century, and Edwards's more earthbound contemporaries gave the inherited messianic complex a special twist. John Adams, who a generation or so earlier would have become a minister instead of a lawyer, put it this way in 1765: "I always consider the settlement of America with Reverence and Wonder—as the Opening of a grand scene and Design in Providence for the Illumination of the Ignorant and Emancipation of the slavish Part of Mankind all over the Earth." Salvation for men like Adams took on a this-worldly meaning.

After independence and the adoption of the Constitution, Revolutionary leaders were even more assertive about their country's redemptive power. If the American nation-state fulfilled the universal principles of the Enlightenment, then the American way was valid for all human beings. "A just and solid republican government maintained here," declared President Jefferson, "will be a standing monument and example for the aim and imitation of the people of other countries."[23]

That national self-regard was reflected with mirror-like accuracy in liberal opinion abroad. "A great revolution has happened," wrote a British Whig, "—a revolution made, not by chopping and changing of power in any of the existing states, but by the appearance of a new state, of a new species, in a new part of the globe."[24] More flattering still, in France and then in Ireland, Norway, Sweden, Belgium, and Latin America, reformers and revolutionaries undertook, in varying degrees, to remake their countries according to the American model. To the far-flung parties of the Enlightenment, the United States was a beacon of freedom for still unliberated societies.

Such praise ratified the national identity that the Revolutionary generation had articulated for their infant republic. Declaring themselves to be the freest society known to history, the Americans heard from foreign admirers that they were indeed so. Seldom have a people received as good a press as did the Americans in the eighteenth century. Forced by their Revolution to define their better selves, they expressed their specialness in terms that appealed to humanitarian opinion the world around.


## The Consequences of the Broken Hyphen

Once articulated, the national identity took on a religious character, with its own symbols, holidays, holy texts, sermons, music, sainted heroes, relics, and shrines. A living faith, its forms evolved over time. "The Star-Spangled Banner" dates from the War of 1812; "The pledge to the Flag" from 1892;

the Jefferson Memorial from 1943. Yet these and all other post–eighteenth-century expressions derived from, and reinforced, the Revolutionary foundations of American nationality. The earliest cults centered upon the "Glorious Fourth" and "godlike Washington." They were related, because the Revolutionary generation linked the birth of the Republic to the "Father of His Country." Washington commanded the Continental Armies in the War of Independence, presided over the Constitutional Convention, headed the new instrument of government as its first President, and then retired to private life with republican simplicity. Three years before his death in 1799, Congress made his birthday a national holiday.

Washington's achievements were formidable, yet in turning him into a symbol for the Republic his contemporaries endowed him with a stature both larger and purer than life. "If there are spots in his character, they are like the spots in the sun, only discernible by the magnifying powers of a telescope," rhapsodized the *Pennsylvania Journal.* "Begin with the infant in the cradle; let the first word he lisps be Washington," urged Noah Webster, the leading schoolmaster among the founders. "O Washington! How I do love thy name! . . . great ornament of human kind!" exclaimed the president of Yale. ". . . Thy fame is of sweeter perfume than Arabian spices. Listening angels shall catch the odor, waft it to heaven, and perfume the universe!"

The adoration of Washington in newspapers, poems, plays, sermons, paintings, oratory, biography, and schoolbooks was too much for John Adams. "The history of our Revolution will be one continued lie from one end to the other," he protested. "The essence of the whole will be that Dr. Franklin's electric rod smote the earth and out sprang General Washington." Yet even Adams, jealous of his own role in the Revolution, admitted: "I glory in the character of a Washington, because I know him to be . . . an exemplification of the American character."[25]

More to Adams's liking was the commemoration of Independence Day. In 1783 his own Boston became the first community to designate July 4 an official holiday; shortly thereafter the custom took root in other localities. Feasting, sports, fireworks, and parades made the Fourth a joyous occasion, but two rituals reminded the people of its seriousness. The first was a public reading of the Declaration of Independence, and the second was the delivery of a sermon-like oration. Hundreds of orations delivered during the first eighty years of the Republic read alike. They celebrated America's devotion to liberty, traced its culmination in the Revolution, and urged the people to keep the national faith.[26]

The cults of Washington and the Declaration lost ground to those of Lincoln and the Constitution as a result of the Civil War. Lincoln gave his life, according to the litany, to save the Union based on the Constitution. His contemporaries attached a particular significance to his assassination because of when it happened. He was shot on Thursday night but died the next morning on Good Friday, following Lee's surrender to Grant at Appomattox the previous Palm Sunday. Funeral sermons on Easter called attention, with awe, to parallel events that had transpired in the ancient Holy Land. To the American word had been added a prairie-bred Christlike figure.[27]

To date the crucified Lincoln is still a more religious yet more human symbol than the majestic Washington. Perhaps the difference between the Washington Monument and the Lincoln Memorial, the one dedicated in 1884 and the other in 1922, is due merely to a difference in architectural eras. Whatever the reason, the monument is abstract, without a graven image, whereas the memorial is a shrine, its interior dominated by a gigantic statue of the brooding savior, and adorned with inscribed tablets of his most stirring words. Four years after it was opened to the public, the Secretary of Interior pronounced the Lincoln Memorial consecrated ground.

Although no day has been set aside for it as the Fourth of July has been for the Declaration, the Constitution has received its share of veneration. At the climax of the centennial observance in 1887, held in Independence Hall under the fabled Liberty Bell, President Grover Cleveland paid homage to "this ark of the people's covenant" and called upon his countrymen to remain steadfast in "their sacred trust" to protect it from "impious hands." Such sentiments continued into the next century, so that in 1907 the Harvard historian Albert Bushnell Hart reported: "There is a national reverence for the Federal Constitution akin to that of earlier generations for the Scriptures."

Professor Hart understated the case. Just before World War I a leader of the New York bar declared in utter seriousness:

> "Our great and sacred Constitution," sang this twentieth century David, "serene and inviolable, stretches its beneficent powers over our land—over its lakes and rivers and forests, over every mother's son of us, like the outstretched arm of God himself . . . the people of the United States, creating the first constitutional government ever created, created also a judiciary . . . the people ordained and established one Supreme Court—the most rational, considerate, discerning, veracious, impersonal power—the most candid, unaffected, conscientious, incorruptible power —a power peculiar and unique in the history of the world. . . . O Marvellous Constitution! Magic Parchment! Transforming word! Maker, Monitor, Guardian of Mankind! Thou hast gathered to thy impartial bosom the peoples of the earth, Columbia, and called them equal. . . . I would fight for every line in the Constitution as I would fight for every star in the flag.[28]

That kind of language went out of fashion after World War I, but the spell of the Constitution remained. Franklin D. Roosevelt discovered that fact in the 1930s when he tried to pack the Supreme Court. In the following decade Charles Beard, who had earlier demythologized the Constitution in a monograph on the economic motives of its framers, wrote a stirring defense of their work as "a prophecy of the Republic for the ages."[29] More recently, Watergate revealed that not even a President elected by an unprecedented landslide can tamper with the Highest Law of the Land. The eighteenth-century legacy lives on.

Its hold on the national imagination stands out all the more when America is compared to Canada, Australia, and New Zealand.[30] Like the United States, they are independent, self-governing, representative, modern democracies. Canada and Australia are also like America in that each is a federal union of states; Australia actually modeled its constitution (1901) along the lines of America's. Yet, despite these and other similarities to the United States, none of the three countries has created a patriotic religion out of democracy.

Lord Bryce made that point fifty years ago, and it is still true today. There is no Canadian, Australian, or New Zealand creed based on the Enlightenment. Nor are there any symbols, rituals, myths, or cults in the three countries comparable to those that developed in America. The Australians, Canadians, and New Zealanders read no Declaration of Independence on a Glorious Fourth; recite no Gettysburg Address to remind themselves of an Ordeal of Union; sanctify no native worthies in hagiography and monument; flock to no Freedom Train; and revere no magic parchment, ark, or covenant.

Why not?

None of the three Commonwealth nations has a revolutionary tradition. To prevent another rebellion like the one in the thirteen colonies, Britain granted self-government, then *de facto* and later *de jure* dominion status, to its Canadian, Australian, and New Zealand colonies. Because they did not fight a long anti-colonial war to become independent and united, as did America, they do not view the founding of their respective states as an event that fulfilled their highest national ideals. On the contrary, as an Australian authority has written, "the state . . . expresses no ideals at all."[31] It is simply an instrument to get some things done.

Each of the three Commonwealth nations has its own national legends. The Australians, for example, although an urban people from the start, have idealized the pastoral worker.[32] More important, as a result of participating in World Wars I and II, each of the three Commonwealth nations has developed a keen sense of where it stands among the peoples of the globe. If a foreigner asks a Canadian, Australian, or New Zealander what he is, the answer will be, unambiguously, Canadian, Australian, or New Zealander.

Yet the umbilical cord to the mother country remains. "God Save the Queen" is still sung in the three countries. Their sovereign is still the British monarch. The feeling of being British—a special kind of British but British all the same—is particularly deep among New Zealanders. Where Canadian nationalism is strong, it is usually directed not against England, but against the United States. Even at this late date the only morning newspaper in Victoria, British Columbia, is called *The Daily Colonist.*

Australia has been undergoing a movement for a separate nationality since the Whitlam government took office in 1972. Its objectives include an Australian flag, an Australian anthem, an Australian image, and an Australian bill of rights (a feature that the Australians in 1901 did not borrow from the American Constitution for their own). Thus far the movement has foundered on the hyphen in the Anglo-Australian identity. Even adults receptive to the surge of national self-awareness cannot forget that as children they used to start the school day reciting:

> I love my country
>      the British Empire
> I salute her flag
>      the Union Jack
> I promise cheerfully
>      to obey her laws.

In 1974 the federal parliament adopted "Advance Australia Fair" as a new national anthem, but some state governments defiantly retained "God Save the Queen." Actually, the proposed anthem was not as radical a break with the mother country as the title implies. Two stanzas delighted in the sun and soil and sea and sons of Australia, but the other two stanzas read as follows:

> When gallant Cook from Albion sailed
> To trace wide oceans o'er
> True British courage bore him on
> 'Till he landed on our shore,
> Then here he raised Old England's flag,

The standard of the brave;
With all her faults we love her still,
Britannia rules the wave.
In joyful strains then let us sing
Advance Australia Fair. . . .

Should foreign foe e'er sight our coast
Or dare a foot to land,
We'll rouse to arms like sires of yore
To guard our native strand.
Britannia then shall surely know
Beyond wide ocean's roll
Her sons in fair Australia's land
Still keep a British soul.
In joyful strains then let us sing
Advance Australia Fair.

*British soul*—the only white colonies to cut out from the British Empire besides America were the Irish Free State in 1922 and the Union of South Africa in 1961. Like the Afrikaners, the Irish differed from the English in religion, culture, history, ethnic descent, and ancestral language. Further, although quitting the Commonwealth after enjoying dominion status, the Irish and the Afrikaners nourished bitter memories of British oppression. To become non-British, in short, one first had to be anti-British.

This last was hardly the case on this side of the Atlantic before the imperial crisis developed in the 1760s. The colonists there held no serious political, economic, cultural, or religious grievances against the home government. On the contrary, they were proud to belong to an empire they thought the most enlightened as well as the most powerful in their day. The term American was coming into vogue, but even so the colonists still regarded themselves, including those of non-British descent, as being Americans living under British rule. On top of everything else, there was a strong emotional attachment to the king.

Transcolonial ties, in contrast, were weak. The thirteen colonies each had their own histories, and it was not uncommon to say that one's "country" was Virginia, Massachusetts, or South Carolina. That sense of separateness countered a growing awareness, by the mid-eighteenth century, that Americans shared a new way of life in a new land. When the Albany Congress of 1754 proposed a defense league against the French and Indians, colonial legislatures did not feel sufficient kinship to ratify the plan.[33]

Perhaps John Adams exaggerated the obstacles to national unity in order to magnify the achievement of his generation, but in 1818 he remembered the lack of cohesion as follows:

> The colonies had grown up under constitutions of government so different, there was so great a variety of religions, they were composed of so many different nations, their customs, manners, and habits, had so little resemblance, and their intercourse had been so rare, and their knowledge of each other so imperfect, that to unite them in the same principles in theory and the same system of action, was certainly a very difficult enterprise.[34]

Americans therefore were reluctant revolutionaries. No sentiment for independence existed until Parliament, in the 1760s, tightened the screws on the colonies in order to make them pay their share of the expense for the French and Indian War of the previous decade. Indeed, as late as 1774, Jefferson and Franklin and their contemporaries on this side of the Atlantic, together with Burke and Whigs of his sort on the other, hoped for an arrangement that Britain later adopted for Canada, Australia, and New Zealand. Under its terms the Americans would have had a parliament of their own, but they would have stayed in the Empire, loyal to the monarch.

Only after fighting broke out—and even then fifteen months intervened between Concord and Independence—did events take an irrevocable turn. The Americans gave up on the home country and, in an even more psychologically painful wrench, on the king. By then they also possessed a new nationality, invented by the evolving logic of Revolutionary ideology. Unlike the Canadians, Australians, and New Zealanders, the Americans were forced to break the historic hyphen in their Anglo-American identity.

## The What-Is and the What-Ought-To-Be

"It has been our fate as a nation," Richard Hofstadter remarked, "not to have ideologies but to be one."[35] He summed up a consensus among students of American nationality. The tie that has united Americans is not ancestry, soil, church, soul, or folk; it is civic belief, what Crèvecoeur called *principles*, Tocqueville *reflections*, Bryce *self-assertions*, and Myrdal *creed*.

Given the character of the American Revolution, the bond could hardly have been otherwise. "In its very origin as a nation," wrote Hans Kohn, "the United States was the embodiment of an idea." More than that, the United States was "the first nation to identify itself and to have been identified by others with an idea." The idea stated that a people of diverse origins shared a common attachment to the values and institutions of free society.[36]

Still a force of considerable power, that idea makes Americans the most eighteenth-century people in the world today. Ideologically, in other words, the United States has been the land of the enduring Enlightenment. But as much as individuals, countries often confuse what ideally they wish to be with what they really are. We must therefore distinguish between the prescriptive and descriptive parts of the national identity.

When the Revolutionary generation upheld America's uniqueness, they thought they were describing the country as it actually was. Up to a point, they were correct to think so. In contrast to the Old World, America enjoyed more liberty, more opportunity, more religious toleration, more representative government, and so on across the spectrum of approved eighteenth-century values. More so than in Europe, in short, the American Enlightenment was rooted in reality.

But far from completely so. The person at the center of the touted American identity was the republican citizen, yet neither women nor blacks participated in the full rights of citizenship. The dilemma was there for anyone to see. As Mrs. John Adams wrote to her husband in 1776: "I can not say that I think you very generous to the Ladies, for whilst you are proclaiming peace and good will to Men, Emancipating all Nations, you insist upon retaining an absolute power over Wives."[37] Blacks made the identical point in regard to themselves.

Had there been no prescriptions, though, there could have been no contradictions. The founders established the country's standards, goals, aspirations, what later generations would call the American dream and the American creed, the conscience of America and its civil religion. By whatever name, the prescriptive side of the national identity was an antidote to the complacency of the descriptive. In equating America with an idea—more accurately, with a cluster of ideals—the Revolutionary generation insured that their posterity would be in search of themselves as they ought to be.

George Santayana, who lived on the margins of the American experience, summed it up well in 1920: "To be an American is of itself almost a moral condition." Woodrow Wilson, who placed himself at the heart of the national identity, declared, "Sometimes people call me an idealist. Well, that is the way I know I am an American. . . . America is the only idealistic Nation in the world."[38]

That kind of rhetoric puts off a lot of people today. It was a refuge for scoundrels, charlatans, demagogues, and misguided interventionists in foreign countries. Yet the identification of America with idealism—with promises—has also nourished every genuine reform movement in the history of this country, from the disestablishment of state churches in the half-century after independence to the latest efforts to make the panoply of American rights cover one and all.

Thus almost two hundred years after a Virginia slaveholder wrote the Declaration, a charismatic black civil rights leader intoned: "I still have a dream. It is a dream deeply rooted in the American dream. I have a dream that one day this nation will rise up and live out the true meaning of its creed: 'We hold these truths to be self-evident, that all men are created equal.' "[39]

Invariably, the prescriptive side of the American identity leads back to the eighteenth century—America's Calvary. Martin Luther King, Jr., was saying that, under the terms of the original national compact, every American *ought* to enjoy the rights of the most prized citizenship in the world. He also reminded his countrymen that there can be no rest for a people who have inherited a moral mission. Like Bunyan's Pilgrim, with the Book in his hand and a burden on his back, the American is obliged to carry out a large historical purpose. That is a special kind of identity.

It fell to the United States, both through choice and the operation of forces outside its own territory, to receive tens of millions of immigrants. Their coming tested the professed universality of American nationality. To see how the country met the challenge, we must again begin with the Revolutionary generation. They founded America's immigration and naturalization policies.

# 4 Immigrants from Everywhere

Every country is free to determine the number and kind of immigrants it will take. The exercise of that sovereign power has affected not only the host society but the redistribution of the world's population during the past three centuries. Immigration policy also provides an index to the boundaries that various peoples have fixed to their respective nationalities. Some countries have restricted admission to religious and ethnic groups most like their own, whereas other countries have opened their doors for practically everyone to enter.

This last is what the Revolutionary generation chose to do. They thereby ratified experience under English imperial rule. The thirteen colonies were peopled by "a medley of different nations" because England, in contrast to Spain, Portugal, and France, allowed foreign nationals to settle in its New World possessions. Yet, with respect to the home island, England had been as unreceptive of immigrants as other European powers. The United States, after attaining its own sovereignty, was the first country to decide, as a matter of national policy, that it would be an immigrant-receiving country.

Next to Independence and the Constitution, that turned out to be the Revolutionary generation's most critical decision. Until its repeal by the Johnson-Reed Act, whose national-origins provisions went into effect in 1929, close to thirty-eight million immigrants entered the United States. Their variety made a people already varied in their origins fantastically more so. Through unrestricted immigration the United States grew to be, in fact as well as legend, the classic land of immigration.

The signs of that heritage are all around us. Our politics, economy, and foreign policies; our religions, arts, music, literature, and educational systems; our sports, entertainment, recreation, even the foods we eat—all testify, in some degree, to the great migrations of the nineteenth and twentieth centuries. Some scholars have ranked them as the prime mover in the making of America. Thus, in the introduction to his book on the subject, an eminent historian wrote: "Once I thought to write a history of the immigrants in America. Then I discovered that the immigrants *were* American history."[1]

Not everyone has shared that understanding of the national past. In the 1930s President Franklin D. Roosevelt thought it necessary to tell a convention of the Daughters of the American Revolution: "Remember, remember always, that all of us, and you and I especially, are descended from immigrants."[2] FDR would not have spoken to the DAR in that way had they agreed. Still other Americans, some for very good scholarly reasons, have rejected the interpretation that the history of the United States is *merely* a history of immigrants.

Yet there is no denying the importance of immigration for keeping alive the original formulation of the national identity. The absorption of tens of millions of newcomers, a process extending over the past two hundred years, raised the question time and again of what a person must do to *become* an American. The most persistent answer, inscribed in every naturalization law since the eighteenth century, is that one must identify with the founding ideals of the Republic.

Thanks to a gift from French liberals in 1886, that concept eventually acquired a symbol of mythological size. Towering 313 feet above the entrance to New York Harbor, the Statue of Liberty is the tallest statue ever built. The French presented it to commemorate Franco-American friendship dating from France's help in the War of Independence; but Americans attached an additional meaning to the monument, "Mother of Exiles," a meaning whose appeal gained special momentum after Congress closed the doors to immigration in the 1920s. By World War II, according to the New York *Times*, the Statue of Liberty had become "Our No. 1 Symbol." Since 1972 the pedestal has housed a shrinelike American Museum of Immigration.[3]

Like every symbol in America's civic religion, the statue's mythic power stems from what people chose to remember and honor from the past. The three things for which it stands, liberty, independence, refuge—more, its fusing the three into a single representation of the United States—reach back to the eighteenth century. The Revolutionary generation initiated the unprecedented policy of unrestricted immigration.

## Let Them Come

The policy followed logically from the universality of the Revolutionary ideology. Tom Paine sounded the keynote. "The old world is overrun with oppression," he declared in 1776; America therefore has the responsibility to "receive the fugitive, and prepare in time an asylum for mankind." Seven years later, in the year that the War of Independence officially ended, George Washington wrote: "The bosom of America is open to receive not only the Opulent and respectable Stranger, but the oppressed and persecuted of all Nations And Religions."[4] In 1790 Congress enacted the most liberal naturalization law then in existence.

There were other reasons besides ideological ones to be hospitable. America's vast expanse was underpopulated; immigrants would help to fill it. America's boundless resources were unexploited; immigrant skills and capital and manpower would contribute to developing them. The builders of the American nation-state were hardheaded men, governed by calculations of self-interest as well as idealism. Immigration promised to make the United States more populous, more wealthy, more powerful.[5]

In the end the case for unrestricted immigration rested on two related faiths. The first relied on the absorptive power of the host society, and the second supposed the adaptability of human beings. Both seemed reasonable to a generation that

believed the birth of their country had begun a New Order of
the Ages. *Taking for granted that America was mankind's
best hope, the founders were confident that immigrants of almost every background, once they chose to come here, would
assent to America's superiority and make its ways their ways.

That was the dominant faith, but there were doubters. We
need not linger over the haters of all things foreign; such hard-
nosed types belonged to an uninfluential minority. Nor need
we be detained by the Alien and Sedition Acts of 1798; those
Federalist party measures were no sooner placed on the statute
books than they were removed by the succeeding anti-
Federalist administration. Before long the Federalist party
would expire.

It was something else, however, when Thomas Jefferson
expressed doubts about immigration. Although committed to
the uniqueness of America, Jefferson was also an elegant
spokesman for the rights of mankind. As the principal drafter
of the Declaration of Independence, he had shown that one
could be both a nationalist and a universalist. Immigration
strained the connection between his two loyalties. Why that
was so, and how Jefferson resolved the tension, demand
attention.

In his *Notes on the State of Virginia* (1782), written while
America was still under the Articles of Confederation, Jefferson dissented from a widespread desire to increase the population through special inducements to immigration. The basis
for his objection was political—more accurately, it was ideological. "Every species of government has its specific principles," he wrote. "Ours perhaps are more peculiar than those
of any other in the universe." Most immigrants would come
from "absolute monarchies," Jefferson warned; and such persons were unlikely to accept the free principles of American
government. Worse still, immigrants would teach their children
the tyrannical maxims of government that they themselves had
"imbibed in their early youth." The safest policy for America,
Jefferson advised, was to let the population grow through
natural increase.

All the same, he drew back from proposing the restriction of mmigration. Jefferson was too much a man of the Enlightenment—too much the universalist—to give in to parochial fears. The natural-rights philosopher believed that human beings ought to be free to choose where they wanted to live. Let the immigrants come if they so desired, Jefferson concluded—but without "the expediency of inviting them by extraordinary encouragements." Hands off; laissez faire. That was precisely the policy that the federal government adopted under the Constitution.[6]

And so the immigrants came, wave after wave, each crest higher than the preceding one. That story has been told many times, but it's worth recalling not only the magnitude but the continuity and dispersion and variety of the peopling of America since the eighteenth century.

*The magnitude.* In 1820 the federal government began to count the number of immigrants annually admitted to the United States. Thanks to that practice, we have a reasonably accurate record of the volume of immigration over the past century and a half. At the beginning of the 1970s the total passed the forty-five million mark. Although easy to cite, the immensity of that statistic is hard for the human mind to grasp. It is sixteen times greater than America's population at the time of the Revolution. It is five times the number of people who now live in the eight Rocky Mountain states. Many good-sized countries—among them Canada and Poland—contain fewer than forty-five million inhabitants. That figure exceeds by far the combined populations of Sweden, Denmark, Norway, Israel, Ireland, and Czechoslovakia. The peopling of America during the nineteenth and twentieth centuries adds up to the largest migration in recorded history.

But fully to appreciate the magnitude of immigration to the United States, one must compare America's experience to that of the world's other major immigrant-receiving countries. The era of heaviest intercontinental migrations in modern times extended from the end of the Napoleonic Wars to the beginning of the Great Depression. From statistics for that period compiled by the countries of reception, scholars estimate that there were around sixty-two million immigrant arrivals. The United States received the greatest share: 60 percent. Its closest competitor, Canada, accounted for 11.5 percent. Other countries ranked as follows: Argentina 10.1 percent, Brazil 7.3 percent, Australia 4.5 percent, New Zealand 3 percent, and South Africa 2.2 percent.

Those are gross figures. To derive the net increase from immigration, one must subtract those immigrants who did not stay permanently. There were many returnees, four out of five in the case of some countries. Once again, for the period ending with the Great Depression, the United States registered the largest gain. Of the thirty-eight million immigrants who entered the United States between 1820 and 1930, twenty-six million took up permanent residence. America's net increase was therefore 70 percent, followed by Argentina's 53 percent, New Zealand's 22 percent, and Australia's 20 percent.[7]

More plainly, whether calculated by net or gross gain, America's intake surpassed the combined intake of all other immigrant-receiving countries.

*The continuity.* Because of the recent immigrant past of many Americans today there is a predisposition to identify immigration with this century. Yet, of the thirty-eight million immigrants between 1820 and 1930, half arrived before 1900. Just over five million entered prior to the Civil War; and by 1860 Boston's population was 36 percent foreign-born, Brooklyn's 39 percent, and New York's 48 percent. After the war, in the peak decade of the 1880s, the United States admitted 5,246,000 immigrants. By then the census takers were enumerating not only immigrants but their native-born children as well, and calling the two groups foreign stock. In 1890 the latter accounted for 68 percent of the people living in Boston, 71 percent in Brooklyn, and 80 percent in New York.

As a result of the restrictive policy of the 1920s followed by the Great Depression and World War II, immigration slowed to a trickle. Indeed, for some years in the 1930s more immigrants returned than entered. The flow resumed after the war, aided first by special legislation and then by the 1965 repeal of the 1920s laws. The proportion of entering immigrants to the American population since 1950 has been lower than the proportion for the era of unrestricted immigration; but the figure is by no means inconsequential. Between 1950 and 1970 the United States received 6,080,000 newcomers, exclusive of around a million Puerto Ricans, who, as United States citizens, were not enumerated in the official statistics as immigrants.[8]

*The dispersion.* Far from coming to rest in the East, the immigrant flow reached deep into America. In 1890, like many a city on the Atlantic seaboard, the proportion of foreign stock in San Francisco was 78 percent, in Salt Lake City 65 percent, in St. Louis 67 percent, in Duluth 75 percent, in Chicago 78 percent, and in Milwaukee 86 percent. Popular opinion does not usually associate immigration with Iowa, Nebraska, Idaho, or Washington, but in the decades after the Civil War the foreign stock in each of those states never fell below 35 percent. Immigrants and their American-born children at the end of the nineteenth century constituted an actual majority, not only in several states east of the Mississippi, but in Minnesota, the Dakotas, Montana, Arizona, Wyoming, Utah, Nevada, and California.

The story was much the same in the twentieth century. According to the 1920 census, Utah's foreign stock of 44 percent was around the same as Pennsylvania's; Minnesota's 65 percent was even higher than New Jersey's 58 percent. The state in 1920 with the highest proportion of foreign stock to its population was not, as one might guess, Rhode Island, Massachusetts, New York, or some other eastern industrial state—it was North Dakota, where only one person out of three was a native American of native American parentage.[9]

Only the race-torn southern states failed to attract a substantial number of nineteenth- and twentieth-century immigrants. In the 1930s well over half of America's three thousand counties contained multiethnic populations. The most homogeneous counties were located in the more inaccessible areas of the Rockies, Appalachians, Ozarks, and a strip that ran across the southern parts of Ohio, Indiana, and Illinois into Kansas and Missouri.[10]

The wide distribution of immigrants in the United States differs from the experience of other countries. Brazil is divided into twenty-two states, four territories, and a federal district; but between 1878 and 1937, 55 percent of its immigrants settled in the single state of São Paulo. Furthermore, almost half the immigrants to Brazil were from Italy and Spain, and 71 percent of the Italians and 78 percent of the Spanish concentrated in São Paulo. Canada, whose large stretches are still underpopulated, had a similar experience. The bulk of its immigrants from Britain and France took up residence, respectively, in the British and French regions of Canada.[11]

*The variety.* "You cannot spill a drop of American blood," wrote Herman Melville in 1849, "without spilling the blood of the whole world." Many migrations later in 1911, statisticians for the federal government reported that some sixty different ethnic groups lived all over the United States. Nor was it so very long ago, according to a reliable survey published in the 1920s, that there was an immigrant press of over a thousand newspapers in more than thirty different foreign languages. The people who read that press are removed from their current descendants by a mere one and two generations. Were Melville to come back to America today, he would find an even smaller fraction of the American people than in his own day who can point to the original settlers as their own Romulus and Remus.

Other major immigrant-receiving countries also have varied populations, but they have drawn their immigrants "disproportionately from a few favored ethnic backgrounds." As late as 1921, 83 percent of Canada's population came from two groups: the British and the French. Down through World War II, nine out of ten Australians were of English, Scottish, or Irish descent and birth. In a century of immigration, Brazil received three-fourths of its immigrants from Portugal, Spain, and Italy. The latter two countries alone provided Argentina with 76 percent of its newcomers.[12]

In the United States on the other hand, for the 150-year span between 1820 and 1970, only one country supplied as much as 15 percent of the immigrants. That country was Germany. To equal the percentage that Italy and Spain contributed to Argentina's immigration, we have to add seven other countries to Germany: Italy (11.4 percent), Britain (10.5 percent), Ireland (10.3 percent), Austria-Hungary (from which came a lot of different ethnic groups 9.4 percent), Canada (8.8 percent), the USSR (7.4 percent), and Mexico (3.6 percent). Two dozen and more countries accounted for the remaining 25 percent of the immigrants to the United States. If their percentages were small, their numbers were considerable. Sweden sent over 1,267,574 persons; Greece 588,160; the predominantly black West Indies 544,688; China 450,900; Japan, Turkey, Portugal, and Denmark each in excess of 350,000.[13]

Small wonder that the concern for identity persisted in the United States. In addition to the Revolutionary heritage of a nation earnestly in the making, the population mix changed so much and so often that Americans could never take for granted their alikeness. Unceasing immigration called for continuing reaffirmations of the eighteenth-century national compact.

## Kinship through Naturalization

Even while doubting the benefits of immigration in 1782, Jefferson was unequivocal in stating that immigrants who selected America as the new homeland were "entitled to all the rights of citizenship." His contemporaries agreed. Besides being just, a policy to that effect would attract immigrants, prevent the formation of an alien class, and carry out America's mission as an asylum. Above all, it would join the foreign- and native-born in a common American nationality.

Machinery to implement those objectives was defective. The Parliamentary Act of 1740 for the naturalization of aliens in the British colonies lapsed with Independence, and the various state naturalization laws bred confusion. Therefore, in 1787 the Philadelphia Convention authorized Congress, under Article I, Section 8, of the Constitution, "to establish an uniform Rule of Naturalization." Congress did so almost immediately.

The sole disagreement was over the residence requirement. The Naturalization Act of 1790 set it at two years, the Act of 1795 at five years, and the Act of 1798 at fourteen years. The last-named measure was punitive, for the majority Federalist party had devised it to limit the voting power and also to discourage the immigration of political refugees sympathetic both to the French Revolution and anti-Federalists. It was repealed by the opposition party in 1802, and the succeeding law remained in effect for over a century.

The 1802 Act restored the five-year residence requirement, a period judged sufficient for newcomers to familiarize themselves with American life, to show intent to remain here, and to demonstrate they were persons of "good moral character." Also, in reducing the probationary period from fourteen to five years, the founders hoped to make clear to the world that the United States welcomed immigrants. Shall "we refuse to the unhappy fugitives from distress that hospitality which the savages of the wilderness extended to our fathers arriving in this land?" asked President Jefferson in 1802. "Shall oppressed humanity find no asylum on this globe?"[14]

But if the naturalization process was meant to be quick and hospitable, it was also demanding. Before an alien could become an American citizen, he was required, "on oath or affirmation," to foreswear allegiance to "the prince, potentate, state, or sovereignty" of which he had been subject or citizen. Americans could have only one national loyalty. Toward that end, a candidate for citizenship had to declare, either on affirmation or oath, that he would "support the constitution of the United States." More than that, he was obliged to prove to the satisfaction of the presiding magistrate that he was "attached to the principles of the constitution." To become an American, in short, one had to be a republican. The requirement was so severe that an aristocratic candidate had to "make an express renunciation of his title or order of nobility."[15]

No other country of the time had a law like the Act of 1802. In England, whose jurisprudence the Americans knew well, naturalization was not a popular right administered by the nearest court but an occasional gift from the monarch bestowed through special parliamentary act. The proceedings were expensive, there was no residence requirement, and the only persons eligible were Protestants who could take the sacraments in the Church of England.

All that and more reflected not only the English Reformation but England's feudal past. Naturalization did not bestow citizenship; all Englishmen, the native-born as well as the naturalized, were subjects of the monarch. It was to the *person* of the monach, and to the latter's heirs and successors as well, that a naturalized subject swore an oath of allegiance. And one did not have to prove that one was a monarchist in principle, or renounce one's previous nationality, or give up one's title of nobility if one had one. In England, and elsewhere in the Old World, naturalization was not an ideological matter.[16]

Only America considered it so. The Naturalization Act of 1802 was, in essence, a loyalty oath to the ideals of the Enlightenment, to which the American nationality had been linked since the War of Independence. And at the center of that nationality was the American citizen. A minority of the founders would have liked to prohibit the naturalized from holding office, a practice which was then in force in England and would last until 1870. But that proposal was defeated. Except for limiting the presidency to native-born Americans, a decision made at the Constitutional Convention of 1787, the founders established the principle of indivisible citizenship.

It is hard to imagine a naturalization procedure that could have been more faithful to the eighteenth-century bond. Later comers were brought into the original compact by requiring their assent to its terms, with the result that the test for becoming an American remained republican belief. In the nineteenth century the word democracy replaced the word republic—hence the title of Alexis de Tocqueville's great book, *Democracy in America*. But the two words were alike in that each was a name for the civic culture whose authority and legitimacy derived from the masses of its citizens. The pride in that identity was such, Tocqueville commented dryly, that Americans "are not very remote from believing themselves to be a distinct species of mankind."[17]

*Distinct*—but much less insular than other peoples. The assumption of America's naturalization policy, that immigrants were free to change their nationality, ran counter to the then prevailing doctrine, a doctrine both ancient and feudal in origin, that a person owed perpetual allegiance to his sovereign. All European nation-states and principalities, well into the nineteenth century, held to that doctrine, whether they based their respective nationalities on place of birth (*jus soli*), like Britain, or on parentage (*jus sanguinis*), like France. The same was true outside Europe. In 1880 the Chinese minister to the United States, presumably speaking for his emperor, informed the American Secretary of State: "All persons renouncing their country and allegiance, or devising the means thereof, shall be beheaded."[18]

As an immigrant-receiving country, the United States came into conflict with countries that were not. One of the causes of the War of 1812 was the British navy's impressment of American sailors of British birth. Refusing to recognize the American law of naturalization, his majesty's government declared that it was "highly criminal" for a subject to sever his allegiance to the monarch. A half-century later, during the Fenian movement, Britain and the United States again clashed when Dublin's courts disregarded the American citizenship of naturalized Irishmen.

Congress responded in 1868 by stating what America had long assumed; namely, that "the right of expatriation is a natural and inherent right of all people, indispensable to the enjoyment of the rights of life, liberty, and the pursuit of happiness." Without assenting to that language, Parliament by an act of 1870 conceded that a British subject ceased to be one after he voluntarily accepted naturalization from a foreign

state. About the same time, the United States negotiated treaties with other sovereign powers to secure a like concession.
Eventually, a good part of the world that called itself free came
around to the principle, first enunciated by the Americans,
that expatriation was a basic human right.[19]

In the meantime, millions of people went to the United
States and changed their national identity. They also publicized
the experience in innumerable letters to friends and relatives
in the old country, and also in autobiographies, novels, poems,
speeches, and magazine articles. Their message was that
America stood for a fresh start in a free society. Titles of popular works tell the story: *The Promised Land, An Immigrant's
Faith in Democracy, The Making of an American, Triumphant
Democracy, From Alien to Citizen.*

Immigrants who made good in this country often gave the
impression that it was easy to become an American. Thus, in
a burst of rhapsodic rhetoric, a naturalized Englishwoman of
the 1820s declared:

> For what is it to be American? Is it to have drawn the
> first breath in Maine, in Pennsylvania, in Florida, or in
> Missouri? Pshaw! . . . Hence with such paltry, pettifogging
> . . . calculations of nativities! *They* are American who,
> having complied with the constitutional regulations of the
> United States . . . wed the principles of America's Declara-
> tion to their hearts and render the duties of American
> citizens practically in their lives.[20]

Immigrants of that sort were Americans before they got off
the boat.

What they said pleased established Americans. The latter
wanted adopted Americans to keep the faith. Beginning in the
1880s, that faith was taught in Americanization courses that
public schools, churches, synagogues, and other voluntary associations organized for prospective citizens. Early in this
century the federal government joined the effort. In 1915, at
a ceremony for five thousand newly naturalized citizens in
Philadelphia, President Woodrow Wilson said: "You have
taken an oath of allegiance to a great ideal, to a great body
of principles, to a great hope of the human race."[21]

Yet the process of shedding one national allegiance for another was not that final, that automatic, or that clean. Close to one out of three immigrants returned to their native countries. Many others lived out their lives in the United States without applying for citizenship. Still others were rounded up by corrupt political machines before elections and fraudulently naturalized by cynical judges. Notwithstanding the title of Andrew Carnegie's best-known book, democracy was not always triumphant.

Nor was the changing of nativities unfailingly painless. The difficulties of learning a new language were considerable. And what if one did not believe in democratic values? Many immigrants landed in America, not because of the pull of its ideals, but because of a harsh push from the home country. Other immigrants approved of America but balked at the naturalization requirement that they "renounce for ever all allegiance and fidelity" to the honored sovereign under whom they had been born. America was hospitable, provided newcomers accepted its terms. The republican identity was exacting.

In critical times, moreover, nativists projected their anxieties onto the foreign-born. In the 1790s crisis over the threat of the French Revolution, America's first Red Scare, the Federalist party extended the residence requirement for naturalization to fourteen years. In the next xenophobic eruption, which grew out of the sectional crisis of the 1850s, the Know-Nothing party demanded that the period of naturalization be lengthened to twenty-one years.

The fear of outsiders, as old as mankind itself, took a special form in America because of the centrality of citizenship in the national identity. Seldom in the 1790s and the 1850s did nativists object to immigrants because they belonged to allegedly inferior stocks. That kind of hostility waited until the theory of Anglo-Saxon exclusiveness was formulated in the late nineteenth century. Until then nativists inveighed against alien *ideas*.

Federalists accused sympathizers of the French Revolution of mistaking license for liberty. Sixty years later the Know-Nothings charged Catholic immigrants with being too authoritarian to appreciate freedom. The French Revolution and the Roman Church were ideological rivals to the American ideology—and, hence, threats to the American nationality. Nativists of both periods turned Jefferson's doubts into certitudes. America's republicanism was so peculiar that immigrants from unfree societies could be nothing but sores on the body politic.[22]

But political nativism was hardly the norm in America between the Revolution and the Civil War. It was a patriotism turned sour, and such success as it enjoyed was short-lived. The Naturalization Act of 1798 was no sooner signed by a Federalist President than the incoming Democratic-Republican President had it repealed. When nativism revived a half-century later, the Know-Nothings failed in the demand to change the naturalization procedure. More important still, after the Know-Nothing candidate for President in 1856 carried a mere fifth of the popular vote, the party fell apart as quickly as it had been put together and passed from the political scene.

Like the Federalists before them, the Know-Nothings foundered on the creed they professed to defend. That was the point of the following letter that Abraham Lincoln wrote to a friend in the mid-1850s:

> I am not a Know-Nothing. That is certain. How could I be? How can any one who abhors the oppression of negroes, be in favor of degrading classes of white people? Our progress in degeneracy appears to me to be pretty rapid. As a nation, we began by declaring that "all men are created equal." We now practically read it "all men are created equal, except negroes." When the Know-Nothings get control, it will read "all men are created equal, except negroes and foreigners and catholics." When it comes to this I shall prefer emigrating to some country where they make no pretense of loving liberty,—to Russia, for instance, where despotism can be taken pure, and without the base alloy of hypocrisy.[23]

The major leader of the soon-to-be dominant political party in the North spoke for a good many constituents who took seriously the founding generation's values. But if to such people the Know-Nothing party's narrow nationalism was unacceptable, there remained a prejudice from which not even they were free. Tucked away in Lincoln's letter was a reminder of the seemingly unremovable and original stain in the American identity: "the oppression of negroes."

## The Dilemma of Color

The first people in the Americas to strike blows against slavery, which took root throughout the Western hemisphere after 1600, were Americans of the Revolutionary era. That they did so then is unsurprising. Men who fought for their own liberty perceived the injustice of—more, they felt guilty about—denying freedom to others. Each of the northern states initiated a process of gradual but mandatory emancipation, except for Massachusetts, which abolished slavery outright in 1783. Four years later the Congress of the Confederation forbade involuntary servitude in the huge territory from which the future states of Ohio, Indiana, Michigan, Illinois, and Wisconsin would be carved.

But such blows, however well intentioned and broadly aimed, missed the main target.

Of some 500,000 bound blacks in 1776, all but 50 thousand or so lived in the South. There—despite expressions of guilt, the founding of many antislavery societies, the passage of state laws allowing masters to manumit their slaves, and 10,000 actual manumissions in Virginia by the 1790s—the peculiar institution emerged intact from the Revolutionary era. The profitability of unfree labor to planters was by no means the sole reason. Southern whites balked at living on terms of equality with a black population that was at least half their own size and even outnumbered them in some localities.[24]

The continuation of black bondage after the founding of the Republic gave foreign critics their best opportunity to mock Americans for boasting that their country was the freest in existence. Under "which of the tyrannical governments of

Europe," asked the influential *Edinburgh Review* in 1820, "is every sixth man a Slave, whom his fellow-creatures may buy and sell and torture?" No wonder Lincoln said of slavery: "I hate it because it deprives our republican example of its just influence in the world."[25]

The founders had inherited the awful institution, but they also designed their own form of racism. More specifically, the Naturalization Act of 1802, like the preceding Acts of 1798, 1795, and 1790, restricted eligibility to "any alien, being a free white person." What alien nonwhites did Congress mean to bar from citizenship? The law did not say, and that question would trouble the courts well into this century. Most likely, legislators had in mind the peoples with whom whites had come into contact in the New World: Indians, Africans, and West Indians of African and mixed African descent.

Although European science had just begun to classify humanity by race, there is no evidence that such scholarship influenced the drawing of a color line in America. What is even more to the point, the lawmakers of 1802 gave no explanation at all for what they did. There was no debate in the Senate or House over the white-person phrase, even though it clearly contradicted the American contention that the right of expatriation, which was intimately tied to naturalization, belonged to all kinds of people.

Congress was silent probably because it thought that the reason for the phrase was self-evident. The reason was white superiority. Notwithstanding considerable research, scholars still disagree about the seventeenth-century and earlier origins of color prejudice. But whatever the ultimate bases, by 1802 white superiority was a grass-roots conviction, having grown out of a two-centuries-long history in which whites had enslaved Africans and conquered Indians.[26]

That experience was not to be easily undone. On the contrary, early in the nineteenth century the federal government adopted the policy of removing the Indian tribes to western lands outside the areas of white settlement. It did so by making treaties with the tribes, on the theory that they were foreign nations, but not quite like England, France, and other

similar powers. The Indian tribes were, in Chief Justice John
Marshall's words (1831), "domestic dependent nations . . . in
a state of pupilage . . . to the United States." Their status was
like "that of a ward to a guardian."[27]

Concurrently, even antislavery advocates favored the voluntary removal of free blacks to an African settlement that later
became the Republic of Liberia. The plan appealed to William
Lloyd Garrison for a while; Lincoln did not give up hopes for
colonization until the final draft of the Emancipation Proclamation. He was mindful that the condition of free blacks had
been deteriorating for some thirty years; in some states they
lost the franchise where earlier they had had the right to vote.
Shortly before the firing on Fort Sumter, Chief Justice Taney
stated in the Dred Scott case that blacks were never meant to
be, nor could they ever become, citizens of the United States.[28]

Without a counterargument of moral compulsion, there
could have been no effective challenge to the doctrine that
America was a white man's country. But such an argument
existed. Besides bequeathing their race consciousness, the Revolutionary generation released the idea, as Lincoln testified
many times, that America was synonymous with immediate
liberty. That legacy provided posterity with a moral yardstick
to measure the distance between actualities and professions.
Therein lay the creative tension, and self-renewing mechanism,
in the national identity. To live up to their better selves,
Americans had to square the what-is with the what-ought-to-be.

This last is what the antislavery movement was all about.
Beginning in the 1830s, and based on the natural-rights premise that blood was supposed to be irrelevant to American
nationality, the movement eventuated in the Civil War amendments that freed the slaves and made them American citizens.
Where the Constitution led, the law followed. By an act of
1870 Congress declared: "The naturalization laws are hereby
extended to aliens of African nativity, and to persons of African descent."[29] The latter phrase was inserted largely for the
benefit of immigrants from the West Indies.

The three Civil War amendments to the Constitution, reinforced by the 1870 change in the 1802 Naturalization Act,

brought the American creed into line with itself. But much else besides logic was involved in extending the values of the Enlightenment to blacks. Several hundred thousand people died in the process, the Civil War claiming more American lives than World Wars I and II combined. That blood-bath proved, if it needed further proof, the stubbornness of color prejudice in the national identity.

Still further, in 1870 Congress had a chance to eliminate altogether the white-person phrase from the naturalization law. Sumner of Massachusetts, together with Trumbull of Illinois and other radical Republican leaders, urged that course. But Congress retained the term, deferring to feelings of anti-Chinese colleagues from the western states. Officially, American nationality after the Civil War had room for only two kinds of people, white and black.[30]

Congress may have thought its intent clear, but many naturalization cases revealed that the term white was cloudy. Was the test skin color? Then lots of Japanese could claim to be lighter than the darkest Italians. Was the criterion membership in the Aryan race? If so, reputable anthropologists taught that Hindus were the original Aryans. Or did white simply refer to the indigenous peoples of Europe? By that standard, the courts should have withheld naturalization, which they did not, from Jews, Hungarians, Finns, and Armenians.[31]

There was an additional source of confusion. Individual aliens were naturalized in the courts, but groups through treaty or special act of Congress. The latter procedures, unbound by the statutory requirements of racial eligibility, extended American citizenship to people neither white nor black. To say that is also to say that the 1802 color line, amended in 1870 to a double line, wavered and broke at many points.[32]

The earliest instances concerned the indigenous peoples of America. For some eighty years after the Constitution's adoption, the United States offered collective citizenship to Indian tribes that agreed to live by the ways of the dominant group. The policy of dealing with the tribes as foreign nations officially ended with the Grant administration, and a movement arose to induce Indians to give up being what they were and become fully part of American society. Short of that alternative, reformers thought, the indigenous peoples would either die out or live as wretched dependents on reservations. After a decade of agitation and debate, Congress passed the Dawes Act of 1887. It promised citizenship to Indians whose tribes dissolved their legal entities and divided their lands into homestead size plots of private ownership. The objective was the creation of independent persons who regarded themselves as Americans.

Logically, that goal should have included individuals who chose it for themselves. But it did not. In the Elk case of 1884, which originated in Nebraska, the Supreme Court denied citizenship to a self-supporting, taxpaying, militia-serving Indian living in Omaha. Having been born on tribal lands, which by law were not subject to American jurisdiction, John Elk could not claim to be a native-born citizen under the Fourteenth Amendment. Besides, the law dealt collectively with American Indians.

The criterion shifted to race for Indian immigrants from Canada. Not only full-blooded Indians but those with one Indian parent were ineligible for naturalization. In the ruling case, *In re Camille* (1880), the United States circuit court observed that the applicant, born in British Columbia of a white father and an Indian mother, was "as much an Indian as a white person, and might be classed with one race as properly as the other. Strictly speaking, he belongs to neither." To qualify for American citizenship, Frank Camille would have had to be "nearer white than non-white," a judicial maxim dating from pre–Civil War cases involving the status of American mulattoes.

Mexican Indians came under still another standard. In the Rodriguez case of 1897, the United States district court for western Texas overruled a lower court for withholding naturalization from a nonwhite Mexican applicant. His color was irrelevant, explained the court, because the United States earlier had granted citizenship to all Mexicans living in the territories acquired from Mexico by treaty in 1848 and 1853.

That precedent was binding, despite *In re Camille* or the statutory requirement of naturalization that an applicant be white or black.[33]

The color line also followed an irregular course with regard to the Chinese. By the Burlingame Treaty of 1868 between the United States and China, the nationals of each country were free to settle in the other. In the same year Congress declared expatriation to be a natural right of all people. But there was some confusion as to whether members of "the Mongolian race" were eligible for American citizenship. Some courts thought not, but others naturalized Chinese applicants.

To impose a uniform rule on the whole of the United States, Congress in 1882 forbade the courts to make citizens of Chinese aliens. That should have settled the matter. It did not. Judges in New York and New Jersey, in contrast to those in California, went on naturalizing the Chinese. Additionally, the courts were asked to decide the status of the American-born children of Chinese parents. Since the latter could not become citizens, argued out-and-out racists, the law should also with-hold citizenship from their equally "obnoxious" offspring.

Eventually, in the *Fong Yue Ting* and *Wong Kim Ark* decisions of 1893 and 1898, the Supreme Court ruled that the American-born children were citizens of the United States by virtue of the Fourteenth Amendment. Their immigrant parents, however, were another matter; for they "have never been allowed, by our laws, to acquire our nationality." Not only the 1882 statute but the general law of naturalization applied only to the white and black races.[34]

It took some twenty-five years before the highest tribunal of the land rendered an opinion on the status of the Chinese. Even then the final word had not been spoken. For one thing, power over naturalization resided not only in the judiciary but in the legislative branch as well. For another, unforeseen events moved both Congress and the courts in unexpected directions. The annexation of Hawaii is a case in point.

In 1889 the Supreme Court of Utah refused naturalization to a native Hawaiian, presumably of Polynesian stock, on the grounds that he belonged to neither the Caucasian nor the

African race. By an act of 1900, however, Congress conferred American citizenship on the former citizens of the Republic of Hawaii, which the United States had annexed two years before. The Hawaiians included persons of Chinese birth, and the courts judged them to come under the 1900 Act. They were thus exempt from the racial barrier, in contrast to their brethren who had settled on the mainland.[35]

Subsequently, Congress breached the color line in two other important instances. In 1917 it granted citizenship to the people of Puerto Rico, which the United States had acquired from Spain two decades earlier. Some Puerto Ricans were of American Indian origin. In 1924, frustrated over the failure of the Dawes Act to break up the Indian tribes, Congress made citizens of all Indians born in the United States, whether they lived on tribal lands or among whites.

Ironically, this last measure was enacted in a virulently racist decade. The Johnson-Reed Act restricted immigration to a little more than 150,000 persons a year, assigning the largest quotas to "Nordic" countries, and excluding all immigrants from Asia. Concurrently, the Supreme Court declared that Japanese and Hindus were ineligible for naturalization. Until then the lower courts had admitted persons from both groups as "free white persons."[36]

To even the most charitable historian of nationality, America's past racial preferences are a marvel in whimsicality. The general naturalization law, originally designed for whites, made a later exception for only blacks. Special measures extended citizenship to Mexican and American but not to Canadian Indians; to Puerto Ricans but not to Filipinos (except for those who served in World War I); to Hawaiians but not to Chinese or Japanese unless they were citizens of Hawaii before its annexation. For years legal opinion divided over the "whiteness" of Hindus, Parsees, Koreans, and Japanese until, finally, the higher courts decided that none of the four was *really* white. All the while the Fourteenth Amendment elevated American-born children over their proscribed immigrant parents.

The only way to straighten out that system—non-system, to be exact—was to discard it and start anew. A beginning was made after World War II broke out. The timing was hardly coincidental; Commissioner of Immigration and Naturalization Earl G. Harrison remarked that the United States was like Nazi Germany in making racial distinctions for naturalization. Unwilling for moral reasons to travel in that company, the United States also realized that its policy injured the conduct of the war. At the same time, scholars were all but unanimous, as they had not been in the past, in condemning racism as unscientific.

To cement the good-neighbor policy of the Roosevelt administration, the Nationality Act of 1940 permitted the naturalization of all the indigenous peoples of the Western hemisphere. A few years later, mindful of the need for allies in the war against Japan, Congress dropped the bars against the Chinese, Filipinos, and peoples of India. A congressional witness, Dr. Taraknath Das, a history professor at the College of the City of New York who had been naturalized a decade before the United States Supreme Court declared Hindus ineligible, told receptive legislators: "If this war is for world unity and world freedom, then the United States cannot practice double standards of international morality—one for the whites and the other for the Asiatics."[37]

The United States came out of World War II, however, with a naturalization policy that still stigmatized many peoples of color. The ensuing cold war spurred the repeal of remaining discriminations; America was competing against Communist countries for the loyalty of emerging nations in the nonwhite world. In 1952 an act stated that the "right of a person to become a naturalized citizen of the United States shall not be denied or abridged because of race."[38]

Despite the cant of certain political and intellectual circles, racial prejudice has been no stranger to humanity outside America and the other First World countries. The Soviet Union and China know the ugly virus, as do Venezuela and Fiji, Uganda and Iraq, India, Indonesia, Malaysia, and other areas of the Third World. Even the Brazilians, often said to be exempt, make invidious distinctions based on color.[39]

The most effective antidote against prejudice has been a higher conscience that pronounces it morally wrong. People have had to be taught not to hate. Therein lies the significance of the American creed. Had there been no creed, Gunnar Myrdal reminded us, there would have been no dilemma in regard to color. A country that claims to embody the democratic ideal cannot, if it means to be true to itself, brand human beings inferior because of how they look.

It took a long time to eliminate that dilemma from America's naturalization laws. Let no one minimize the difficulties of the achievement. Significantly, the greatest gains resulted from the urgencies of the Civil War, World War II, and the cold war. Yet color prejudice had lain uneasily on the American conscience, for how else is one to account for the bewildering exceptions to the color line? Australia, in its formerly all-white naturalization policy, made no such concessions. But that country did not carry the burden of a national identity deriving from the Enlightenment's universal values.

## The Oneness of Citizenship, the Particularism of Ethnicity

When it was common in the 1960s to say that the United States never did anything well, critics liked to equate the history of immigration with the history of intolerance. America did in fact have reason to feel ashamed. The anti-Catholicism of the 1850s; the California riots against the Chinese in the 1870s; the American Protective Association's nativism of the 1890s; the anti-German-American hysteria of World War I;  the Ku Klux Klan obscenities of the 1920s; the internment of Japanese-Americans during World War II—those and other bouts of bigotry accompanied the process of absorbing immigrants.

But the pathologies were not the whole story. America absorbed, over the past three centuries, close to fifty million immigrants and their even more numerous descendants. Given the existence of a very imperfect world, that ingathering is a historical achievement of genuine size. Despite explosive tensions and immense difficulties and the nastiness of human nature, America took in more people, and more different kinds of people, than any other country. And they are still coming, more than three million a decade, not counting Puerto Rican migrants to the mainland or innumerable illegal entrants.

As expressed in the naturalization process, the creed offered a common nationality to newcomers of extraordinarily different origins. The touchstone of that nationality was citizenship, and the character of that citizenship was ideological. To become an American one had to link one's future to the future of a free society. That is still the prerequisite for naturalization, whose laws are now fully color blind.

The creed was, and remains, an instrument of civic homogenization. That is why it has been taught to tens of millions of schoolchildren. "It may be an easy thing to make a Republic," observed an educational reformer in 1849; "but it is a very laborious thing to make Republicans."[40] To this day, despite the battering of the recent past, the creed retains the power of a surrogate religion. But ethnic loyalties persist, as they did in the past, among men and women who believe in that religion. Citizenship is indivisible; culture turned out to be particularistic.

Does the one contradict the other? In the first century of independence, only a minority of nativists thought so. Ethnic diversity was accepted as a condition of American life, and many writers linked it to the role of the United States as a refuge. "We have extended our open arms to all lands, and their superabundant population has found a welcome to our shores," wrote the author of a popular New York City guidebook in 1850. "All races, from the 'green isle of the ocean' to the scorching sands of the desert, may find their representatives in this comprehensive emporium."[41]

At the end of the last century, however, theories began to proliferate about the kind of ethnic mix that best suited America. All of them grew out of the debate that took place between the 1890s and 1920s over immigration restriction. Each, therefore, was a partisan statement. The most important—the melting pot, Anglo-Saxon supremacy, and cultural pluralism—are worth reviewing in historical context.

# 5  The Melting Pot

The melting-pot concept dissolved in the discontents of the late 1960s. Not only did it antagonize white ethnics, blacks, Chicanos, Indians, and Puerto Ricans; radicals attacked it as another example of repressive America. Meanwhile, interest in ethnicity revived in the media, academia, the foundations, and government. By the time the President signed the Ethnic Heritage Studies Programs Act of 1972, hardly anyone had a good word to say for the melting pot.

The few who did took the position that all the social movements of the day were destroying American unity. Eric Hoffer, the San Francisco longshoreman-writer, was the most widely read spokesman for that point of view. He advised minorities to join the mainstream, condemned radical intellectuals for wanting to remake the world in their own image, and lauded the United States as the only successful mass society in history. Defiantly, Hoffer attributed the achievement to traditional values: the work ethic, technological innovation, self-reliance, civility, cleanliness, order, self-discipline, love of country, and "the process of amalgamation in the melting pot."[1]

Both sides to the controversy gave the impression that an old American symbol was at issue. Actually, during the greater part of the national past, the melting pot was known in only its literal sense; namely, as a vessel in which inanimate substances—not human beings—were fused or melted. It was so defined in Noah Webster's dictionaries, which since 1806 had been compiling American additions to the English language. And that rendering remained the common usage into the next century.

None of the standard works on the history of the American language include the term at all. It found no place in Sir William Craigie's *Dictionary of American English* (4 vols., 1936–44) or in Mitford Mathews's *Dictionary of Americanisms* (2 vols., 1951). H. L. Mencken, though sensitive to the influence of immigration, mentioned it in neither the original (1936) edition nor two supplements to his celebrated *American Language*.

Yet the *idea* of the melting pot, as against the *phrase*, was as old as the Republic. From Crèvecoeur in the 1780s through succeeding generations into the next century, writers urged the need to "amalgamate," "fuse," "blend," "smelt," and even "melt" America's different ethnic groups into a "composite" people. Still other writers took the opposite tack of hailing America as "this nation of many nations." Both groups of intellectuals and the models they projected deserve attention. But the phrase itself, "the melting pot," became a national symbol only in this century.

## A Great Play, Mr. Zangwill

Not until 1934, with the publication of the second edition of *Webster's New International Dictionary of the English Language*, did lexicographers say of the melting pot: "The United States as a place of amalgamation of races and mores." The entry attributed that meaning to "a phrase coined by Israel Zangwill as the title of a play (1908) treating of immigration problems." But the next edition of *Webster's New International*, copyrighted in 1961, dropped the attribution; and at present no one knows for sure who originated the phrase. If not Zangwill, the fact remains that his four-act drama on intermarriage, which caught the public fancy in the years before World War I, made the melting pot a common expression of American speech.

*The Melting-Pot* takes place in immigrant New York City. David Quixano, a Russian-born Jew, and Vera Revendal, a Russian-born Christian, fall in love. Despite the opposition of their relatives, they plan to marry, until they learn that Vera's father, a colonel in the tsar's army, had been personally responsible for the slaughter of David's family in the Kishinev pogrom of 1903. The marriage is put off, but in the end not only love, but the "American crucible" as well, evaporate the awful "shadow of Kishinev."

Zangwill pulled out the stops in developing his theme. The attractive young couple are reconciled on the roof garden of a settlement house where the idealistic Vera is a resident and David's brilliant new symphony on the American dream has just been successfully performed. It is the final scene. The set contains a view of Lower Manhattan and the Statue of Liberty against the backdrop of a stirring sunset. David and Vera, standing hand in hand, speak:

VERA: Look! How beautiful the sunset is after the storm! (DAVID *turns. The sunset, which has begun to grow beautiful just after* VERA'S *entrance, has now reached its most magnificent moment; below there are narrow lines of saffron and pale gold, but above the whole sky is one glory of burning flame.*)

DAVID (*prophetically exalted by the spectacle*): It is the fires of God round His Crucible. (*He drops her hand and points downward.*) There she lies, the great Melting-Pot—listen! Can't you hear the roaring and the bubbling? There gapes her mouth (*he points east*)—the harbour where a thousand mammoth feeders come from the ends of the world to pour in their human freight. Ah, what a stirring and a seething! Celt and Latin, Slav and Teuton, Greek and Syrian,—black and yellow—

VERA (*softly nestling to him*): Jew and Gentile—

DAVID: Yes, East and West, and North and South, the palm and the pine, the pole and the equator, the crescent and the cross—how the great Alchemist melts and fuses them with his purging flame! Here shall they all unite to build the Republic of Man and the Kingdom of God. Ah, Vera, what is the glory of Rome and Jerusalem where all nations and races come to worship and look back, compared with the glory of America, where all races and nations come to labour and look forward! (*He raises his hands in benediction over the shining city.*) Peace, peace, to all ye unborn millions, fated to fill this giant continent—the God of our *children* give you Peace. (*An instant's solemn pause. The sunset is swiftly fading, and the vast panorama is suffused with a more restful twilight, to which the many-gleaming lights of the town add the tender poetry of the night. Far back, like a lonely, guiding star, twinkles over the darkening water the torch of the Statue of Liberty. From below comes up the softened sound of voices and instruments joining in "My Country, 'tis of Thee." The curtain falls slowly.*)

Zangwill dramatized a process that had gone on and would go on. Intermarriage was in the American tradition. But the author of *The Melting-Pot* was saying a good deal more than that. He was saying that the authentic, the best, the real American ought to be an American of mixed ancestry. Zangwill made intermarriage a cause. Its success depended, obviously, on the disappearance of ethnic groups and their institutions.

Zangwill received help toward that end from no less a person than the President of the United States. When *The Melting-Pot* opened on 5 October 1908 in the Columbia Theater, Washington, D.C., the audience included Theodore Roosevelt and members of his official family. At the end of the performance, when the author was called up to the stage, the President shouted from his box: "That's a great play, Mr. Zangwill, that's a great play." To the author's wife, who had joined him in the presidential box, Roosevelt said: "*This* is the stuff." A week later, while Zangwill was preparing his work for publication, he wrote to Roosevelt for permission to dedicate *The Melting-Pot* to him. Roosevelt consented, writing back: "I do not know when I have seen a play that stirred me as much."[2]

Launched with the most favorable publicity, *The Melting-Pot* went on to become a huge popular success. After showing in the nation's capital, it ran for six months in Chicago, and then for 136 performances in New York City. Thereafter, for close to a decade, it played in dozens of cities across America. In 1914 it was produced in London, again before full houses and admiring audiences. Lord Bryce joined Theodore Roosevelt in praising *The Melting-Pot*, as had already Jane Addams, Hamlin Garland, Booth Tarkington, Augustus Thomas, Brand Whitlock, Burns Mantle, Constance Skinner, and many other prominent figures in politics and the arts.

In 1926 the New York *Herald Tribune* said of Zangwill: "Seldom has an author so molded thought by the instrumentality of a single phrase." If not the originator of the phrase, Zangwill was its most important popularizer. His play affected the thinking of a larger number of people than those who saw it performed on the professional stage. Widely reviewed in newspapers and magazines on both sides of the Atlantic, and published in 1909, it became a text in schools and colleges, and amateur theatrical groups often produced it. "Oh," wrote a Connecticut teacher, "oh, it is splendid to see the little Citizens—Latins, Celts, Jews and Gentiles, all repeat it understandingly." To keep up with the continuing demand, Zangwill's publisher (Macmillan) reprinted the book at least once a year until the United States entered World War I in 1917.[3]

And yet, when Zangwill composed his ode to America as "God's Crucible," he was a Zionist of thirteen years' standing. Critics pointed out the contradiction between his being, simultaneously, a Jewish nationalist and a militant assimilationist. Nor was that the sole paradox in a man who said of himself that he embodied "violent contraries." Zangwill took pride in his controversial twistings and turnings. As a character in another of his plays said for the author: "Ah, sir, the human heart contains four chambers, so surely there is room for contradictions."[4]

Zangwill felt pulled in different directions because he touched base in different cultures without fully belonging to any of them. More emphatically, *The Melting-Pot*'s author was a classically marginal figure. And although his prophecy of a mixed American "race" must of course stand or fall according to the evidence, one cannot altogether separate the man from the historical significance of his work. Zangwill's makeup affected his ability to add an influential phrase to the language of American nationality.

## The Writer as Lay Priest

When Israel Zangwill died in 1926 at sixty-two in his native England, obituary writers on both sides of the Atlantic mourned the passing of "the Disraeli of modern letters." He was the first English Jew after Lord Beaconsfield to make his mark in literature and by far the best-known Jewish writer of his generation in the English-speaking world. Turning out a book a year for more than thirty years, Zangwill was primarily a playwright and novelist, but he also wrote poetry, short stories, history, travel accounts, literary criticism, and political journalism. His admirers thought him the equal of Arnold Bennett, John Galsworthy, G. K. Chesterton, H. G. Wells, Bernard Shaw, and other Victorian-Edwardian notables. To Theodore Roosevelt's way of thinking, Zangwill was much the better playwright than Shaw or Ibsen.

Roosevelt had a taste for moralizers, and Zangwill approached his craft as a holy calling. "The true man of letters," he wrote in 1896, "was and must always be a lay priest, even though he seems not to be religious in the popular sense."[5] Many another intellectual of that time also viewed the writer as society's conscience; Victorians looked upon literature as very serious business. To men of Zangwill's background, though, it took on a particular urgency.

Born in the London ghetto of poor Russian immigrants in 1864, Zangwill belonged to a generation of men and women compelled to create a new identity for themselves. Parliament, by a historic act in 1858, had granted complete civil rights to Jews. They welcomed the emancipatory act, but the invitation to enter English society as equals placed them under severe strain. They could no longer go on thinking, as they had done for centuries, that they and their hosts were peoples apart. Legal emancipation forced England's Jews to come to terms with their Englishness.

Elsewhere in the Old World and for the same reasons, Jews also had to reconsider who they were. First in France, then in other countries, legislation raised Jews to full citizenship. Except for the Roman destruction of the second Temple, wrote

Zangwill, no era in the history of the Diaspora was more radically upsetting than that of emancipation. At issue was whether Jews could be true to themselves while they tried to be like others.

The resolution of that question, as Zangwill knew from personal experience, sometimes drove a wedge between fathers and sons. He grew to manhood in the Whitechapel district of London's East End, an immigrant community much like New York City's Lower East Side. In both there was a generational conflict over the degree to which Jews should accommodate to the host society. Zangwill's father Moses, a devoutly Orthodox, Yiddish-speaking peddler, saw no reason to make any adaptations at all, and chose to spend the last years of his life in Palestine. It is said that he disapproved of his anglicized son.

For his own part, the son yearned to be both English and Jewish. Zangwill attended Jews' Free School in Whitechapel, Lord Rothschild's institution for the children of poor immigrants, and then taught there while commuting to the University of London, from which he earned a degree in 1884, with honors in English, French, and Moral and Mental Science. At the university he formed, for the first time, associations and friendships with non-Jews. The circle widened as Zangwill, in the 1890s, achieved a reputation as "one of the foremost writers" of his native land. Eventually, he not only moved out of the ghetto but also outgrew many of its taboos and commandments.[6]

In 1903, just before his fortieth birthday, Zangwill married an English Christian, Edith Ayrton, herself a writer and the daughter of a liberal professor. Shortly thereafter, in a newspaper interview, Zangwill said: "With Israelitish stiffneckedness we have spurned intermarriage, the only natural process by which two alien races can be welded into one. To speak most dispassionately, we have in the long run got only what we deserved." The newspaper reporter described him, sympathetically, as "the very archetype of his race—shrewd, witty, wise, and patient; spare of form and bent of shoulder, and with a face that suggests nothing so much as one of those sculptured gargoyles in a mediaeval cathedral."[7]

But the outsider who wanted to become part of English life no more accepted the Christianity of the host people than he did the Orthodox Judaism of his father. Zangwill's religion was humanism. One of his plays proposed the creation of a new church, with Mazzini and Emerson and Swinburne as saints to transcend the creedal and ancestral differences that had long divided mankind. Mrs. Zangwill shared her husband's faith. Their first son was neither baptized nor circumcised. Initiated into no tribe or sect, the infant belonged to humanity.[8]

Actually, Zangwill had given up Judaism years before marrying. With Heine he liked to say that it "was not a religion, but a misfortune." That rejection of his heritage notwithstanding, Zangwill remained intensely absorbed in things Jewish. "I can never forget," he said at the height of his literary fame, "that I am one of the Children of the Ghetto."

Whenever Zangwill spoke of the ghetto, he had in mind time as well as place. "The ghetto looks back to Sinai," he declared, "and forward to the millennium." According to his reading of history, Jewish life fell into two major eras, the biblical and the ghetto. The latter was breaking up, Zangwill wrote again and again, and Jewish lay priests like himself must prepare the way for the future.

The way was confusing, for the ghettos of the Old World, defenseless against the forces of modernity, had turned into a battleground for contending messiahs. Zangwill warned Jews against following the lead of Moses Mendelssohn, whose children had converted to Christianity; of Ferdinand Lassalle, the father of German socialism; of Heinrich Heine, who had made a religion out of art; of Disraeli, the high prophet of Tory patriotism. Their dispensations rested on the assumption that someone was superior to someone else—the Christian to the Jew, the worker to the capitalist, the aesthete to the philistine, and the aristocrat to the people.[9]

Such distinctions ran counter to Zangwill's universalism. In addition to a creedless church to which everyone could belong, he and his wife found substitutes for their respecive ancestral faiths in the peace and feminist movements. Neither cause pitted one group or class against another; and, transnational in scope, both promised to extend the family of mankind.

But however inclusive his sympathies—and Zangwill's interests were very large—Jews were his primary concern. The major part of his literary work was about them. For that output he had a larger American than British audience; indeed, the book that first brought him widespread acclaim—a novel about English Jewish life called *Children of the Ghetto* (1892) —was commissioned by the Jewish Publication Society of America to dispel unflattering Jewish stereotypes. Zangwill, then twenty-eight, had re-created the world in which he had grown up. He followed his initial triumph with *The King of the Schnorrers, Ghetto Tragedies, Dreamers of the Ghetto,* and *Ghetto Comedies.* In 1899 *Children of the Ghetto* was produced as a play in New York, and in that year Zangwill visited the United States for the first time.

Dependent on Jews for his literary materials, Zangwill's principal political cause was also Jewish. In 1895, as a result of the Dreyfus Affair, he joined Theodor Herzl and others in founding the Zionist movement. But he came to believe that neither the Arabs nor the Turkish government, to which Palestine belonged, would ever give up the ancient homeland to the Jews. In 1905, together with like-minded secessionists from the Seventh Zionist Congress, Zangwill set up the Jewish Territorial Organization to establish a Jewish state *wherever* possible. For a while he thought British East Africa a probability. When condemned for betraying the original movement, Zangwill replied that he was no less a Zionist because he regarded Palestine as irretrievable. "Our Messiah is Zionism," he assured an audience in Manchester, England; "we shall know again what it is to love mountains and rivers that are our own."[10]

Three years later, while still involved in that cause, his *Melting-Pot* opened in Washington, D.C.

And so we come back to the puzzle with which we started— namely, Zangwill's recommendations, at one and the same time, that the Jews form their own national state and that they

disappear through intermarriage. Zangwill explained that the
first proposal was for persons who did not care to remain in
their respective countries or who could not, as in pogrom-
ridden Russia, whereas the second applied to men and women
who wanted to stay where they were. By that formula Zangwill
solved to his satisfaction the Jewish problem, which he had defined as the inability or unwillingness to stop being Jewish in
the post-ghetto era.

## The Ethnic Apparition

From Zangwill's point of view, *The Melting-Pot* could not
have come out at a better time. The American people were
then engaged in a debate over the immigrant problem. In 1911,
while Zangwill's play was being shown across America, the
Government Printing Office published a forty-one-volume report by the Dillingham Commission on Immigration. Its major
point was that the new immigrants, from southern and eastern
Europe, threatened both American society and the American
stock. The implications of that conclusion culminated in the
next decade in restrictive legislation.[11]

But until then the immigration policy of the United States
was an open question. It consisted of two parts. First, were
the new immigrants to blame for the social disorders of the
American city—for slums, congestion, poverty, broken families, juvenile delinquency, crime, prostitution, drunkenness,
mental illness, illiteracy? Second, were the new immigrants so
different from the old in cultural background and physical appearance as to make their absorption impossible?

Restrictionists answered yes to both questions and urged
Congress to close the doors to immigration. Anti-restrictionists
argued that the old and the new immigrants shared a common
humanity; that the most recent newcomers were not the causes
but the victims of urban decay; and that the host people could
best solve the problems of the city through housing reform,

better schools, higher wages, fewer hours of work, trade union-
ization, industrial insurance, and other progressive measures.
Between the restrictionists and anti-restrictionists lay a large
body of opinion, probably representative of most Americans,
who had yet to make up their minds about what to do but were
apprehensive about the possible effects of the new immigration
on America's future.

The best index to their mentality was *The American Scene*,
an account by Henry James of his visit to the United States in
1904–5. An expatriate since the 1860s, James had settled in
the Old World because the New had been "too vague, and,
above all, too uniform" to provide him with the "diversity of
type" he needed as "a story-seeker and picture-maker." The
ethnic variety he found in America almost a half-century later
should therefore have appealed to the artist in James. Instead,
it overwhelmed him.

*The American Scene* abounded in such expressions as "re-
morseless Italian," "depths of the Orient," " 'Slav' origin," "rays
of the Croatian," "Moldavian eye," "Galician cheek," "hard
glitter of Israel," "unprecedented accents." Not only at "terri-
ble little Ellis Island," but everywhere he traveled outside the
South, James was haunted by "the 'ethnic' apparition." Worse
still, in the presence of "the ubiquitous alien," he felt "a chill
in his heart" and "a sense of dispossession." He had grown
up in New York City and had lived in Boston; the one was
now under "the Hebrew conquest" and the other under "an
Irish yoke." Astonished to find an Armenian immigrant in the
New Hampshire woods, and feeling alien to Italo-American
workers in the New Jersey countryside, James complained that
elsewhere in the world a man could take a "rural walk in his
England or his Italy, his Germany or his France"—but not "in
the land of universal brotherhood" The sense of dispossession
was so great that James yearned for "the luxury of some such
close and sweet and whole national consciousness as that of
the Switzer and the Scot."[12]

In comparison to H. G. Wells, another British visitor to the
United States at the beginning of the century, James's reactions

to the American population mix were very mild indeed. An Anglo-Saxon supremacist, Wells urged restriction on his American friends and was astonished that so few of them shared his view that the new immigrants were polluting the American bloodstream.[13] James, having neither Wells's racist certitudes nor his socialist fondness for solving problems through radical legislation, went back to England without telling the United States what to do.

But in his apprehensions over the ethnic apparition, the self-called "expatriated observer" and "brooding critic" expressed the feelings of millions of old-stock Americans. As a result of the new immigration, James asked, what was to become of the Americans "ethnically . . . physiognomically, linguistically, *personally*"?[14]

Zangwill, in contrast to James and Wells, assured Americans that the alien influx from southern and eastern Europe was not a threat or even a cause for worry. Progressive reformers like Theodore Roosevelt were capable of coping, rationally and humanely, with the economic and social dislocations of the modern city. Meanwhile, the melting pot would thaw disturbing ethnic differences and forge a common American race. Some twenty years later the *Literary Digest* said of Zangwill: "He made a phrase that long postponed restricted immigration in America."[15]

Neither Zangwill nor any other person affected legislation to that extent. His play served a political purpose in an age that liked writers to translate urgent public issues into human terms. Zangwill's personal anxiety over the Jewish problem meshed with the American public's concern over the immigration problem. He succeeded in dramatizing that problem, as Hamlin Garland did the farm problem, Upton Sinclair the labor problem, Frank Norris the trust problem, and Winston Churchill (the American) the problem of political corruption.

Their solution was something else. Many a reader, though moved by Upton Sinclair's novel about the disintegration of a working-class family in Chicago's stockyards, rejected the Socialist author's call for a classless America. Just so with *The Melting-Pot*: one could be sympathetic to Zangwill's young immigrant couple in New York City without endorsing his crusade for intermarriage. The response to *The Melting-Pot* was many-sided.[16]

## Protean Appeal

The oratorical and oracular finale of *The Melting-Pot* was typical of the play as a whole, and Zangwill was criticized for composing a tract for the times rather than an enduring work of art. His harshest critics were Britons who cared for none of his plays. "Nonsense, nonsense, nonsense"—that is how G. K. Chesterton dismissed *The Melting-Pot*. John Palmer, who, years before, had promised never to attend another of Zangwill's plays, remarked that *The Melting-Pot* achieved "the limit of vulgarity and silliness." A. B. Walkley, the London *Times* prestigious drama critic, also expressed contempt. "Romantic claptrap," he wrote, "this rhapsodising over music and crucibles and statues of Liberty."

The thin-skinned Zangwill retorted that it was wrong to think that the only worthwhile art was "art for art's sake." On occasion he himself had written works in that spirit, he noted, but *The Melting-Pot* was not the less artistic because it dealt with a great social problem. Zangwill scorned the likes of Walkley, "the library-fed man of letters," for not understanding what liberty meant to someone who had been hunted down in a Russian cellar by a murderous mob. One of the functions of art, the lay priest maintained, was to make vivid the highest aspirations of mankind.[17]

Most reviewers agreed with Zangwill rather than with Chesterton and Walkley. Burns Mantle was so moved by *The Melting-Pot's* idealism that he called it "Something of a master work." Percy Hammond liked it because it "is all so sincere, so certainly from the heart, that it thrills with conviction." Still another Chicagoan praised it for being "a mighty prophecy, an eloquent plea." The *English Review* testified that it "laps the pulse strings of our humanity, refreshing as the 'gentle dew from heaven.' " The *Athenaeum* thought Zangwill right for "using the stage as the preacher does the pulpit."[18]

The sharpest rebuttal to Walkley came from Augustus Thomas, one of America's better-known playwrights, who wrote that "Mr. Zangwill's 'rhapsodizing' over music and crucibles and statues of Liberty is a very effective use of a most potent symbolism. . . . I have never seen men and women more sincerely stirred than the audience that was present . . . when I saw 'The Melting Pot.' . . . The impulses awakened by the Zangwill play were those of wide human sympathy, charity and compassion; and for my own part I would rather retire from the theater, and retire from all direct or indirect association with journalism, than write down the employment of these factors by Mr. Zangwill as mere claptrap."[19]

But in the battle among the critics, which continued as long as *The Melting-Pot* continued to be performed and read, the issue turned less on Zangwill's technique than on his message. "Not since Walt Whitman wrote *Leaves of Grass* have we had so inspiring a picture of America—" exclaimed Holbrook Jackson in 1914. Another admirer alluded to an even more popular American classic when he said that Zangwill's work was "calculated to do for the Jewish race what Uncle Tom's Cabin did for the coloured man." Jane Addams reached back in her comparison to the authors of the Declaration of Independence and of the Constitution, declaring that *The Melting-Pot* performs "a great service to America by reminding us of the high hopes of the founders of the Republic."[20]

This extravagant praise—placing the British playwright in the American pantheon alongside such democratic saints as Walt Whitman, Harriet Beecher Stowe, and Thomas Jefferson —raises the question of what, precisely, Zangwill's message was. Jefferson believed in amalgamation (for whites only), but Stowe did not, and Whitman praised ethnic variety. Clearly, not everyone who liked *The Melting-Pot* believed in a mixed American race. Zangwill's play contained additional themes that pleased reviewers and accounted for its enthusiastic reception among the public.

For example, in an article called "Plays That Make People Think," the *American Magazine*, edited by Lincoln Steffens, thanked Zangwill for calling attention to a social problem that really mattered to Americans. "What are we going to do with our immigrants?" that publication asked in a review of *The Melting-Pot*. It offered no answer other than the observation that "no thoughtful person will deny that the social future of this country depends largely upon the answer to that question." Zangwill's play succeeded, among many persons, because it was a "problem play."[21]

It was appealing, too, for celebrating America's superiority over Europe. Like previous foreign admirers since the eighteenth-century Enlightenment, Zangwill identified the New World with democracy and the Old with aristocracy. Vera's brutal father and empty-headed mother, the Baron and Baroness Revendal, stood for a social order where the upper classes devour the lower. In contrast, David spoke for a humane society. He decorated his room with the American flag, hummed the national anthem on the street, and dedicated his symphony to the American promise of a fresh start for everyone.

Not even Thomas Jefferson had drawn a more striking polarity between America and Europe, and Zangwill's portrait of the United States embarrassed American reviewers at the same time that it pleased them. Here is how the *Independent* put it: "*The Melting-Pot*, written by an English Hebrew, is altogether American, more American than Americans, for even on the Fourth of July we hardly dare be so unqualifiedly optimistic over the future of the country, so wildly enthusiastic about the success of our great experiment of amalgamation, as Mr. Zangwill is. But it will do us good in this case to see ourselves as others see us, to learn how the fair Goddess of Liberty looks to those who have fled to her protection from Russian pogroms."[22]

Therein lay another reason for *The Melting-Pot*'s success. Civilized opinion had for years deplored Russia's murderous policies against Jews, and audiences were therefore prepared to sympathize with Zangwill's young refugee who keeps the

American faith. Indeed, the playwright's loathing for the Kishinev massacre, expressed in speeches by David Quixano and his Christian bride-to-be, was no stronger than the Roosevelt administration's earlier and official condemnation of the barbaric event.

Americans were also receptive to Zangwill's attacking their homegrown plutocracy. Quincy Davenport, Jr., a cynical millionaire who apes the European aristocracy and tries to force Vera to marry him, is a stock villain. He and his kind were popular targets during the Progressive era. Theodore Roosevelt captured the public imagination as a trust-busting President, and a generation of muckraking journalists equated big money with dirty money. So did *The Melting-Pot*. When Davenport offered to produce David's symphony, David refused and indicted the rich for "undoing the work of Washington and Lincoln, vulgarizing your high heritage, and turning the last and noblest hope of humanity into a caricature."

The most obvious key to Zangwill's protean appeal was that Jane Addams and Theodore Roosevelt could both endorse his work. Roosevelt opposed "hyphenated Americanism," declaring that immigrants and their descendants must slough off their heritage and be loyal only to the United States. He was an amalgamationist. But Miss Addams, who devoted her life to immigrants at Chicago's Hull House, was a pluralist. She believed that not only the newcomers, but America as well, would profit by the preservation of ancestral cultures. She liked Zangwill's work because its author shared her faith in democracy.[23]

Some reviewers denounced Zangwill for asserting that the real American did not as yet exist and would have to wait until the Davids and Veras of the United States mated. "This extraordinary idea of the function of America emanates, of course, from an author who is himself foreign in nationality and alien in race," objected Clayton Hamilton in the *Forum*. "It might be instructive to Mr. Zangwill to look up the ancestry of certain representative Americans of the past." To Hamilton and men of his point of view, "the present pouring in of alien millions is fraught with menace to our future." That hostility would lead, by the 1920s, to the triumph of restrictive legislation.[24]

But the strongest criticism of Zangwill's views on intermarriage came from the American Jewish press and pulpit. He was ridiculed for holding, simultaneously, such diverse views as Zionism, Jewish territorialism, and assimilation. More important, he was condemned for proposing the extinction of American Jews in the melting pot. "Not for this did prophets sing and martyrs die," the *American Hebrew* protested in an editorial devoted to Zangwill's play. "Not for this have the million refugees from Russia sought America." Zangwill's talent as a writer made his message all the more dangerous. "*The Melting Pot* is certainly lighted by the intellectual fires of a God-given genius," a Jewish reviewer observed; but "that is all the worse for you and me, brother, who are to be cast into and dissolved in the crucible."[25]

As with Walkley and others who dismissed his play as bogus art, Zangwill answered back to critics who deplored it as objectionable sociology. In an Afterword to the revised (1914) edition of *The Melting-Pot*, he defended himself against the charge of inconsistency. Those Jews who wanted to live in Palestine or work for still another homeland should do so, Zangwill said; but Jews who intended to live in America should accept the absorption that David Quixano advocates. Zangwill saw no reason why he had to offer "a panacea for the Jewish problem, universally applicable."[26]

But the essential quarrel between the British playwright and his critics was not his ability to juggle the claims of Zionism and assimilation—it was the survival of Jews as Jews in America.

Zangwill complained that he had been misunderstood on the subject of intermarriage. In 1914 he wrote: "The action of the crucible is . . . not exclusively physical—a consideration primarily important as regards the Jew. The Jew may be Americanized and the American Judaised without any gamic interaction." Two years later, when World War I raised hyphenated Americanism to a new level as a political issue, Zangwill observed that the resurgence of ancestral loyalties "has only made the majority of Americans more conscious than ever of their Americanism, more determined than ever to be a non-European and politically homogeneous people. I say politically homogeneous"—he emphasized the point—"because the actual physical fusion is a long process and is not even necessary, any more than it is necessary in Britain for Welshmen to marry Highland women."[27]

These reservations nowhere appear in the texts of either the original or the revised editions of *The Melting-Pot*. The play's central theme is Vera's and David's union. Her parents oppose it because David is a Jew, and his uncle is against it because Vera is a Christian. And not only in the final scene, but throughout the play, David talks incessantly about the American crucible. To it he dedicates his life and the symphony that will make him a famous composer.

"No, uncle," the young musical genius exclaims, "the real American has not yet arrived. He is only in the Crucible, I tell you—he will be the fusion of all races, the coming superman. Ah, what a glorious Finale for my symphony—if I can only write it."

That vision was unambiguous, as was Zangwill's prediction in the Afterword that Americans "will ultimately harden into a homogeneity of race, if not even of belief." He granted that continuing immigration and the persistence of both the synagogue and anti-Semitism would slow down the process of homogenization for Jews, but their melting-pot fate was inevitable. "Once America slams her doors [to immigration]," Zangwill concluded in the Afterword, "the crucible will roar like a closed furnace."[28]

And yet we cannot discount his disclaimer that there need be no "gamic interaction" for Jews. Zangwill was confused. In his violent contraries he veered between wanting to be a Jew and not wanting to be a Jew. The prophet of universalism never reconciled his philosophy with his background. He belonged to a generation of English Jews that struggled, painfully, to devise alternatives to the tight little communities that Jews had been obliged to build and nourish in the ghetto era. Men of that sort were unsure of their identity. One of Zangwill's

alternatives was national regeneration through a Jewish state, and the other was disappearance into the melting pot.
In the end he despaired of both.

## Disillusionment and Renunciation

Zangwill was born into a Victorian world that had faith in unlimited progress, and he died in a decade of embittered intellectuals. The turning point was World War I. Zangwill was a Tolstoyan pacifist but he supported England against Germany—despite the hateful alliance with tsarist Russia—in the hope that a better world would emerge from the peace. The shape of post–world War I society shattered that hope and, ultimately, his faith in mankind.

In a speech in New York City's Carnegie Hall in 1923, Zangwill pronounced political Zionism "dead." The "small people" who had succeeded Theodor Herzl as leaders of the movement, Zangwill said, would never be able to dislodge the Arabs from Palestine. By that time, too, the founder of the Jewish territorialist movement had also given up the dream of creating a Jewish state somewhere else in the world. For his criticism of Zionist leaders, and also for his urging "a Jewish vote in the United States," Zangwill was denounced by Samuel Untermyer, Louis Marshall, and other Jewish leaders in America.

He was no less disenchanted with the United States. "If America had not gone into the war," he wrote in the 1920s, "a draw would have resulted and militarism would have been killed instead of reviving it in other countries." For the League of Nations he had contempt. It was a "League of Damnations" that had been "palmed off on" Woodrow Wilson in exchange for an unjust treaty. Zangwill also deplored America's stand on war reparations as "isolationist."

More dismaying still was the rise of the Ku Klux Klan. In a polemic against Dr. Hiram Evans, the Klan's Imperial Wizard, Zangwill scornfully remarked that under Evans's "Nordic dispensation" Christ himself would be turned back at Ellis Island. But Zangwill knew that it was not just the hooded knights but the American people speaking through a large majority in their Congress who approved the passage of immigration restriction laws on the theory of Anglo-Saxon superiority. Disillusioned with the United States for forsaking its founding ideals, the author of *The Melting-Pot* called for a revival of the Judaism he had rejected as a youth. Moses Zangwill's son had come full cycle.[29]

His death a few years later was a public event. New York City's most prestigious newspaper ran his obituary on the first page, and Carnegie Hall was hired for a mass memorial meeting. But in death, as well as in life, Israel Zangwill was a controversial figure. Which of his many books, it was asked, were likely to last? Few obituary writers selected Zangwill's most famous play. As the New York *Times* put it in an editorial: "The country and the Immigration law are far away from that pious belief, expressed in the play about which such a hullabaloo was made here some twenty years ago, that the melting pot is 'God's crucible.' "[30]

*Pious belief*—the epitaph was cruel but the choice of language was not altogether inappropriate for a writer who had thought of himself as a lay priest. The work that in 1908 Theodore Roosevelt called a great work had its moment and then fell to the level of a period piece. Nobody recognized better than the Victorian dreamer of the ghetto himself that he was dated. Israel Zangwill died after a nervous breakdown, irritated, as he said, with "the whole human race."[31]


## The Melting Pot before and after Zangwill

In the debate over the immigration bill of 1924, many a congressman said he was voting for restriction because the melting pot had failed to weld America's ethnic groups into a homogeneous people. Despite that repudiation, Zangwill's metaphor survived, and in the 1950s *Funk and Wagnall's* still defined it as the "Nickname for the United States of America." Dictionary-makers aside, to whom in particular did it appeal? And why?

Before turning to that question, we must first establish the fact that American writers anticipated Zangwill's amalgamationist vision. Four stand out not only because of their stature but also because of the frequency with which historians quoted them: J. Hector St. John de Crèvecoeur, Ralph Waldo Emerson, Frederick Jackson Turner, and Theodore Roosevelt. Together, they span the years of the national experience down to the appearance of Zangwill's play. Further, each used words similar to those in *The Melting-Pot*, and Emerson came close to coining the figure of speech later attributed to Zangwill.

"I could point out to you a family," wrote Crèvecoeur during the Revolutionary era, "whose grandfather was an Englishman, whose wife was Dutch, whose son married a French woman, and whose present four sons now have four wives of different nations." Crèvecoeur, himself born in France, married a native American of English stock. His conclusion about the new nation-state? "Here individuals of all nations are melted into a new race of men."[32]

Emerson, appalled by the anti-Irish-Catholic feelings of his fellow New Englanders, entered the following protest in his journal: "I hate the narrowness of the Native American Party. It is the dog in the manger. It is precisely opposite to all the dictates of love and magnanimity, and therefore, of course, opposite to true wisdom." Then, in a soaring passage that surpassed Crèvecoeur's apostrophe to intermarriage, the Transcendentalist declared:

> Man is the most composite of all creatures. . . . As in the old burning of the Temple at Corinth, by the melting and intermixture of silver and gold and other metals a new compound more precious than any, called the Corinthian brass, was formed, so in this continent,—asylum of all nations—the energy of Irish, Germans, Swedes, Poles, and Cossacks, and all the European tribes—of the Africans, and of the Polynesians—will construct a new race, a new

religion, a new state, a new literature, which will be as vigorous as the new Europe which came out of the smelting-pot of the Dark Ages, or that which earlier emerged from . . . barbarism. *La Nature aime les croisements.*[33]

For some thirty-five years until his retirement in 1924, Professor Frederick Jackson Turner taught that "the evolution of a composite nationality" was basic to understanding American history. First at the University of Wisconsin and then at Harvard, he emphasized the role of the frontier in that development. The most famous of his essays (1893), whose major ideas he repeated in the next three decades, maintained: "In the crucible of the frontier, the immigrants were Americanized, liberated, and fused into a mixed race, English in neither nationality nor characteristics."[34]

Theodore Roosevelt, in a history of the West that Turner reviewed, had made a similar point in 1889:

> . . . it is well always to remember that at the day when we began our career as a nation we already differed from our kinsmen of Britain in blood as well as in name. . . . The modern Englishman is descended from a Low-Dutch stock, which, when it went to Britain, received into itself an enormous infusion of Celtic, a much smaller infusion of Norse and Danish, and also a certain infusion of Norman-French blood. When this new English stock came to America it mingled with and absorbed into itself immigrants from many European lands, and the process has gone on ever since.

Proud of his own mixed ancestry, Roosevelt later said: "We Americans are the children of the crucible." He was delighted to have the author of *The Melting-Pot* dedicate his book to him.[35]

Clearly, Zangwill was correct in thinking that there had been support for the melting-pot concept well before he put it into dramatic form. But we must distinguish between the normative and descriptive parts of that concept. Like Emerson before him, Zangwill celebrated a process that he thought Americans ought to encourage. Roosevelt and Turner and Crèvecoeur, in contrast, not only praised the amalgamation but believed it to be a widespread reality.

Did the evidence support them?

The absence of eighteenth-century statistics makes it impossible to determine just how much intermarriage took place in Crèvecoeur's America. Yet, on the basis of what his contemporaries wrote about New England, New York, Pennsylvania, South Carolina, and the southern backcountry, it seemed to be more customary than not for persons of different ethnic groups to marry their respective sort. Actually, in scattered passages of his own writing, Crèvecoeur made that observation of English, Scottish, Dutch, Swedish, and French communities with which he was familiar. The most careful history of the subject thus far concluded: "In the late eighteenth century the idea that the 'American' was a 'new man' by reason of physical amalgamation was the exceptional opinion of a romantic French immigrant."[36]

Ralph Waldo Emerson did not confuse his personal preference with the conditions he saw around him. Until the large migration from Ireland after 1845, Bostonians formed the most homogeneously English-derived population of any large American city. A generation later, according to statistics compiled at the time, the Catholic newcomers had a lower rate of intermarriage than even the city's few blacks. The Irish and the host people clashed for social and intellectual as well as religious reasons; and the resulting divide reinforced in both groups "the natural tendency to mate with their own kind."[37]

That practice lasted well beyond the initial Yankee-Irish confrontation. The first Catholic President of the United States, whose paternal great-grandfather made the immigrant crossing in 1850, was a fourth-generation Bostonian of unmixed Irish descent. In contrast to Theodore Roosevelt's devotion to the crucible, John Fitzgerald Kennedy summed up his understanding of America in a book by the title *A Nation of Immigrants.*

Turner and Roosevelt asserted that new western areas had been much more hospitable to the fusing process than old eastern cities. But neither man offered supporting evidence, and a quarter-century after Turner's death in 1932, the interpretation failed "objective tests" of a computer-based history of a frontier county, Trempealeau, Wisconsin. Its population consisted of native Americans from eastern states and of immigrants and their descendants from Germany, Norway, Poland, Bohemia, Scotland, Switzerland, Ireland, and England. Except for the last named, who *seem* immediately to have merged with the native Americans, the others settled among their own kind and established their separate churches, festivals, clubs, games, stores, and the like. The press took such diversity for granted in reporting the county's news.

At the end of the thirty-year period examined (1850–80), Trempealeau's ethnic groups had yet to form a common religious, social, and cultural life. This was contrary to the Turner-Roosevelt thesis, as was the rate of intermarriage. In 1880 an overwhelming majority were still choosing mates from their group. By that criterion, "the melting pot in Trempealeau worked slowly in the early years."[38]

Actually, Trempealeau County was very much like Turner's own Portage, Wisconsin, where he was born in 1861 and grew up. The population, divided equally between the native- and foreign-born, was a mosaic rather than an amalgamation of different ethnic groups. Turner himself, in a reminiscing mood shortly before he retired from Harvard, described the Portage of his youth as:

> a mixture of raftsmen from the "pineries,"—(the "pinery road" ran by my door), of Irish (in the "bloody first" ward), Pomeranian immigrants (we stoned each other), in old country garbs, driving their cows to their own "Common," of Scotch with "Caledonia" near by; of Welsh (with "Cambria" adjacent); with Germans some of them university-trained (the Bierhall of Carl Haertel was the town club house); of Yankees from Vermont and Maine and Conn. Chiefly, of New York-Yankees, of Southerners (a few relatively); a few negroes; many Norwegians and Swiss, some Englishmen, and one or two Italians. As a local editor and leader of his party, my father reported the community life . . . harmonized the rival tongues and interests of the various towns of the county, and helped to

shepherd a very composite flock. My school fellows were
from all these varied classes and nationalities, and we all
"got on together" in this forming . . . society.

It remains to be said that the frontier historian married a Mid-
westerner of his own New England origins.[39]

But Turner's Portage and the then contemporary Trempealeau—as well as the Boston of John Kennedy's forebears—
belonged to the era of unrestricted immigration. And here we
must return to Israel Zangwill, whose death coincided with
the end of that era. To what extent did the amalgamationist
ideal persist in the next half-century? To what degree was it
realized? Both questions require qualified answers. Not only
have Americans held ambivalent attitudes toward mixed marriage; the data for such unions in the last fifty years are so
fragmentary and elusive that we do not have a full picture
of what went on.

This much can be said, however, with reasonable certainty.
First, the ideal lived on as evidenced by the popularity of
*Abie's Irish Rose* (the play broke all pre-1930s box office
records) and of subsequent movies, novels, and TV shows
treating the same theme. Second, sociological studies reveal
that the descendants of immigrants intermarried much more
frequently than did the foreign-born. Third, the most common
form of such unions took place within the ancestral religion,
so much so that in the 1940s scholars referred to the emergence of a "triple melting-pot," one each for Protestants,
Catholics, and Jews. Fourth, since World War II it has been
by no means unusual for persons to marry outside the faith.
This last applies even to Jews, who, at the beginning of the
twentieth century, had the lowest rate of intermarriage of
immigrant groups from Europe.

It is therefore incorrect to state flatly, as some writers have,
that the melting pot never happened. Millions of Americans
of mixed ancestry know otherwise. Intermarriage did occur,
and is still occurring, and anyone who doubts it has only to
look around. Indeed, the phenomenon's sharp increase among
Jews since the early 1960s has caused some Jewish leaders to
fear for the group's survival.[40]

But if applicable to many individuals, the melting pot is an inappropriate label for American society. It denies the legitimacy, and value, of ethnic groups. It underestimates the strength of family, religious, ethnic, and racial constraints against intermarriage. It deprecates the right to marry inside as well as outside the group. Were mixed ancestry the sole measure, a Theodore Roosevelt, but not a John Kennedy, would be an admissible American type.

Not even in its own terms does the amalgamationist credo stand up. Zangwill assumed that a single stock would issue from mixed marriage beds, but experience has proved the opposite. The unions between Irish Catholics and German Catholics, or between Swedish Lutherans and Yankee Congregationalists, or between Russian and German Jews—plus all other combinations—have added further variations to the American population mix.

Far more important than intermarriage, Zangwill's metaphor survived his death as a symbol of homogenization through institutions. The school was held to be the most important. Typically, in a 1927 presidential address to the National Education Association, the Illinois superintendent of public instruction said: "the great American school system is the very pit of this melting pot. Here the ancient foreign prejudices are melted out of the youth and the best that was brought and the best that is here are fused together." Forty years later a widely adopted American history textbook claimed that, as a result of the educational and other institutions, by "the middle of the twentieth century the melting process was astonishingly complete."[41]

As the decades passed, Americans also invoked the melting pot as a symbol of diversity. That had not been Zangwill's major emphasis; he was less interested in what went into the crucible than in what came out of it. Still, he did stress its varied ingredients, and it was not uncommon after 1950 for historians to refer to the melting pot solely in that way. Further, in the post–World War II struggle to revise the immigration laws, reformers equated the melting pot with America's original policy of welcome to strangers from everywhere.[42]

The laws were no sooner repealed in the mid-1960s than self-called "unmeltable ethnics" denounced the melting-pot concept as "genocidal." Hyperbole aside, and their mistaking Israel Zangwill's phrase for an Anglo-Saxon invention, the opponents won their point, as evidenced by the passage of the Ethnic Heritage Studies Programs Act of 1972. Officially, the United States is not, nor ought it to be, a melting pot. And there, at present, the matter rests.

## The One and the Many

Seen in the long shadow of history, the melting-pot concept was a response to the problem of the One and the Many. But if as old as human thought itself, that problem had special significance for a country whose Great Seal contained the words, *E pluribus unum.* The Revolutionary generation adopted the motto for their newly founded nation-state, a political union of thirteen former colonies that merged into one without giving up their legal identities.

Insofar as ethnic groups were concerned, eighteenth-century law was silent, except about peoples of color. That large and tragic exception, the original stain in American nationality, was eventually but not easily removed from the Constitution and the statute books. Meanwhile, white immigrants of all antecedents, but as individuals not groups, were welcomed to a common citizenship on condition that they accept the civic culture of the founding people.

Zangwill's version of American nationality was based less on that bond than on genes. He was candid in stating that, by dissolving the Many into One, intermarriage would solve the Jewish problem. Yet, as Crèvecoeur and Emerson and Turner and Roosevelt demonstrated, a person did not have to belong to a persecuted group to favor the benign power of the crucible's homogenizing fires. The preference of the One over the Many had multiple appeal.

It also expressed itself in different ways. When Congress closed the doors to immigration after World War I, a large majority of its members maintained, in contrast to the melting pot's advocates, that the perfected One already existed, in the form of the Anglo-Saxon American. The Many, therefore, had to conform to him. It is to that doctrine of American nationality, and also to the then competing theory of cultural pluralism, that we turn next.

# 6 Two Doctrines of Group Survival

The irreconcilable issue between Anglo-Saxon supremacists and cultural pluralists was whether the United States was to be dominated by men and women of colonial descent or reconstituted into a Swiss-like federation of equal ancestral groups. No one could mistake the controversy as a family quarrel. As against the old stock in the supremacist camp, all but a few cultural pluralists were of recent immigrant origin. And the longer the confrontation lasted, the more ideological differences hardened.

Yet the antagonists also resembled each other. Neither respected the universalist view that human beings were basically alike. To their way of looking at things, mankind was divided into a multitude of tribes, each with a special folk psyche and stubborn consciousness of kind. And what was, ought to be. Supremacists and pluralists subscribed to the adage that ancestry determined destiny.

Israel Zangwill's most unyielding opponents came from their ranks. On one level, they criticized the melting pot as an impracticable proposal; on a deeper level, they feared it as an invitation to self-annihilation. Supremacists and pluralists were group survivalists—with opposing prescriptions for America as a whole but equally determined that their respective groups endure in all their specialness.

Their cleverest polemicists understood that resolve in the other. Thus, in his *Melting-Pot Mistake* (1926), Professor Henry Pratt Fairchild found it useful to quote Rabbi Joel Blau's warning against disappearing into the crucible: "The chief duty that a people owes both to itself and the world is reverence for its own soul, the mystic centre of its being."

What Jews held most dearly, Fairchild went on to say, was no less true for charter Americans like himself.

There ended the comparability of the two positions. In contrast to the Jewish clergyman, who was willing to live and let live, the old-stock sociologist was averse to sharing America with anyone not his sort. Personal taste aside, he objected to Jews and every other new-immigrant type as endangering "the American nationality itself." Fairchild, who would shortly be elected president of the American Eugenics Society, ended his influential book by saying: "A preponderating influence of foreigners . . . takes away from a people its most precious possession—its soul."[1]

The Johnson-Reed Act of 1924 left no doubt as to which survivalistic doctrine triumphed. Reducing immigration to a trickle and sifting newcomers by national origin, it gave meager admission quotas to southern and eastern European countries, larger ones to Nordic western and northern Europe, and the largest to Britain and Northern Ireland. More plainly, the law stated that the dominant group preferred that future citizens be most like their Anglo-Saxon selves.

Of the several reasons for that psycho-genetic redefinition of American nationality, none was more emotional than the old stock's anxiety that the new groups would take America away from them. Yet the fear of displacement had existed before without resulting in the tribalistic backlash of the 1920s. It is also worth remembering that Anglo-Saxons first defined themselves as a uniquely liberal, confident, hospitable people. The transformation of their self-image was crucial for closing the gates.

## From Anglo-Saxon Inclusiveness to Exclusiveness

The Anglo-Saxon complex entered American thought during the movement to acquire the southwest and northwest in the 1840s. Imported from England, where it had emerged in Parliament's struggle against the Crown, the complex stated that the English had a genius for self-government and political liberty. American expansionists of that descent claimed those characteristics for themselves, and added that their country had a "manifest destiny" to expand the geographical area of freedom. Accordingly, in the New York *Herald*'s words of 1845, the United States was fulfilling a grand historical design in stretching "Anglo-Saxon free institutions . . . to the shores of the Pacific."

More than messianism, of course, propelled the westward surge. Commercial greed mingled with land hunger and a southern desire to extend slavery. Dreams of military glory also played an important role. Expansionists spoiled to oust England by force from the disputed Oregon territory and had their war against Mexico along the Rio Grande. Aggressive nationalism was in the saddle.

But Anglo-Saxons said they were an absorbing as well as a warrior people. American conquests must culminate, said one congressman, in "elevating those who have been misgoverned and oppressed to the rank of freemen." In that spirit, condescending but inclusive, the United States offered citizenship to the people acquired from Mexico, some of whom were of mixed Indian-Spanish descent. America was "destined to expand by assimilating."[2]

That emphasis distinguished the Anglo-Saxonists of the 1840s not only from those of Henry Pratt Fairchild's later generation but also from most of the Old World nationalists of the mid-nineteenth century. Whether German, Italian, Polish, French, Rumanian, Greek, Serbian, Slovenian, Czech, or even English, none claimed that theirs was uniquely an assimilating people. On the contrary, they accented the impermeable boundaries between their kind and others: language, religion, place, tradition, history, customs—above all, descent, *folk*.[3]

In contrast, the Anglo-Saxonists of the 1840s added a rhetorical gloss to the eighteenth-century conception of American nationality as a matter of citizenship in a democracy. Apart from the expansionist movement (and not all expansionists were Anglo-Saxonists), Americans before the Civil War seldom called themselves Anglo-Saxons. Doing so would have drawn them closer to the English than they then felt. The memory of the Revolution was still alive, as was that of the War of 1812, and diplomatic relations with the former home country remained abrasive through the 1860s. Additionally, American writers and artists and educators were engaged in a self-conscious effort to create a culture independent of England's.

It is true that from the Yankee heartland of New England, subject to huge Irish immigration in the 1840s and 1850s, Anglo-Saxon folk cried out against a Celtic invasion. Yet such references were rare. The major Know-Nothing objection to the Irish was that they were Catholic and therefore hostile to American democratic institutions. And even those accusations were limited to a largely ineffectual minority. No more than in the case of ethnic descent, did a majority believe that religion was a bar to American nationality.

A new breed of Anglo-Saxonists challenged all that in the half-century after 1880. Consisting of white southern supremacists, imperialists, and immigration restrictionists, they argued that some groups were less capable than others of becoming part of the American people. Their exclusiveness drew a line against southern blacks, then against Orientals, and finally, but with greater difficulty, against the variety of new immigrants from southern and eastern Europe.[4]

The new Anglo-Saxonism coincided with the emergence of history and the social sciences as academic disciplines. Not all men in those fields were racists, but many of their leaders were. The conventional wisdom of their day, influenced by the theory of evolution, sanctioned the classification of mankind into races according to their fitness. Accordingly, scholars arranged America's ancestral groups in hierarchical order, placing Anglo-Saxons and their Nordic cousins from northern and western Europe on top, and southern and eastern Europeans and Orientals and blacks on the bottom. The ranking was grounded in the then scientific understanding that moral and intellectual characteristics, not just physical ones, were inherited from generation to generation. For that reason, contended the new Anglo-Saxonists, some nations progressed while others fell behind into "the beaten men of beaten races." Such notions were eventually to be congenial to a society that, between 1880 and 1920, was transformed by urbanization, industrialization, and immigration. In 1896 newcomers from southern and eastern Europe surpassed, for the first time, arrivals from northern and western Europe. The gap between the two streams widened with the passing of years. By 1907, for every person entering from the old areas, four were being admitted from the new. A quarter-century earlier, when the first signs appeared that a major demographic shift was in the making, the ratio had been just the reverse.

The more the population changed, according to Anglo-Saxonists, the more the American landscape spoiled. But for the influx of inferior types, the explanation went, the country would be free of slums, poverty, strikes, radicalism, broken homes, drunkenness, crime, prostitution, gambling, illiteracy, and corrupt political machines. What made the picture uglier still was the nostalgic view that no serious social problems had existed when, earlier, an essentially small-town and rural America drew its people from Nordic Europe. The conclusion followed that only through racially selective laws of admission could the country escape further deterioration.

But until the passage of such legislation after World War I, what was one to do about unwanted stocks already living here? The Anglo-Saxonist Edward A. Freeman, Regius Professor of Modern History at Oxford University, told an American academic audience in 1881: "The best remedy for whatever is amiss in America would be if every Irishman should kill a negro and be hanged for it." Few if any Americans thought the Englishman funny, any more than a decade later they took seriously Henry Adams's fantasy of "helping the London mob to pull up . . . Rothschild on a lamp-post in Piccadilly."[5]

The preferred Anglo-Saxonist solution was assimilation. Later called Americanization, it asked newcomers to rid themselves of their ancestral customs and loyalties and memories and languages and take on the ways of the host people. America the great absorber would assist the process through jobs, citizenship, the press, and the schools. But in the end the hard-

est task fell to the foreign-born and their children, a task requiring, in the words of New York City's superintendent of
schools, *"absolute forgetfulness of all obligations or connections with other countries because of descent or birth."*[6]

The most charitable publicists came out for intermarriage,
not only among the newcomers but also between the latter and
the old stock, "so as in the course of time to form one homogeneous people." Professor Richmond Mayo-Smith of Columbia University, the author of those words, was the proud
descendant of seventeenth-century New Englanders. No more
than other Anglo-Saxonists of his generation (Mayo-Smith was
born in 1854) did he have in mind the melting-pot ideal of
creating a new type and culture. The national character was
fixed, according to Mayo-Smith, and needed no immigrant
modifications. Intermarriage, by breaking up ethnic communities, would reinforce the already existing and "one American
nationality."[7]

Anglo-Saxonist assimilators like Mayo-Smith thought themselves reasonable and hospitable. Their ancestors had colo-
nized America and given the country its language and independence and nationality and government and laws. By the
very act of immigration later comers signified that they believed America superior to their native lands. Why then should
they want to perpetuate their different group identities in the
new country, and especially when the host people was willing
to share its own with them?

Such questions overlooked the strength of other peoples'
ancestral ties. Also their pride. And for every decent Mayo-
Smith, many others sternly lectured the newcomers on their
unworthiness. Typically, in 1909 an Americanizing educator
compared the new with the old immigrants in these words:
"Illiterate, docile, lacking in self-reliance and initiative, and
not possessing the Anglo-Teutonic conceptions of law, order,
and government, their coming has served to dilute tremen-
dously our national stock, and to corrupt our civic life."[8] Un-
derstandably, non–Anglo-Saxons did not take kindly to the
invitation that they disappear.

On the contrary, during World War I, they agitated to free their Ireland, their Poland, their Hungary, their Lithuania, their Czechoslovakia, their Yugoslavia, and their Palestine. Such goals corresponded to America's official war aim of promoting the self-determination of unfree nations abroad, but immigrants were also then subject to a stepped-up, coercive, win-the-war, undivided-loyalty, Americanization program. From all quarters, reaching as high as the White House, the word went out that the United States had no room for hyphenated types. Absolute forgetfulness of ancestry was the price of becoming an American.[9]

The matter reached a decisive stage in the next decade. When Herbert Hoover and Al Smith ran for President in 1928, the electorate turned them into polar symbols. The one denoted small-town-rural America, old stock, Protestant, and prohibitionist. The other typified big-city America, new stock, Catholic and Jewish, and wet. Hoover won the election for many reasons, but Smith lost largely because his candidacy frightened crossroads Americans into thinking that their survival was at stake.

Walter Lippmann, in many ways the most perceptive observer of the twenties, summed up the basic issue. "Here is no trivial conflict," he wrote of Al Smith's supporters and assailants. "Here are the new people, clamoring to be admitted to America, and there are the older people defending their household gods. The rise of Al Smith has made the conflict plain, and his career has come to involve a major aspect of the destiny of American civilization." Lippmann refused to say which of the two Americas was better. "But one can say that they do not understand each other," he concluded, "and that neither has learned that to live it must let live."[10]

The 1928 campaign was a replay of the long struggle over adjusting the immigration laws to the new racial learning. To reduce the flow from southern and eastern Europe, in the 1890s Anglo-Saxonists proposed that immigrants be able to read as a condition of entering the United States. Finally enacted in 1917 over President Wilson's veto, the literacy test proved to be ineffective, and Congress resorted to the quota system. A law in 1921 limited annual immigration from a country to 3 percent of the number of its emigrants living in the United States according to the census of 1910. But that arrangement gave large quotas to the new immigrants, so in 1924 the Johnson-Reed Act pushed the census year back to 1890, when the old immigrants outnumbered the new.

The 1924 quotas were meant to be temporary until a committee of experts prepared permanent quotas based, not only on the foreign born, but on native Americans as well. This was to be done by breaking down the "racial" composition of the American people as they were in 1920, that is, into those who were of English origin, German origin, Italian origin, and so on. Then each national origin group was to receive a quota equal to the proportion of the number of its people in America in 1920 to the white census of that year. Total immigration each year was to be limited to 150,000-odd persons.

Thus, Italians, who were said to constitute roughly 4 percent of the white American population in 1920, were to get roughly 4 percent of 150,000, or an annual quota of just under 6,000. Great Britain and Northern Ireland, which were said to have contributed just over 40 percent of the people to the white American population in 1920, were to receive roughly 40 percent of 150,000, or a little more than 65,000 as their combined annual quota. Asians were to be excluded altogether.

This ambitious effort called for complicated mathematics and guessing; the census figures on national origins were unavailable for the early years, and how were persons of mixed descent, of whom there were many, to be listed? Further, when government statisticians presented their findings to the House in 1927, a bitter debate broke out between Anglo-Saxons and their Nordic cousins. The proposed British quota, derived in large part from the estimated natural increase of the colonial population, was roughly double that of 1924, while the quotas for Germany and the Scandinavian countries fell by half.

The oldest stock had now made it plain whose blood they thought the most superior of all. And they had the votes to get their way. After two postponements to allow for the election of a Republican President and minor quota revisions for the Nordic relatives, the national origins plan went into effect in 1929. Radically altering the concept of American nationality, it announced that the real American was of Anglo-Saxon derivation.

That doctrine had circulated for close to forty years, promulgated in newspapers, magazines, books, and a forty-one-volume government report. But it had been checked by powerful constraints: America's image of itself as an asylum; its cosmopolitan nationality; and the Progressive movement's faith in democratic reform. All succumbed to the disillusionment and xenophobia following World War I. Besides closing the doors to immigration, America rejected the Treaty of Versailles, the League of Nations, and the World Court. Meanwhile, the Justice Department cracked down on foreign-born Anarchists and Bolsheviks, Henry Ford launched an anti-Semitic crusade, and the fanatically Anglo-Saxonist Ku Klux Klan took on new life.

Against that background the Johnson-Reed Act passed. For more than three decades an assortment of nativists—Yankee bluebloods, southern demagogues, labor leaders, social scientists, and disillusioned reformers—had tried in vain to keep out the new immigrants. Suddenly, assisted by the post–World War I revulsion for all things foreign, the survivalists' arguments triumphed; to restore America to what it had been before being overrun by the minions of the Pope and the Elders of Zion, free of booze and gangsters, of slums and revolutionaries, in short, a paradise of Protestant Nordics living on farms and in small towns.

Some congressmen said they voted for restriction to protect American labor and to give the country a breathing spell to assimilate an already large number of foreigners. Yet those reasons, however sincerely they may have been held, did not account for the distinctions in the national origins plan. Nor

was the denial convincing that the quotas were not discriminatory but simply a reflection of the population as it existed in
1920. Too many congressmen were frank in saying what was
really on their minds in approving the Johnson-Reed Act.

In a speech before his colleagues, Senator Ellison DuRant
Smith of South Carolina asked: "Who is an American? Is he an
immigrant from Italy? Is he an immigrant from Germany? If
you were to go abroad and some one were to meet you and
say, 'I met a typical American,' what would flash into your
mind as a typical American, the typical representative of that
new nation? Would it be the son of an Italian immigrant, the
son of a German immigrant, the son of any of the breeds from
the Orient, the son of the denizens of Africa?"

To all those questions Smith answered, of course, no.
"Thank God we have in America," he explained, "perhaps the
largest percentage of any country in the world of the pure,
unadulterated Anglo-Saxon stock; certainly the greatest of any
nation in the Nordic breed." To contend that America was
"an asylum for the oppressed of all countries," Smith warned,
was to threaten "the preservation of that splendid stock that
has characterized us."[11]

Like other like-minded senators, Smith cited the supremacist writings of Madison Grant. A wealthy New Yorker of
colonial stock who moved in respected scientific circles, Grant
was chairman of the New York Zoological Society, councillor
of the American Geographical Society, and trustee of the
American Museum of Natural History. In his *Passing of the
Great Race* (1916), which went into three editions by 1923,
he wrote with utter seriousness about Jesus Christ's Nordic
descent on his mother's side. Fiorello H. La Guardia, then
representing polyglot but predominantly Italo-American East
Harlem, marveled at his congressional colleagues' "fixed ob-
session on Anglo-Saxon superiority."[12]

For the next two decades there was silence. The greatest
folk migration in recorded history came to an almost dead
stop, and almost no one seemed to care. As a result of the
Great Depression and World War II, few Americans considered immigration a relevant issue. But the McCarran-Walter

Act of 1952, which codified existing legislation except for amendments assigning quotas to Asian countries, aroused a nationwide movement to repeal the exclusiveness that marred the statute books.

The demand reflected profound changes that had taken place since the 1920s. For one thing, the descendants of the new immigrants were strong enough to speak up in their own behalf and to put pressure on their Democratic party. For another, a new generation of scholars discredited the formerly accepted proofs for the doctrine of Anglo-Saxon supremacy. For still another, America was no longer isolationist and had to show an unprejudiced face to the world. Above all and beyond everything else, Nazi Germany demonstrated the appalling consequences of equating nationality with Nordic blood.[13]

What finally cleared the way was the election in 1960 of the country's first Irish-Catholic President. While still a junior senator from Massachusetts, John F. Kennedy took up the fight for repeal. He entered the White House with that pledge but died before carrying it out. The triumph of reversing the racist reversal of the 1920s fell to his successor. Congress in 1965 wrote a new immigration law which admitted newcomers according to the skills they had and America needed, and also with the purpose of reuniting families.

President Lyndon Johnson signed the new bill in the Statue of Liberty. The Anglo-Saxonist-inspired national origins system "has been un-American in the highest sense," he said, "because it has been untrue to the faith that brought thousands to these shores even before we were a country. Today, with my signature, this system is abolished."[14] Officially, America stood, once again, for a nationality based on democratic belief.

Madison Grant and Henry Pratt Fairchild did not live to see their precepts come tumbling down. Nor did they leave behind any scholarly heirs of stature. Some of their early twentieth-century opponents, however, were still around. None felt more vindicated nor commanded more respect than the long-lived theoretician of cultural pluralism: Horace Meyer Kallen.

## Cultural Pluralism

Horace Kallen belonged to a long line of writers who perceived that ethnic diversity was a given in American life. Tom
Paine had that perception, so did the more provincial John
Adams, and such otherwise different members of the Revolutionary generation as Charleston's David Ramsay and New
Haven's Timothy Dwight. In the middle of the nineteenth century, Walt Whitman apostrophized "this nation of many nations," at the same time that Herman Melville was exulting:
"On this Western Hemisphere all tribes and people are forming into one federal whole."

Immigrant leaders joined the chorus in celebrating the country as one yet many. In a lecture to a Berlin audience in 1854,
for example, the Swiss-born Philip Schaff called attention to
America's "ethnographic panorama," pointing out that the
"English, Scotch, Irish, Germans of all provinces, Swiss, Dutch,
French, Spaniards, Italians, Swedes, Norwegians, Poles, Mag-
yars, with their well-known national virtues and weaknesses,
have peaceably settled down together in political and social
equality." Nowhere in the Old World, Schaff emphasized, could
one find such "a wonderful mixture of all nations under
heaven."

Many persons thought that nineteenth-century America
countenanced dual cultural allegiances. Carl Schurz, the Forty-
Eighter who distinguished himself in America as journalist,
reformer, senator, Civil War general, minister to Spain, and
cabinet officer in the Hayes administration, in a speech delivered in German at the Chicago World's Fair of 1893, urged
fellow immigrants to honor both the old and new fatherland.
Not only would they be wholer persons for it, he reasoned,
but also better citizens of the United States. "The German-
American can accomplish great things for the development of
the great composite nation of the new world," Schurz said, "if
in his works and deeds he combines and welds the best that is
in the German character with the best that is in the American."[15]

*Composite nation, nation of nations, federal whole, ethno-
graphic panorama*—these and similar phrases common in the
last century were coined in pride, not defensiveness. Schurz
inserted the hyphen between German and American without
fear of attack for advocating a hyphenated nationality. Nineteenth-century nativists, to be sure, protested: "We have had
enough of 'Young Irelands,' 'Young Germanys,' and 'Young
Italys.' " But not until the passions engendered by World War
I did the idea become official that to become an American one
had to forget one's origins.

Therein lay a crucial difference between Horace Kallen's
generation and Carl Schurz's and Philip Schaff's. Very much
on the defensive, Kallen proposed cultural pluralism as an
alternative to both the melting-pot concept and the doctrine of
Anglo-Saxon supremacy. Again unlike Schurz and Schaff, Kallen justified his multiethnic view of America in a *theory* of
group relations. What others before him had taken for granted
and mentioned in a phrase or sentence or paragraph, Kallen
elaborated in detail over and again.

His first major publication was a two-part article for the
*Nation* magazine, "Democracy *versus* the Melting Pot"
(1915). Then came a book of essays under the title *Culture
and Democracy in the United States* (1924), in which Kallen
coined the term cultural pluralism. Thereafter, for some five
decades, Kallen restated, to some extent clarified, and defended his original position in numerous books, articles, and
lectures. *Cultural Pluralism and the American Idea* (1956),
Kallen's most elegant statement, appeared when he was
seventy-four. He was to live into his nineties.

Although trained as an academic philosopher, Kallen was
an action intellectual who addressed himself to the large public concerns of the day. He graduated from Harvard in 1903,
then returned there to take a doctorate in 1908. After teaching at Harvard, Princeton, and the University of Wisconsin,
and serving on Colonel House's staff planning the peace, he
joined the faculty of the New School for Social Research,
where he remained for fifty-one years until his retirement in

1969. A prize student of William James, with many distinguished students and disciples of his own, and the colleague of John Dewey and other notables, Kallen ranked among the major scholar-intellectuals of his long life.

Perhaps even more relevant than his imposing credentials, the father of cultural pluralism was a born-again Jewish survivalist. Born in Germany in 1882, the son of an Orthodox rabbi, Kallen arrived with his family in Boston when he was five. His father wanted him to become a rabbi, but Kallen broke with Judaism after his bar mitzvah. For the next few years, while under the influence of Yankee public school teachers, the boy fully identified with the host people. Harvard spun him in another direction, for it was there that he studied the Jewish component in Western civilization and the Old Testament basis for Puritanism. Kallen then re-embraced his ancestral heritage, a conversion to which he remained faithful for the rest of his life.

Kallen called himself a Hebraist rather than a Judaist. The later term referred to the Jewish religion, and Kallen was a nonbeliever, whereas the former signified to him "the total biography of the Jewish soul." More plainly, the rabbi's born-again son developed into, unlike his Orthodox father (from whom he was and continued to be estranged), a secular Jewish nationalist. From there it was a short step to his joining the recently founded, and then unpopular, American Zionist movement.

A cultural rather than a political Zionist, Kallen followed the lead of Ahad Ha'am. The Russian Hebraist argued that the gravest threat in the Diaspora was not anti-Semitism, as Theodor Herzl maintained, but loss of identity through assimilation, and that only a spiritually vitalizing center in Palestine could enable Western Jews to preserve their distinctiveness as a people. An identical line of reasoning led other men besides Kallen into Zionism, among them the soon-to-be Supreme Court Justice Louis D. Brandeis, who warned in 1915: "Assimilation is national suicide."

The behavior of other groups strengthened Kallen's Zionist resolve. He had occasion to observe, while teaching at the University of Wisconsin before World War I, that the persistence of ethnicity was as true of the Midwest as of his own New England. The region's German, Swedish, Norwegian, and Irish communities particularly impressed him, and he attributed their cohesion to cultural influences from the overseas home country. America's Jews must follow suit, for Kallen was certain that a Jewish Palestine was indispensable to his people's quest for a pluralist civilization in the United States.

Ideological considerations aside, Kallen's group consciousness was accentuated by anti-Semitism. The barriers were going up when he entered academic life, and in one of his reminiscences he asserted that Princeton let him go after learning that he was a Jew. Later, at the University of Wisconsin, he heard the same disparaging remarks about his kind. Even in the home of his favorite Harvard professor, Kallen felt that Mrs. William James thought "that somehow a Jew . . . Jews were outsiders, they didn't belong."[16]

Those words, which Kallen spoke when he was in his eighties, are a key to his life and thought. Like Israel Zangwill, about whom he wrote contemptuously, the rabbi's rebellious son was a marginal man. He called for a revival of fellow Jewish feeling, yet felt as strange in the Reform temple as in the Orthodox synagogue. He was proud to be a Harvard graduate, yet had lived on the edges of student life, Harvard having been dominated in his time by upper-class Yankees who viewed their Jewish classmates in much the fashion of Mrs. James. Not even as a distinguished professor later on did Kallen swim with the mainstream. The New School for Social Research was founded in New York City during World War I as an alternative to existing institutions of higher learning.

Shortly before Kallen wrote his *Nation* articles, Professor Emily Greene Balch of Wellesley College, in a book called *Our Slavic Fellow Citizens* (1910), reported a conversation with a Polish-American priest whose statement contained the germ of cultural pluralism. He said:

America was empty, open to all comers alike. There is no reason for the English to usurp the name of American. They

should be called Yankees if anything. That is the name
of English-Americans. There is no such thing as an
American nation. Poles form a nation, but the United
States is a country, under one government, inhabited by
representatives of different nations. As to the future, I have
. . . no idea what it will bring. I do not think that there
will be amalgamation, one race composed of many. The
Poles, Bohemians, and so forth, remain such, generation
after generation. Switzerland has been a republic for
centuries, but never has brought her people to use one
language. For myself, I do favor one language for the United
States, *either English or some other*, to be used by every
one, but there is no reason why people should not also have
another language; that is an advantage, for it opens more
avenues to Europe and elsewhere.[17]

Like the Polish-American priest, Kallen denied that there
was a uniform American nationality. Nor was it necessary or
desirable to create one through either the agency of the melting pot or of Anglo-Saxonization. Instead, nationality groups
in the United States must keep alive their consciousness of
kind by retaining their languages and cultures and group
associations. Cultural differences could be "orchestrated,"
Kallen was confident, into a harmonious symphony. The ancestral language would be spoken in the ancestral community,
but English would remain the country's official language, and
everyone would accept and work within the democratic polity.

Kallen defended pluralism in three ways.

The first revolved around what he called the "inalienability"
of a person's "psycho-physical inheritance." In perhaps his
most quoted words: "Men may change their clothes, their politics, their wives, their religions, their philosophies, to greater
or lesser extent: they cannot change their grandfathers." More
plainly, Kallen believed that once a Jew always a Jew. The
same was true for Poles, Italians, Germans, Irishmen, Swedes,
Englishmen, and every other psycho-physical type in the
United States.

A second defense was philosophical. Borrowing from
William James's *A Pluralistic Universe*, Kallen derided the no-

tion, which had a long history, that the One is better than the Many—that there should be one god, one religion, one culture, one system of ethics, and so on. The insistence on sameness was not only undesirable, Kallen emphasized; it was unrealistic. Human beings are by nature unalike, and the most sensible social arrangement is to let them express their uniqueness.

Kallen's third defense was political. He contended that the American Idea guaranteed the equality of all persons, that the United States had prospered in proportion to its diversity. Cultural pluralism faithfully expressed the Revolutionary generation's ideal of *E pluribus unum*. Unlike unitary nation-states, Kallen went on, the United States was constitutionally a federal union. How appropriate therefore that it should be "in the process of becoming . . . also . . . a cooperation of cultural diversities, . . . a federation or commonwealth of national cultures."

If Kallen had made a plea merely for toleration, there would be no rational basis for the criticism he has received. But he expressed much more than the need to accept and respect differences. The father of cultural pluralism had drawn up a blueprint for America in which Jews, Poles, Greeks, Ukrainians, Czechs, and so on would each have their own American transcontinental community. And he meant the arrangement to be permanent, not a way-station for immigrants. As a model he pointed to Switzerland, "the most successful democracy in the world"; it was a cultural federation of the German, French, and Italian nationalities.[18]

In a review of *Culture and Democracy in the United States* in 1924, Bertrand Russell asked two questions that remain pertinent today. Is cultural pluralism desirable? Is it realizable? The distinguished English philosopher answered yes to the first question and no to the second.

Kallen wrote in 1915 that the implementation of his plan depended solely on the assent of what he termed the dominant classes in America. Almost no one from that sector came to his aid. Nicholas Roosevelt, reviewing Kallen's 1924 book in a long essay for the New York *Times*, warned that cultural pluralism would "result in the Balkanization of these United States." What is more, he objected to Kallen's premise that everyone in America was an ethnic. Calling himself an "American-American," Roosevelt claimed that there were millions of other like-minded persons, and that it was among them that the true national character had existed, still existed, and ought to exist.

The then influential critic Brander Matthews made the same point maliciously. No American-American, he wrote, could take seriously the philosophy of "an unassimilated alien, who refuses all assimilation, and who denies that there is any American type to which he could be assimilated." Only a man of that sort, ignorant of what this country was all about, could propose "Making America a Racial Crazy-Quilt." Matthews's review appeared, like Roosevelt's, in the same year that the Johnson-Reed Act passed.[19]

Nor were Jewish educators appreciative of Kallen's ideas. About the same time that he was first formulating his position, a movement began in New York City for supplemental Jewish education, offered after public school hours, so that children could grow up both Jewish and American. The movement's leaders, disciples of John Dewey, stood for pluralism, but not for Kallen's federation of nationalities. The latter would Balkanize America, they thought. Worse still, Kallen's certitude that a man could change everything but his grandfathers appalled them. What was the difference between that position and the racism of the Madison Grant school?[20]

At the beginning of his half-century advocacy for cultural pluralism, Kallen's supporters were of two sorts: Zionists and non-Jewish but philo-Semitic intellectuals fascinated by the ethnic diversity of American urban life. Cultural pluralism appealed to the one as a rationale for Jewish survival and to the other as a more exciting alternative than the bland homogeneity of both the melting pot and Anglo-Saxon conformity. Neither sort in the 1910s and 1920s was numerous or influential.[21]

In the post–World War II era, the term cultural pluralism won increasing favor among sociologists, historians, educators, clergymen, and officials of organizations fighting prejudice. Few of them, however, believed in the desirability of a federation of nationalities, let alone that the United States was in the process of becoming one. Pluralism was their way of saying that America was ethnically diverse. From that it followed that Americans ought to have a proper regard for one another's differences. The assumption was that all Americans, whatever their antecedents, shared the common national culture.

As for ethnic identity, later pluralists maintained, in contrast to Kallen, that it was a matter of personal choice, not genetic determinism. Thus, in the 1940s, two educational leaders wrote that in a democracy it was up to individuals to decide whether to identify with their ethnic group or "lose themselves in the population as a whole." Two decades later, the country's major historian of immigration expressed himself similarly, saying that the ethnic group could help a person to "assert his distinctive individuality if he wishes to do so."[22]

Such statements implied that there would be enough voluntary members for the ethnic group to survive, but some scholars prophesied that it would ultimately dissolve. The city was to be its solvent, according to the famous Chicago school of sociology. Laboriously, with the help of census returns and street maps, they showed how immigrant groups first settled in neighborhoods of their own and then dispersed throughout the city and into the suburbs, a process ending in the "disintegration of the group and the absorption of the individual into the American population." At the close of World War II, two leaders of the Chicago school announced that, except for people of color, ethnic groups were on the point of finally disappearing.[23]

It would be hard to conceive a more premature pronouncement. The movement to repeal the discriminatory immigration laws soon revealed that there was still a lot of life (and fight) in ethnic groups. Then came the white-ethnic revival. In 1972, at a party honoring him on his ninetieth birthday at the New School for Social Research, Horace Kallen said that time had vindicated him. "It takes about 50 years for an idea to break through and become vogue," he mused. "No one likes an intruder, particularly when he is upsetting the commonplace."[24]

That did not mean—to come back to Bertrand Russell's second question—that cultural pluralism had been realized, that America had become a federation of nationalities. No organization today can legitimately claim to speak for the whole of America's Jews, or blacks, or Poles, or Italians, or Irish, or what have you. There are important differences within each of their communities. Not even in a given city has any ethnic group created an organic community for all the persons who are said to belong. More generally, Kallen never fully recognized the degree to which *the ethnic group is itself pluralistic*.

This last has been as true of the Jews as of any other group. At the same time that Kallen was first publicizing his model, a coalition of New York City's Jewish leaders founded the *Kehillah*, the Hebrew word for community, in the hope of making it the sole voice for the city's Jews. Many things favored the success of the experiment—the Jewish communal experience in Europe, brilliant intellectual leadership, sound administrators, money, the cooperation of "uptown" (German) and "downtown" (eastern European) spokesmen, and the threat of an anti-Semitic police commissioner to crack down on Jews.

But the experiment was soon abandoned. It had assumed that a community already existed and that it was merely necessary to organize it. The short and contentious history of the *Kehillah* proved that assumption false. Enormous differences existed among Jews—political, occupational, economic, educational, linguistic, and even religious; and such differences the Jews chose to express through widely varying associations. Only in a figurative sense, the *Kehillah* leaders discovered, could one talk of *a* Jewish community in New York City. There were limits to the cohesiveness of ethnicity.[25]

The practicability of Kallen's federation of nationalities foundered on other realities. It depended on continuing immigration to keep alive the Old World cultures that had been transplanted to the New; restrictive legislation cut off that renewing force. Kallen placed the highest value on the

preservation of the ancestral language (his family, parenthetically, spoke German at home, not Yiddish or Hebrew); experience demonstrated that that part of the cultural heritage could
be transmitted to only a minority of persons in the second and
third generations. Above all, even within Kallen's own ethnic
group, which had a very low rate of intermarriage in 1924,
men and women were to mate in such a way as to change the
grandfathers of their posterity.

Kallen himself married outside the group. His wife, the
daughter of a Methodist minister and hymn writer, observed
Jewish ceremonials more faithfully than did her husband, and
this pleased him because he believed that a successful marriage
with a non-Jew depended on the latter's becoming Jewish. By
that formula Kallen did not change his grandfathers, but where
did it leave Mrs. Kallen? Or their daughter and her husband,
a nonbelieving Quaker? Their son, despite a Quaker grandfather and a Methodist great-grandfather, was brought up in
the tradition of his Jewish grandparent.[26]

This genealogical footnote reveals that the boundaries of
cultural pluralism were more fluid in life than in theory. Actually, Kallen's view on intermarriage was identical to that of
Richmond Mayo-Smith, who also expected the outgroup spouse
to fuse with his group. However ironical, the agreement between the Anglo-Saxonist assimilator and the Jewish cultural
pluralist was neither surprising nor coincidental. Each was a
spokesman for the survival of his folk.

## Pluralism without Fences

Kallen narrowed lines of pluralist thought stemming from
William James and Charles William Eliot.[27] He maintained
with them that reality was diverse; that multiple cultures enriched the United States; that democracy sanctioned the right
to be different; and that the "sniveling cant" (James's phrase)
of Anglo-Saxon conformity denied not only the American experience but life itself. As a survivalist in search of a rationale,

however, Kallen created a synthesis more rigid than either Eliot's or James's.

Their ideas stemmed from securer personal roots. Eliot, Harvard's president for forty years until his retirement in 1909, brought a patrimonial concern to national affairs, a concern shared by his socially prominent and renowned professor of psychology and philosophy. Neither man went through an ethnic-identity crisis; nor did they fear for the extinction of their old stock. The role of cultural mediator, as against that of group advocate, came easily to the Cambridge duo.

They therefore wore fewer blinders than the embattled younger man they influenced. Although a pragmatist in most respects, Kallen was an absolutist in asserting that ethnic traits were fixed once and for all. James damned all absolutes in the belief that nothing stayed forever the same. Notwithstanding his student's writings on the subject, James had a greater relish for the quirkiness of experience. Where Kallen stressed the ancestral group's indelible "physical inheritance," James delighted in telling friends he had fathered a "wonderfully beautiful Jewish-looking" son.[28] Less interested in groups than Kallen, James believed that the more individuals departed from type the more they proved their individuality.

For his own part, Eliot understood better than Kallen the degree to which the United States changed ethnic groups. Succeeding waves of newcomers since the eighteenth century had been absorbed, he wrote, in proportion to habits of mind they substituted for those brought from nondemocratic lands. More specifically, America's religious toleration, economic well-being, and manhood suffrage educated immigrants in freedom and turned them into "serviceable citizens of a republic." Without that peculiarly American transformation in nationality, the country would have been a collection of separated ancestral communities.

Eliot derived pluralism from tested processes in the national past, not from differently formed Switzerland and the requirements of cultural Zionism. At the height of the World War I drive against hyphenated Americanism, he upheld the traditional position that it was sufficient for newcomers to accept "the common ideals, hopes, and aims of the heterogeneous peoples assembled on the territory of the United States." That done, citizens were free, as previously, to retain the ancestral heritage, including "an affectionate regard for the old country from which the original immigrant into America took his resolute departure."[29]

The emphasis on process as exemplified by Eliot and James culminated in Emily Greene Balch's detailed study of Slavic immigrants. She observed that they developed a stronger group solidarity in the United States than they had known in their peasant villages. Kallen missed that point, and also another made by Balch; namely, that the old stock Kallen thought everlastingly English was no longer English in speech, bearing, values, manners, or physique, but a new "national type" shaped by American circumstances. As the old had changed, Balch predicted, so would the newer stocks. In contrast to Kallen, the Wellesley social scientist saw ethnicity as an evolving phenomenon.

Randolph Bourne, though Kallen's admirer, also perceived the dynamic elements in American pluralism. An Anglo-Saxon who said he found his "true friends not among his own race but among the acclimatized" intellectuals of other origins, the cosmopolitan Bourne proved by example that group souls were not all that unpierceable. Also, he noted that the "more objectively American" a group became, the more it felt "German or Scandinavian or Bohemian or Polish." Understanding like Balch the extent to which ethnic groups were made in America, Bourne expected the future to remake them in as yet unknown ways.[30]

Kallen's blueprint strayed from the Jamesian tenet that a pluralist universe moves. One of his favorite metaphors for transnational America, "mosaic," was a static figure of speech. That of "orchestra" was less so, yet also evoked a prearranged harmony immune to outside forces, events, or historical time. Violations of pragmatic principles aside, Kallen's original formulation refused to grant that ethnic affiliation was voluntary. He thought it "natural," given, ascribed, predetermined.

The father of cultural pluralism knew little about the history of group identity in the United States. The fault was not altogether his, for throughout the better part of his career as a philosopher, the history of immigration consisted largely of filiopietistic works. There is now, however, a reliable body of scholarship. Its findings demonstrate what Kallen's ethnic system minimized: the looseness of experience.

# 7 The Looseness of Experience

*Ethnicity in Comparative Context*

Few Americans today stop to consider that a majority of the roughly 150 independent countries in the world are also multiethnic. They range in size from tiny Singapore to Yugoslavia to Nigeria to the Soviet Union to India. Closer to home Canada has been fostering a policy since 1971 of "multiculturalism within a bilingual framework." Even the state of Israel, despite an ancient Jewish folk identity, wrestles with the problem of the One and the Many as it tries to absorb a bewildering variety of newcomers from almost everywhere.[1]

In this as in other respects, the march of twentieth-century events has altered the place of the United States in the scheme of things. It is therefore no longer enough for Americans to define themselves, as did succeeding generations after the Revolution, only in contrast to ethnically homogeneous countries. The latter still exist but their proportion has dwindled since World War II. To know itself in a rapidly changing world, America also has to compare itself with other ethnically diverse countries.

A little over a half-century ago, Horace Kallen wanted to redo America along Swiss lines. In our own day, at the height of the white-ethnic revival Congressman Roman Pucinski, the co-author of the Ethnic Heritage Studies Programs Act, pointed to the Soviet Union as a model. Neither proposal won significant support, but both highlight the kind of multiethnic country that the United States is and is not.

Switzerland and the Soviet Union are multiethnic *states*. The USSR is divided into fifty-three republics, districts, and regions, each named for the dominant nationality in the area. Those and still other peoples, furthermore, are represented in the Soviet of Nationalities, the country's upper legislative house. Although Switzerland's twenty-two cantons are unnamed by nationality, and some of them are neither wholly French, German, nor Italian, the Swiss Federal Republic unites those three historic groups. Two representatives per canton make up Switzerland's upper house, the State Council, and each canton has veto power over federal legislation through the referendum.

It hardly needs saying that the American federal union has no constitutional arrangements for ethnic groups. The Senate is neither a Soviet of Nationalities nor a Swiss State Council, not only because the founders designed it to be something else, but also because no state belongs even unofficially to a single group. As for the smaller congressional districts, some are predominantly black, Jewish, Polish, Italian, or Irish, but most contain an ethnic mix. No more than the Senate, therefore, is the House a house of nationalities.

Those differences reflect the different ways by which America, Switzerland, and the Soviet Union became multiethnic. The Swiss Constitution of 1848 provided for a voluntary federation of cantons that had existed for centuries. To this day the numerical proportion of Switzerland's three constituent groups has remained substantially the same. For its own part, the Soviet Constitution of 1924 brought into the government scores of stocks whom a long line of Great Russian tsars had conquered. At present those stocks together are as large as the Great Russians.

The United States owes the greater part of its diversity not to federation like Switzerland or to conquest like the Soviet Union but to mass migrations of the last three centuries. Less than 2 percent of the present American population derives from Indian tribes and pre-1848 Mexicans conquered in the Southwest. Another 10 percent have distant ancestors who were brought involuntarily from Africa and the West Indies. All other Americans descend directly or remotely from immigrants unless they are themselves immigrants.

But the peopling of America from the outside has a larger significance than numbers. For over three centuries streams of succeeding newcomers from different parts of the world have been pouring into and changing the ethnic composition of the American mix. In the Soviet Union and Switzerland, by contrast, the lack of large-scale immigration has kept the population relatively static. To put the matter in another way, immigration made America's ethnic experience perpetually fluid. We seem always to have been a people in the process of becoming.

Once arrived in this country, furthermore, incoming groups did not come to rest in a permanent place. Here again the comparative context is instructive. The peoples of the Soviet Union, and those of the Swiss Federal Republic as well, each inhabit a territory on which their kind have lived for longer than anyone can remember. This last is true in all countries whose diversity is not a product of mass immigration. The Walloons and Flemings in Belgium; the Czechs, Slovakians, and Carpatho-Ukrainians in Czechoslovakia; the Serbs, Croats, Slovenes, Montenegrins, and Macedonians in Yugoslavia; the Ibos, Hausas, Yorubas, and Fulani in Nigeria; the Kikuyu, Luo, Masai, and Kamba in Kenya; plus scores of peoples in India, Indonesia, and other decolonized new nations in the Third World—all inhabit defined territories of their own.

The connection between land and ancestry is of a different order in the United States. Neighborhoods developed in which one or another ethnic group predominated, but rarely did a group remain in the same quarter for many generations. On the contrary, the history of American cities records that groups succeeded each other in the typical neighborhood. Even Chicago, said to be the most residentially separated city in the country, has conformed to that historical process since its incorporation in the second quarter of the last century.[2]

Although a full history of residential succession has yet to be written, we know that it was often accompanied by group tension and conflict. The new pluralists of our day are simply the latest groups to defend their "residential turf" against "territorial aggressors." Their unhappiness is understandable—who likes to be displaced?—but they err in celebrating the "old neighborhood" as if it were really old. Today what is often Polish, Jewish, or Italian used to be German, Irish, or Swedish, just as many a currently Puerto Rican, black, and Mexican neighborhood was formerly Jewish, Polish, or Italian.

Now as previously such neighborhoods are widely scattered, again distinguishing the United States from the Soviet Union and other countries where nationalities concentrate on a land uniquely theirs. The American situation could have turned out to be like that had public policy wished it to be so. But in a historic refusal in 1818, which involved a petition from the Irish societies of New York and Philadelphia for a western land grant, Congress established the principle that the federal government would assist no overseas group to establish a homeland away from home.

No precedent possessed profounder consequences for how immigrants distributed themselves in the United States. Congress foresaw that if the Irish were to receive a grant, the Germans might be next, followed by other groups. The result would transform the federal union into a confederation of nationalities. Not only objectionable in itself, that arrangement was contrary to the understanding that the law dealt with immigrants as individuals. By those terms no one was subject to special privileges or special disabilities.[3]

The United States is also significantly less multilingual than many other multiethnic countries. Today as in the past few Americans beyond the second generation speak or even know the language of their immigrant forebears. The passing of the ancestral tongue has been so general in United States history that one might think it resulted from widespread suppression. However, only a few state legislatures moved in that direction, at the end of the last century, and their coercive laws were quickly repealed because of popular opposition.[4]

Four long-range factors were far more damaging to the generational continuity of the ancestral language: the absence of an ancestral homeland in this country; the influence of the public schools; the power of English as an international lingua franca; and the unwillingness of government to accept immigrant languages (except for Spanish recently in some quarters) as American languages. This last did not prevent immigrants from speaking and writing and reading their respective languages, but the American-born children grew up believing that the officially unapproved parental tongue was not American.

In Switzerland, on the other hand, the law regards German, French, Italian, and (recently) Romansch as equally "Swiss." Ancestral languages flourish with governmental approval not only there but in other countries that became ethnically diverse for reasons other than mass immigration: the Soviet Union, Yugoslavia, Czechoslovakia, Belgium, together with dozens of decolonized new nations in the Third World. In all such countries the peoples predated the formation of their respective states, and the state had no prudent choice but to sanction their peoples' linguistic autonomy.

It is often said that Americans would be culturally richer had they retained their ancestral languages. The statement is self-evidently true, yet multilingual societies have their own shortcomings. Like many a new African state, India, with fourteen major languages and several hundred dialects, faces formidable problems in creating a common national identity. Even countries less complicated linguistically, like Canada and Yugoslavia, teeter between separatism and nationhood.

Nor are multilingual societies, except for Switzerland, linguistic democracies. Along with the officially sanctioned ancestral language there is usually an official-official language— Russian in the Soviet Union, Serbo-Croatian in Yugoslavia, French in Senegal, Hindi (and English) in India, Portuguese in Mozambique, English in Nigeria; and the top positions usually fall to persons fluent in the official-official language. Typically, Singapore recognizes Chinese, Malay, and Tamil, yet its leaders deal with each other and the world in the lingua franca that Singaporeans of all three origins must learn in school: English.

The purpose of this brief comparative survey is not to chide anyone but to show that America has vaguer ethnic boundaries than countries whose diversity derives from federation, conquest, or colonialism followed by decolonization. Although significantly different from each other, such countries are also in some degree or another what the United States is not and has never been: a union of nationalities. The Constitution does not recognize nationalities; none lives in a historic homeland of its own; and all but a few have lost their original languages.

All the same, ethnic diversity has characterized America from the beginning. Neither prescribed nor proscribed by law, the ethnic group originated with members who affiliated of their own will; and the collectivity held together to the degree it satisfied varied needs for belonging: religious, educational, fraternal, matrimonial, political, economic, or the need for protection against discrimination. Meanwhile, the state stood aside, silently acknowledging that voluntarism was liberty's way of identification.

## Old Roots, New Growths

Among the issues raised by the surge in ethnicity since the 1960s, none has been subject to greater distortion than the character of group identity. New pluralists look upon it as immutable and are fond of saying that, now that the nightmare of the melting pot is over, Americans are awakening to the same consciousness of kind as their respective immigrant and slave ancestors. The implication is that Old World roots count for everything and New World growths for nothing.

That view runs counter to the experience of native-born Americans who journey overseas in search of their origins. Usually, American blacks discover that they are not simply Gambian, American Irish that they are not merely Irish, American Japanese that they are not wholly Japanese, American Jews that they are not really Israeli, American Greeks that they are not just Greek. What is equally revealing, seldom do hosts regard visitors as being quite like themselves. The two differ in speech, values, behavior, attitudes, and manner. That they often feel mutual ties of kinship is also true. Yet the knowledge that they stem from a common source has the ironical but understandable effect of making them all the more conscious of the ways in which they have diverged.

Instead of ending in the feeling that at long last one has come home, the overseas quest for self more commonly heightens the awareness that home is where one grew up. Different persons express the perception in different ways. For Anthony Mancini, a New York journalist who traveled through Italy in the early 1970s to find his roots, the moment of illumination occurred when he stood before the house in which his immigrant father had been born. All along the suspicion had been growing that he was more than his origins. Now he was able finally to say why.

"I wasn't underneath *really* Italian," Mancini concluded. "Neither was I just another good old red-blooded American. I was an Italian American—a unique breed, an identity in itself."[5]

It is indeed. Neither Mancini's father nor other immigrants brought it over from the old country. Actually, few of them arrived in the United States fully conscious of being even Italian. They defined themselves, as they had done at home for centuries, by the villages, towns, and provinces from which they came. The immigrants carried to America, in short, diverse local consciousnesses of kind.

They usually settled with their particular sort. Unknowing Americans misunderstood and thought all Little Italies alike when, in fact, they were Calabrian, Sicilian, Neapolitan, Genoese, Piedmontese, Turinese, Abruzzese, or some such other transplanted self-designation. The various *paesani* (countrymen) continued to speak their own dialects, commemorate their special patron saints, and eat their regional foods. They also formed separate clubs and mutual-benefit societies. Had they known the term, they would have called themselves ethnic groups. Nearest countrymen were fellow villagers.

But the newcomers were unable indefinitely to withstand the fluidity of American life. People moved away from the block, neighborhoods changed, and different *paesani* met each other as never before in the old country. Without giving up their local group identities, the immigrants drew together as Italians. An originally reconstituted Palermian or Neapolitan church might become the neighborhood Italian church, just as the local eating place learned to serve the dishes of more than one Italian region.[6]

Emerging leaders of varied backgrounds joined to promote the wider fellow feeling. They founded the Order of the Sons of Italy in America (1905), supported the publication of newspapers in an American Italian rather than dialect, and opposed the bigotry directed against no matter which *paesani* in this country. Meanwhile, politicians, seeing how the Irish succeeded at the polls, strove to weld their kind into an effective voting bloc.

When Fiorello H. La Guardia joined a Republican district club in his native New York City in 1910, leaders referred to "the colony" as if it were a fully awakened interest group. It was not, but the impact of World War I and of subsequent events and issues in the 1920s moved immigrants in that direction. They rallied to Italy's declaration of war against hated Austria; later attacked Woodrow Wilson for preventing Italy from getting Fiume at the peace conference; and still later made common cause against Prohibition and the openly anti-Italian immigration laws. Concurrently, Mussolini's rise to fame filled so many of them with pride that not even La Guardia, the native hero, dared publicly to denounce the man he privately loathed.

La Guardia received close to 90 percent of the Italian vote when he was elected mayor of New York City in 1933. His total plurality in the three-cornered race, by contrast, was a mere 40 percent. Never before had the colony known such solidarity. Its members had been politicized by the grievances of the previous decade and a half, and they also resented the Irish for shutting them out of public life. La Guardia capitalized on such hurts, knowing that his followers hoped to achieve through him a place in the American sun.

"Viva Il Nostro Fiorello La Guardia!"—Long Live Our Fiorello La Guardia! exulted *Il Progresso*, the most popular

Italian-language newspaper in the colony. "Finally the greatest city in the world has an Italian Mayor."[7]

But by the 1930s, with the half-century era of mass immigration over, an American-born generation was changing the group's self-image. Unlike their parents, who learned they were Italian in this country, the children grew up assuming that part of their identity. But they seldom thought themselves only or even primarily Italian and were insulted when others said they were. Formed in large part by the native culture, they wanted to be known as Americans of a particular origin.

The designation in La Guardia's day for their sort was Italo-Americans. It lasted well into the post–World War II period. Today the more common terms are Italian Americans, American Italians, and Americans of Italian descent, although some of the older generation continue to call themselves Italo-Americans. The lack of agreement is not only an index to the current flux but also a reminder that the group's identity is made in the United States and is therefore an American artifact.

Efforts since the 1960s to give it a cultural content took the form of Italian American studies. Now institutionalized on a good many campuses, they have yet to appeal to more than a minority of students and intellectuals.[8] Perhaps the numbers will expand in the years ahead, but whatever that outcome, the ethnic renewal is unlikely to revive the original identities that the immigrants brought from the old country. For if still very strong over there, Italy's regional loyalties sway few Americans.

Such transmutations have been common to America's historic immigrant groups. Initially, the founders knew themselves by different places of local origin. Later, in adjusting to the new environment, they merged as Irish, German, Norwegian, Swedish, Finnish, Polish, Lithuanian, Portuguese, Greek, Albanian, Chinese, or Japanese. Next, the designation "American" appeared either before or after the collective name.[9]

This is not to deny that every group is unique, but rather to puncture the currently fashionable myth that ethnic identity is immutable. Despite considerable differences in other respects, America's historic groups have all enlarged their sense of collective self as a result of living in this country. Consider, for example, such unlike groups as the British and the Jews.

Of all the immigrants in the last century, those from Great Britain were most like the host people. The popular assumption is that they therefore melted on contact into the native American stock. Some did. But it was more customary for the incoming English, Scots, Protestant Irish, and Welsh each to set up their own churches, fraternal orders, benevolent societies, and newspapers. The same was true of both Canadian Scottish and Canadian English immigrants in America. Altogether, the various foreign-born groups numbered around 600,000 in 1850 and 2,000,000 forty years later.

No more than the Italians of this century could they remain permanently apart. Many shared an attachment to the Crown; all except some exclusively Celtic-speaking Welsh valued the common tongue. But the cement that ultimately joined them was an inherited dislike for the Catholic Irish that the latter returned in kind. In America the antagonists clashed at work and in the streets; and the more the Irish rose to power as Democrats after 1870, the more they drove various British into the Republican party.

Matters took a decisive turn during the 1887 celebration of Queen Victoria's Golden Jubilee. Three weeks after the American Irish insulted her majesty's name, her enraged supporters founded the British-American Association. They aimed to defend themselves, as well as the Crown, against the traditional foe. The British had coalesced as an interest group in American politics.

Over a million reinforcements crossed the Atlantic in the next twenty-five years. Many affiliated with the established cultural organizations of their respective groups. When world war broke out in 1914, Americans of British birth and descent responded in much the same fashion as did other immigrant groups. They united to support the country of origin. Theodore Roosevelt included British-Americans in his denunciation of hyphenated Americans.[10]

The influences operating on the Jews were more complicated. They emigrated from more different parts of the world than any other group and yet arrived in America with a tradition of oneness. They were the seed of Abraham and a covenanted community; their Messiah would some day deliver them from the Diaspora and restore them to the holy soil. And for millennia all the others—goyim—had persecuted them for their faith and origin. No other immigrants brought bonds of identity quite like those.

They nevertheless acted like the varied lot they were. Around 2,500,000 Yiddish-speaking people debarked in the United States in the half-century after 1880. They came overwhelmingly from the Russian and Austro-Hungarian empires, and convention is therefore correct in calling them eastern European. Yet that homogenized term obscures the regional points of reference around which the newcomers at first organized their lives in New York and other American cities.

They settled in a manner that the nearby Italian *paesani* would have understood. *Landsman* (countryman) clustered with *landsman* from Russian Poland, Russia proper, the Ukraine, Lithuania, Hungary, Romania, Bessarabia, Bukovina, or Galicia. Those were not merely place names. One *was* a Galician, just as one was a Bukovinian with distinguishable foods, customs, memories, religious rituals, and Yiddish dialect. Next to members of the family, the closest *landsman* was someone who had come over from the same village, town, or city.

Like the immigrant founders of other ethnic groups, Jews turned to their immediate kind for fellowship and help. The result was a proliferation of fraternal orders, burial societies, and associations to aid the sick. Even the *shuls* (synagogues) affiliated by Old World locality. In 1900 there were three hundred congregations in New York City alone. The consciousness of kind was so restrictive that a Lithuanian would no sooner marry a Galician than a Gentile.

But the traditional boundaries succumbed to American pressures making for a larger fellow feeling. Regional customs mingled as various countrymen met in the same trades and as families moved from first areas of settlement into mixed Jewish neighborhoods. Local *shuls* gave way to the larger Orthodox synagogue; the many charities joined in federation; and an American Yiddish evolved with the help of the press and theater. By World War I, despite many lingering divisions, an eastern European Jewish entity had come into being in America.

The then established Jews stood apart from it. Their kind, who had arrived earlier from German-speaking central Europe, numbered around 300,000 when the Yiddish-speaking influx began in the 1880s. Having homogenized their local differences of origin, the various Germans supported a common set of social, charitable, and religious institutions. They were also much more well to do than the largely working-class newcomers from eastern Europe.

The two sorts divided sharply over the question of what it meant to be Jewish. To the eastern Europeans, the Jews were a people as well as a religious group. To the German Jews, as the central tenet of their Reform Judaism had proclaimed in 1885, the Jews were simply one religious denomination among others in America. Eastern Europeans regarded that creed as not Jewish at all, and the more so because Reform temples conducted services in English on Sunday, seated men and women together, had organs and choirs, and did not offer up prayers for a return to Palestine. For their own part, the Reform regarded their unassimilated Orthodox brethren as outlandish. Small wonder that all efforts failed, just before and during World War I, to create a single voice for the Jews in America.

No such unity has occurred since then, but the old distinctions steadily lost ground after the close of mass immigration. In the years between the two world wars, the Reform temple attracted the children and grandchildren of eastern European immigrants. Similarly, German Jews affiliated with the Conservative synagogue, which stands between Reform and Orthodoxy. By the end of the Great Depression the American-born were also pooling their efforts to raise funds for all Jewish philanthropies.

Anti-Semitism drew people closer together still. Indeed, from the end of World War I to the end of World War II, the major communal effort focused on protecting Jewish rights. In that effort American Jews formed an alliance, which is still strong, with the liberal forces in American politics. But the best index to the power of anti-Semitism to close ranks was the revised Reform platform of 1937; it stated that the Jews were not just a religious group but a historic people as well. By 1948 even non-Zionists, appalled by the Holocaust, justified the creation of the state of Israel as a refuge for European survivors.

A steep decline in anti-Semitism over the next two decades raised fresh questions about the group's identity. In newly inhabited suburbs across the country, families found an answer in one or another of the growing number of temples. As for the nonaffiliated, they understood their kind to be one of America's established ethnic groups. In both cases the memory had dimmed that the points of reference were once a hamlet, town, or province between the Rhine and the old Russian Pale. When Jews looked fondly abroad, it was to Israel, which also happened to be an American ally in the cold war. Its brilliant victory on the battlefield in 1967, celebrated in the United States by non-Jews as well as Jews, seemed to lay to rest the image of the Jews as victims.

Then came the Yom Kippur War. A growing number of young people have since given serious study to their heritage, yet the cultural renewal still affects relatively few persons. The majority of all ages have been far more concerned with safeguarding Israel's survival in a hostile world. They approach the task not as Galicians, Bavarians, Lithuanians, or Bukovinians, but as American Jews. For as much as their group consciousness intensified because of events in the Middle East, it had expanded since their ancestors immigrated to the United States.[11]

Experience stretched so many ethnicities that the exceptions stand out. Sectarians like the Amish held on to the original identity as long as they managed to insulate themselves from changing American life. The only ones to resemble them are the few Indian tribes that accommodated neither to each other nor to the larger society. More typically, as currently demon-strated by the attempt of various Latinos to form a trans-Hispanic entity, ethnic identification has gone from small to larger collectivities.

Still other Americans, on the other hand, have moved away from ethnicity. They place greatest stress on the religious bond they share with others. Many Catholics of unlike origins so define themselves, but another immigrant-derived church bet-ter illustrates the fusing process involved.

## Lutheranism and the Creation of a Pan-Ethnic Identity

American Lutherans overwhelmingly descend from Ger-man, Norwegian, Swedish, Danish, Finnish, Icelandic, and Slovakian immigrants. Like most American Catholics and Jews, in other words, most American Lutherans belong to the church that their ancestors transplanted from the Old World to the New. But in contrast to Jews and Catholics, hardly any Lutherans of any descent took part in the ethnic revival of the late 1960s and early 1970s.

Revival leaders did not think to ask why. Perhaps they as-sumed that Lutherans had vanished long before into WASP-dom. An unknown number did, yet their disappearance is not a sufficient explanation. The remnant was so sizable that Luth-erans ranked third only to Methodists and Baptists as the largest Protestant denomination in the United States. The re-vival meant little to most of them because, by the 1960s, two centuries of experience had leached and transmuted original ancestral attachments into a pan-ethnic Lutheran identity.

Lutherans first came to America from Sweden and Holland in the seventeenth century, but the church was not firmly planted until tens of thousands of immigrants arrived from southwestern Germany in the next century. They formed the basis for the first American synod, organized in 1748 by the patriarchal Henry Melchior Muhlenberg; and they continued to predominate in the 150 congregations that existed by the time of the Revolution. As a result, Lutheranism in colonial times was as much an ethnic as a religious affiliation.

The formation of that group consciousness was peculiarly American. Rarely had the immigrants considered themselves German in the villages of their native Palatinate and surrounding provinces. There was then no German nation-state or consciousness of kind that transcended the multitude of independent principalities. Such fellow feeling developed much earlier, for good reason, in far-off Pennsylvania, New York, Maryland, Virginia, the Carolinas, and Georgia. There, amidst Scotch-Irish, Scottish, English, and native colonial neighbors, transplanted Palatines and Württembergers came to think of themselves, and were so regarded by others, as German in "nation" because of a shared religion, language, and culture.[12]

Circumstances eventually leached the three bonds of identity. As immigration slowed to a trickle in the half-century after independence, Lutheranism's survival depended more and more on the immigrants' native-American children and grandchildren. Fewer and fewer of them knew the ancestral language; so English was substituted for German in Luther's church. Concurrently, because of the prevailing latitudinarianism, the Augsburg Confession disappeared from synodical references. A few pastors favored union not only with the German Reformed Church but also with non-German churches; and some of the immigrants' descendants actually became Episcopalians, Presbyterians, or Methodists. The patriarch's oldest son, John Peter Gabriel Muhlenberg, a Revolutionary war hero, was first ordained a Lutheran minister and then an Episcopal priest.

To save the situation from further disintegration, religious leaders, beginning in the 1820s, moved to create an "American Lutheranism." They reasoned that, although the native environment had destroyed the German language and culture, Lutheranism's doctrinal distinctiveness could survive as a point of identity in the new Zion. Toward that end they formed the General Synod, founded Gettysburg Seminary, translated holy works (including a hymnology) into the American tongue, and required the Augsburg Confession for ordination. A struggle ensued over amending the Confession, yet both sides to the controversy agreed that Lutheranism, no longer tied to an immigrant culture, must become an American "faith."

That transmutation no sooner emerged than it was contained by a huge number of ultra-confessional immigrants from eastern and northern Germany. The advance guard arrived with their pastors in the late 1830s and 1840s. Already opposed to the doctrinal laxity of their home churches, they denounced American Lutheranism for resting on *merely* the Augsburg Confession.* Equally to the point, they objected to severing the ancestral language from the faith. Apart from their confessional purity, the newcomers were like the Muhlenberg Lutherans of the previous century in thinking themselves an ethno-religious group.

Rejoicing in America's voluntarism, they provided themselves with their own seminaries, colleges, schools, publications, and church organizations. One branch, containing the nucleus of the Buffalo Synod, organized the Synod of Exiles from the Lutheran Church of Prussia. Another branch, consisting of Saxons who first settled in and near St. Louis, formed in 1847 the German Evangelical Lutheran Synod of Missouri, Ohio, and Other States. Before long the Missouri Synod would include close to a third of American Lutherans.

Other nineteenth-century tides of Lutheran immigration, from Scandinavia and Austria-Hungary, also beat back the Americanist course set by the General Synod. The Swedes, Norwegians, Danes, Finns, Icelanders, and Slovakians set up synods in their own names and languages. Further, as among the Germans, each group had its doctrinal and other disputes,

---

*In addition to the Unaltered Augsburg Confession, the newcomers demanded "acceptance of all the symbolical books of the Evangelical Lutheran church as a true and correct statement and exposition of the Word of God, to wit: the three Ecumenical Creeds (the Apostles' Creed, the Nicaean Creed, the Athanasian Creed), the Unaltered Augsburg Confession, the Apology of the Augsburg Confession, the Smalcald Articles, the Large Catechism of Luther, the Small Catechism of Luther, and the Formula of Concord." Quoted in Carl Mauelshagen, *American Lutheranism Surrenders to Forces of Conservatism* (Athens, Ga., 1936), p. 118.

sometimes deriving from the different places of origin in the old country. The result was the creation of still more synods. All went their separate ways, each maintaining that only it stood for the true Lutheranism of its ethnic group.[13]

There matters stood until World War I brought an effective close to the era of mass Lutheran immigration. In the next half-century, as had been true in the half-century following the Revolution, the leaching process came into play. Two world wars against Germany, a growing secularism and ecumenicism, and the homogenizing influences of the mass media accelerated it. More than anything else, by the 1960s as in the 1820s, the church was no longer an immigrant church based on the ancestral language and culture.

Once again the native-born undertook to make Lutheran identity entirely a matter of faith. This time, unlike the General Synod in the second quarter of the nineteenth century, the thrust cut across all ancestral boundaries save Slovakian. Institutionally, major mergers within national groups prepared the way. The next step took place in the early 1960s when, after more than a decade of negotiations, two trans-ethnic consolidations came into being, each embracing around a third of the Lutherans in the country.

Their official designations were instructive. One was named the American Lutheran Church and the other the Lutheran Church in America. Although the latter absorbed the primary Swedish synod and the former the major Norwegian synod, neither church defined itself in ethnic terms. Both contained larger German and smaller Danish synods. The major difference between the two was that the Lutheran Church in America was more ecumenical than the American Lutheran Church with regard to other Protestant churches.[14]

The predominantly German-American Missouri Synod, speaking for roughly a third of the Lutherans, refused to enter either merger. That was in character. Missouri had led the fight in the 1840s against the first Americanization movement in the church. Yet, in the decades beginning with World War I, not even Missouri could stand fully intact against forces demanding accommodation.

To protect itself against the hostility to all things German during World War I, Missouri dropped the name of the fatherland from its designation. By the Great Depression its famed parochial schools, which had taught the ancestral language and culture as well as religion for close to a century, enrolled many fewer of the synod's young than did the public schools. World War II further weakened ties with Germany, and in the following decades the native-born were thrown back more and more on the distinctiveness of Missouri's doctrinal purity.[15]

In 1969 they elected a president of non-German origin for the first time in the synod's 122-year history. The group was then locked in controversy over certain modernist tendencies, and the Reverend J. A. O. Preus, who happened to be of Norwegian descent, led a faction that was as confessionally demanding as Missouri's Saxon founders. He and his followers cracked down on a minority of liberal dissidents who, after failing to overcome the denomination's conservatives, seceded in 1976 to form their own Lutheran church.

Besides dividing over points of religious belief, the parties clashed because of differences in personality, life-style, and world view. That such factors came into play, along with a desire for power, should surprise no one familiar with sectarian infighting.[16] But given the character of Missouri's history, the 1960–70s struggle was exceptional for the factors that *were not involved*. Neither the German language nor the relationship to the German fatherland was important in defining the issues and deciding the outcome.

Not even the most ardently trans-American Lutherans claim that all ethnicity has disappeared from the institution that Muhlenberg planted in colonial America. The three major bodies have yet to absorb a few independent Finnish, German, Slovakian, and Norwegian synods. Further, Missouri still has a German-American flavor. And despite the mergers and proclamations of the 1960s and 1970s, feelings of ethnic identity linger, in varying degrees, among members of both the Lutheran Church in America and the American Lutheran Church.

But the ethnic attachment has changed from what it used to be in the period of mass Lutheran immigration and just beyond. Descent and faith were then so closely joined that they formed a seamless whole. Today that is the case for only a minority. The majority have separated the two attributes; more, they have subordinated one to the other. Lutheranism has come to signify, in other words, less an ethnic than a religious identification.

The contemporary white-ethnic movement therefore seemed irrelevant to most Lutherans. Their respective resurgences—German, Swedish, Norwegian—occurred earlier this century; by the 1960s the majority reached a point where they were ready to institutionalize a pan-Lutheran group consciousness that corresponded to their American experience. What is more, few of their kind lived in big cities with a large black presence, which contributed in no small part to triggering off the ethnic revival among Catholics and Jews.

## Hands Off

It is hard to draw a line between when and when not to legislate. But if the past has anything to teach the present, the country would be better off if government understood when to leave things alone. A case in point is the Ethnic Heritage Studies Programs Act that ethnic ideologues secured from Congress in 1972. The law sanctioned the sponsors' claim that their own intense feelings of ethnicity applied to Americans as a whole.

Many a congressman knew better, but the pressures were too strong to resist. Since ethnicity was in and riding high, why risk standing in the way of a seemingly unimportant bill? Besides, there would be times when one would need the votes of colleagues to satisfy the demands of special interest groups in one's own constituency. By either line of reasoning, the sensible course was to give in and go along.

The view from Washington did harm to the understanding of group life in America. Congressmen in 1972 would have damaged the truth just as much had they enacted a heritage bill on the premise that the Lutheran mergers of the 1960s were the American norm. More emphatically, the most prudent decision would have been to pass no law at all; for when it comes to the experience of ethnic groups, there is no single norm.

How could there be? Different groups, depending on who they are, when they came here, where they settled, how they adjusted, what they thought of others and others of them, have different characteristics. That all groups have also known similar *patterns* of experience is true, but that does not signify that all have reached the same points of development. Even within a single group, as instanced at present by such extremes as fourth-generation Jews living in the suburbs and Brooklyn's recent Hasidic arrivals, the disparities in behavior and outlook are enormous.

A statute penalizing congressmen for failing to do their homework would fall very short of spurring them to accomplish the task at hand. For even if they learned to distinguish among heritages, they would go on legislating for groups without concern for the individuals who are said to belong to them. Lawmakers cannot bother with individuals, because the business of lawmaking bodies is with groups, farmers and manufacturers, exporters and importers, trade unionists and bankers, and on and on.

A discussion of the wisdom of legislative intervention in the economy can be left to others. For the purposes of our inquiry it is enough to say that, with the unhappy exception of "peoples of color," the law has customarily left individuals alone to define their ethnic as well as religious identities. The past decade departed from the tradition, and by way of concluding and summarizing this essay, let us return to the revival and consider the relation of ethnicity to individuality.

# 8    Liberty Means Choice

## Degrees of Affiliation

Revival leaders not only maintained that group self-identification was unchanging but that individuals had equally strong ethnic ties. Both errors stemmed from the kind of thinking that had led Horace Kallen astray earlier in the century. The concern for the group was so consuming that revival leaders shut their eyes to, or were genuinely unaware of, differences in individual experience, taste, and choice.

In either case, they fostered the misconception that white ethnics thought of themselves as ethnic all the time. Perhaps a few new pluralist intellectuals did, but the rank and file also identified themselves by religion, sex, age, occupation, education, income, politics, and region. Nor is it reasonable to suppose that ethnics were exempt from thinking of themselves as tall, short, fat, skinny, beautiful, ugly, outgoing, shy, happy, depressed, homebodies, swingers, football fans, music lovers, and on and on. The point is so obvious that one wonders if new pluralists truly appreciated the variety of the human condition. Ethnicity is important, but other things as well are involved in the question, Who am I?

The new pluralism also went too far in asserting that Americans were ethnics all. Here again a truth was pushed to the extreme and distorted. According to a survey conducted by the United States Bureau of the Census in the early 1970s, over half the whites identified themselves by "origin or descent." But close to 80,000,000 persons did not. Statistics aside, anyone who traveled around the country knew that some individuals felt more ethnic than others.[1]

Such was the case even among men and women of the same origin in a single city. In a survey of Milwaukee's Polish-Americans, Professor Donald E. Pienkos found that 48 percent of his sample affiliated with the group and 52 percent did not. High school and college students had the weakest ties. Those with the strongest included individuals of three sorts: "the elderly, less educated, more conservative who reside in heavily Polish neighborhoods"; businessmen and community officials servicing the group; and an educated minority determined to resist "general trends toward assimilation."[2]

Unpublished findings of the National Opinion Research Center reveal both higher and lower figures for the members of groups other than the one Professor Pienkos examined. Thus, when asked, "How important is your ethnic background to you?" 76 percent of the Jews, 43 percent of the Italians, and 32 percent of the Irish responded, "extremely important or quite important."[3] It is a matter of simple arithmetic to extrapolate from those answers the not insignificant proportion of individuals for whom the question was less or much less important.

The differences in the figures reported by the Census Bureau, the Milwaukee study, and the National Opinion Research Center are a reminder that percentages can convey a false precision. Nevertheless, whatever the disparities in techniques and in decimal-point returns, each of the samples confirmed that Americans were unalike in the intensity of their ethnic feelings. To put the matter more strongly, the three surveys agreed that the range of such feelings was considerable.

Moreover, within each of us there is a tugging and a pulling among the several things each of us is. No survey is likely to render that reality in human terms, a matter best left to both biographers and psychologists who credit every personality as unique. Yet, in the following words of an experienced people-watcher, we catch a glimpse of the ambiguities and ironies to which ethnics are subject:

> Minorities are in fact often divided as to what rights they really want, or think they want. Even individual

members of minorities are often divided within themselves, and change in mood from year to year or month to month, or even at different times of the day. A partly integrated society forces versatility in role-playing in an unusual degree on minority members. I have observed both in faraway countries and nearer at home certain minority people playing one role in the presence of local majority people, a second role, equally artificial, in the presence of more militant members of their own minority, and a third role, more natural, with their own friends, all minority people but none of them aggressively minoritarian. (That is a point too: minorities are not being minorities, or thinking of themselves as minorities, all the time.) In the first context these people may sound like social integrationists; in the second they may behave as if they were at heart secessionists; and in the third they may show themselves to be on the whole economic integrationists, with not much more taste for social integration in the full sense than for secession. But the conviction with which they adopt these roles will vary according to mood, the previous day's news, or even the rumors of the day itself.[4]

The obstacles to classifying Americans are such that one is tempted not to try. Still, with respect to scale of ethnic identification among individuals, there is now as in the past a configuration. Beyond the affiliation that others might ascribe to them, immigrants and their descendants fall into one of four categories:

*Total identifiers* live out their lives entirely within the ethnic group. They reside with their own kind, go to school with their own kind, work with their own kind, pray with their own kind, eat the food of their own kind, relax with their own kind, marry their own kind, and vote and campaign for their own kind. But the persons who do so willingly constitute a tiny fraction of the population. More commonly, total identifiers are recent immigrants who, for reasons of poverty and prejudice, have no choice but to live completely by themselves.

*Partial identifiers* take their ethnicity in measured and selective doses. It is usually most important to them in primary associations, but they are apt to define themselves in non-ethnic terms at work, in the community, or at college. The more such individuals play autonomous roles, the more they see themselves as being more than solely ethnic. They constitute a majority of Americans who retain ties to their ancestry.

*Disaffiliates* grew up in ethnic or ethno-religious neighborhoods but cannot go home again because they have chosen not to. They are most often found in the worlds of academia, the media, and show business. They are intellectuals, in a word. In a witty and combative article Andrew Greeley wrote that they are the same as ethnic groups.[5] That they constitute a tribe of their own is true. They have their own values, rituals, heroes, ways of bringing up children, and so on. Yet, unlike members of ethnic groups, disaffiliates are not tied together by a common ancestry. They number in the many millions and are likely to remain numerous when one considers the extraordinarily high percentage of Americans who go to college.

*Hybrids* cannot identify themselves through a single stock. They are of mixed ancestry and come from families that, for a long time, have intermarried. In a course at the University of Chicago on ethnicity in American history, there are students in whom the ethnicity has been so completely washed out that they have a hard time getting hold of the concept. Some of them even resent it, thinking that it is a mark of bigotry to sort out people according to their origins. Often these students are westerners, particularly from California, where it is usual to describe one's self as originating from Iowa, Pennsylvania, or some other eastern state. Such Americans are, in literal fact, products of the melting pot.[6]

Each of these categories calls for refinements. It is extremely hard to place people in a fluid society and for people to place themselves in it. Perhaps that is why America engenders more alienation than societies where everyone knows exactly where he or she fits. But such were the places from which masses of immigrants were uprooted and set in motion. In adjusting to America they, and later their progeny, fashioned ties of belonging appropriate to changing conditions. The process is likely to go on, for where boundaries are loose there is freedom to choose.

## Persisting Dilemma

It is now a given that blacks form one of many groups in America, yet bitter memories prevent them from viewing themselves as comparable to others in a pluralist democracy. None but their kind was brought to the New World in chains; defined as things in the national compact; fought over in the country's only civil war; needful of special Constitutional amendments; or set apart from everyone else by the supreme tribunal of the land. Throughout their history in America others have told blacks who they were.

Forced bondage destroyed ties to what they had been. Men and women did not arrive from the dark continent in the seventeenth and eighteenth centuries as undifferentiated Africans. They came as Ashanti, Ibo, Yoruba, Wolof, or members of still other tribes, with cultural and linguistic differences that were as significant as those that marked off incoming groups from Europe. The latter were each free, however, to nourish their distinctive ways. Slavery stripped Africans of most of theirs, and before long they came to know themselves only by common color and inferior status.

In the two centuries after the first emancipations of the Revolutionary era, free blacks struggled to fashion a new identity. Not the least of the difficulties was the choice of an appropriate name for their kind. It shifted from African in the eighteenth century to colored and Afro-American in the nineteenth, back to colored early in the twentieth and then to Negro and most recently to black. No immigrant group experienced the same confusion or designated itself by so gross a category as race or continent.[7]

The name mattered less, W. E. B. Du Bois noted, than the place blacks occupied in America. Although like Horace Kallen a Harvard Ph.D. (1895) and a student of William James, Du Bois did not define the position in pluralist terms. A few years after leaving Harvard he wrote: "One ever feels his twoness,—an American, a Negro; two souls, two thoughts, two unreconciled strivings; two warring ideals in one dark body." Unable to resolve those dualisms during his long life, Du Bois

died in 1963 both a Communist and a Ghanaian citizen. "I
was not an American," he said before leaving the United States,
but "a colored man in a white world."[8]

In the 1920s some writers and artists of the Harlem Renaissance glimpsed the possibility that Negroes might become equal
participants in multiethnic America. Deriving the hope from
the writings of Charles William Eliot and from the still popular credo of self-determination, such intellectuals traveled the
full distance to pluralism. They numbered few among the
educated classes, whose quest for integration precluded the
cultural distinctiveness of American blacks. Meanwhile, millions of persons rallied to Marcus Garvey's black nationalist
movement. It was not to be the last mass separatist expression.[9]

The anomalous position of blacks is reflected in the literature on ethnicity. An occasional Ralph Waldo Emerson welcomed people of color to his smelting pot, but Israel Zangwill
was less sanguine that racial intermarriage would be common.
Frederick Jackson Turner and Theodore Roosevelt, like Crèvecoeur in the eighteenth century, made no room at all for blacks
in the American crucible. Even the father of cultural pluralism
left them out of his plan for transethnic America. The new
pluralists of our day also drew a color line in their ancestral
mosaic.

But if exceptional in vital respects, the black experience
intersects the immigrant experience at two critical points. The
black identity is also an American artifact; and they have a
vital stake in making the national creed a reality. Indeed, as
the excluded outsiders for so long, they have been the persistent reminder of the liberties that are supposed to include
all American citizens.

The right to affiliate as one chooses is basic. There is considerable disagreement about where blacks now stand in that
respect in comparison to when Martin Luther King, Jr., dramatized the openness of the American dream. Many whites believe that blacks have achieved parity, while a number of blacks
insist that nothing has changed. The truth lies in neither extreme, because neither considers the same persons and both
refer to "the black" as if that term were the singular.

No trend of the past two decades is more striking than the upward mobility of millions of blacks. To a sizable body of individuals who remain trapped in the pathologies of the underclass, freedom of affiliation seems light years away from realization. But for young educated men and women of a growing middle class, options have opened as perhaps never before. The big question is whether the movement will not only continue but also broaden to take in people still outside it.

Forecasting the future of the most persistent dilemma in American history is risky, but recent experience suggests lines of direction. Improving conditions have not only raised expectations for fuller participation but actually brought increasing numbers of blacks closer to the goal of deciding for themselves how they will affiliate and in what degree. And that blacks desire this long deferred quest is apparent. Even Marxians among them concede: "Liberalism, if it amounts to anything, must mean the freedom of the individual to choose his or her allegiances."[10]

## Guides from the Past

Ethnic diversity has been a persistent factor in American history, but it has defied rigid categorization. Significantly, attempts to reduce it to a pat formula have risen in troubled times. Israel Zangwill's melting-pot model, Madison Grant's Anglo-Saxon racism, and Horace Kallen's grand design for a federation of nationalities were single-minded prescriptions for the immigrant problem. Today few persons seriously think that any of the three comprehends the American mix as it actually is or was in all its variety.

An assessment of the new pluralism proposed by the white-ethnic revival must also begin with historical context. There was no sign of a revival when the 1960s opened with the election of the nation's first Catholic President. Kennedy's victory laid to rest an issue that previously divided the old and newer stocks, and the reconciliation moved on to near unanimous approval of repealing the immigration-quota laws. For a brief moment, multiethnic America was at ease with itself.

The decade closed to the tumult of Vietnam and other divisive discontents. Separatist factions, themselves symptoms of a fragmenting society, also contributed to the ungluing process. Normally sanguine persons feared that America would come fully apart. It did not, but the post–World War II era consensuses washed away. Neither the 1972 presidential landslide, nor the end of the war in Southeast Asia, nor the resolution of the Constitutional emergency caused by Watergate brought the American people together again.

Begotten and sustained by the national identity crisis, the new pluralism called for a renewal of traditional ties. Although purporting to describe America as it was and had been, the new pluralism was really a proposal for things as they ought to be. In that respect it stood in a direct line from earlier blueprints. Like Horace Kallen and his followers, the new pluralists wanted to remake the United States into a commonwealth of ethnic groups. Conversely, the advocates of both the melting pot and Anglo-Saxonism hoped, although for different reasons and in different ways, to collapse varied ancestral groups into a uniform American type and culture.

Like many another extreme expression engendered by the troubled 1960s, the revival petered out by the Bicentennial year. Government did not stay permanently interested; the media discovered other newsmaking subjects; foundations addressed themselves to new problems; and academia tamed the movement by conceding ethnic-studies programs to it. Meanwhile, various group leaders turned into themselves, tired, gave up, dropped out, joined the mainstream, or found alternative causes in, among other things, women's liberation and the exhilaration of American sports.

It is next to impossible for the United States to avoid prescriptions. Theories may come and go, but ethnic diversity remains a condition of American life, and the question persists: What is one to make of that condition? Despite the popularity of *Roots* and *Holocaust*, TV will not do as a guide. The nostalgia and *angst* of the 1970s, as in the previous decade, draw attention away from the character of group life in America, the relation of individuals to it, and the common nationality that has historically held together the multiplicity of peoples assembled on this continent-sized country of ours.

Notwithstanding the certitudes of ethnic ideologues, America is not merely a collection of ethnic groups. Nor was it so in the past. There exists now as previously a complex of political, occupational, religious, civic, and neighborhood associations. They sometimes overlap with the ethnic, but the boundaries for the most part are fluid rather than fixed. Neither in practice nor in theory has America's *historic* pluralism consisted of isolated fortresses.

America is home for individuals as well as for groups, and no more than the latter do the former care to be boxed in. For many persons ethnic affiliation strengthens sense of self. Not only life-giving under normal circumstances, that identity provides psychic protection when an encroaching state reduces Americans to categories that are meaningful only to bureaucrats. Most prized when voluntary instead of ascribed, ethnic affiliation leaves room for additional identities appropriate to one's position in life.

Both individual and group rights inhere in America's concept of nationality. Formulated during the Revolution for a people whose development denied them the bond of common origins, it stated that Americans were unique in the liberties they enjoyed as citizens in a free society. Nothing better illustrates that enduring character of the national identity than the now close to 200-year-old naturalization procedure. Upon identifying with the Constitutional principles of the Republic, a candidate becomes a citizen of the United States and therefore an American in nationality. Legally, he shares the new status with all Americans of no matter what descent.

It is easy enough to cite the occasions when that inclusiveness collapsed under one form of bigotry or another. From the Alien and Sedition Acts of the 1790s through the Know-Nothing eruptions of the 1850s through the triumph of Anglo-Saxonist proscriptions in the 1920s through the internment of Japanese-Americans in the 1940s, there is an ugly legacy of hatred, violence, and dangerous and foolish thinking. But the prescriptive part of the national creed, in every instance thus far, provided a resilient and therefore self-correcting mechanism. Without that eighteenth-century given of the liberties which America was supposed to represent, there could have been no basis for saying that the people of this country were Americans all.

Other multiethnic countries make finer distinctions. In the USSR a person takes at age sixteen one of the officially recognized Soviet nationalities by which he will be known on his passport until he dies. Even democratic Canada requires in its census that individuals state their "original" nationality on the father's side, no matter how many generations ago the first paternal ancestor arrived in Canada. When a citizen of Fiji returns from a trip abroad he must declare on his landing permit whether he is by nationality Fijian, Indian, or European.

Should any of those regulations come to be imposed on Americans, the United States will cease to be what it has been. It was the first country in modern history to take the position that expatriation is a basic human right. It thereby served its own interest as the world's leading receiver of immigrants, but it also released a liberating idea for mankind: the idea that nationalities are changeable rather than irrevocable. As with so much else in America, the welcome to newcomers symbolized a fresh start, the chance to begin anew, an opportunity to choose.

At the same time, the terms for becoming a naturalized citizen did not require immigrants to give up their religions, languages, memories, customs, music, foods, or whatever else they cared to preserve in the folk culture. Unlike such countries as Brazil or France, America's definition of nationality was civic rather than cultural. It therefore left space for different ethnic affiliations while upholding to a diverse people the unifying values of the nation's democratic polity and society.

That American conception of self was severely battered in the late 1960s and early 1970s, and though the crisis has receded, the country still has to regain the former sense of wholeness and pride and confidence. Much of the world, meanwhile, remains organized against liberty. America's place in the conflict should be obvious. For two centuries the national identity has rested on the peculiar faith that the One and the Many are not only mutually compatible but essential to freedom. Few other multiethnic countries live by a transcending creed that the members of their constituent tribes or nationalities have willingly chosen.

# Notes

*To avoid wearying and distracting the reader with frequent citations, I have followed the now common practice of combining references, wherever possible, to document a single line of thought.*

## Chapter 1

1. "Six Historians Reflect on What Ails the American Spirit," *Newsweek*, 6 July 1970, pp. 15, 26.

2. Theodore H. White, *The Making of the President 1972* (New York, 1973), p. vii; Daniel P. Moynihan, "The American Experiment," *Public Interest*, Fall 1975, p. 7.

3. *Time*, 8 April 1974, p. 23.

4. C. Vann Woodward, *The Strange Career of Jim Crow* (New York, 1955), p. 124.

5. Samuel Lubell, *The Future of American Politics* (New York, 1952), pp. 58–80; John Higham, *Send These to Me: Jews and Other Immigrants in Urban America* (New York, 1975), p. 193.

6. The greatest single influence after World War II in vitalizing the history of immigration was Professor Oscar Handlin, who received the Pulitzer Prize in history for his *The Uprooted: The Epic Story of the Great Migrations That Made the American People* (Boston, 1951). It was preceded by Handlin's *Boston's Immigrants, 1790–1865: A Study in Acculturation* (Cambridge, Mass., 1941), and followed by *The American People in the Twentieth Century* (Cambridge, Mass., 1954); *Race and Nationality in American Life* (Boston, 1957); *Al Smith and His America* (Boston, 1958); *The Newcomers: Negroes and Puerto Ricans in a Changing Metropolis* (Cambridge, Mass., 1959); *Immigration as a Factor in American History* (Englewood Cliffs, N.J., 1959); *Fire-Bell in the Night: The Crisis in Civil Rights* (Boston, 1964); *Children of the Uprooted* (New York, 1966). For an appreciation of Handlin, see Maldwyn A. Jones, "Oscar Handin," in *Pastmasters: Some Essays on American Historians*, ed. Marcus Cunliffe and Robin W. Winks (New York, 1969), pp. 239–77.

In addition to his own books and articles, Handlin exerted a major influence through his students' work. See, for example, Rowland T. Berthoff, *British Immigrants in Industrial America, 1790–1950* (Cambridge, Mass., 1953); Robert D. Cross, *The Emergence of Liberal*

*Catholicism in America* (Cambridge, Mass., 1958); J. Joseph Huth-macher, *Massachusetts People and Politics, 1919–1933* (Cambridge, Mass., 1959); Arthur Mann, *La Guardia, a Fighter against His Times, 1882–1933* (Philadelphia, 1959); Mann, *La Guardia Comes to Power: 1933* (Philadelphia, 1965); Moses Rischin, *The Promised City: New York's Jews, 1870–1914* (Cambridge, Mass., 1962); William V. Shannon, *The American Irish* (New York, 1963); Barbara M. Solomon, *Ancestors and Immigrants: A Changing New England Tradition* (Cambridge, Mass., 1956).

But the interest in multiethnic sources of American civilization extended beyond the Handlin circle, as demonstrated by Robrt Ernst, *Immigrant Life in New York City, 1825–1863* (New York, 1949); John Higham, *Strangers in the Land: Patterns of American Nativism, 1860–1925* (New Brunswick, N.J., 1955); Will Herberg, *Protestant-Catholic-Jew: An Essay in American Religious Sociology* (Garden City, N.Y., 1955); Edwin O'Connor, *The Last Hurrah* (Boston, 1956); Maldwyn A. Jones, *American Immigration* (Chicago, 1960); Robert A. Dahl, *Who Governs? Democracy and Power in an American City* (New Haven, 1961); Nathan Glazer and Daniel Patrick Moynihan, *Beyond the Melting Pot: The Negroes, Puerto Ricans, Jews, Italians, and Irish of New York City* (Cambridge, Mass., 1963); Milton M. Gordon, *Assimilation in American Life: The Role of Race, Religion, and National Origins* (New York, 1964); E. Digby Baltzell, *The Protestant Establishment: Aristocracy & Caste in America* (New York, 1964).

I could go on and on with citations, but my purpose is not to give a complete bibliography; rather, it is to establish the point that ethnic studies were well under way before the ethnic revival of the late 1960s. As for things black, compare the ample bibliographical essays in the successive editions of John Hope Franklin's classic history, *From Slavery to Freedom: A History of Negro Americans* (New York, 1947, 1956, 1967).

7. Bureau of National Affairs, *State Fair Employment Laws and Their Administration: Texts, Federal State Cooperation, Prohibited Acts* (Washington, D.C., 1964). For a partisan but illuminating analysis of the difference between the two policies for minorities, see Nathan Glazer, *Affimative Discrimination: Ethnic Inequality and Public Policy* (New York, 1975).

8. U.S., President, *Public Papers of the Presidents of the United States* (Washington, D.C.: Office of the *Federal Register*, National Archives and Records Service, 1953–    ), John F. Kennedy, 1962, pp. 470–71.

9. Cf. John Higham, ed., *The Reconstruction of American History* (London, 1962); Reinhold Niebuhr, *The Children of Light and the Children of Darkness: A Vindication of Democracy and a Critique of Its Traditional Defense* (New York, 1944); Arthur M. Schlesinger, Jr., *The Vital Center: The Politics of Freedom* (Boston, 1949); Danie! J. Boorstin, *The Genius of American Politics* (Chicago, 1953); Louis Hartz, *The Liberal Tradition in America: An Interpretation of American Political Thought since the Revolution* (New York, 1955); Rich-

ard Hofstadter, *The Age of Reform: From Bryan to F.D.R.* (New York, 1955); Elting E. Morison, ed., *The American Style: Essays in Value and Performance* (New York, 1958); Daniel Bell, ed., *The New American Right* (New York, 1955); Bell, *The End of Ideology: On the Exhaustion of Political Ideas in the Fifties* (Glencoe, Ill., 1960); Oscar Handlin, ed., *American Principles and Issues: The National Purpose* (New York, 1961).

10. Like many other social movements, we know much more about the origins and peak of the Marxist left of the 1930s than its demise and aftermath. The latter story has yet to be told in all its complexity, and this is no place to attempt it. For the points I have emphasized, see David A. Shannon, *The Decline of American Communism: The Communist Party since 1945* (New York, 1959); Irving Howe and Lewis Coser, *The American Communist Party: A Critical History, 1919–1957* (Boston, 1957), pp. 437–99; "Our Country and Our Culture: A Symposium," *Partisan Review* 19 (1952): 282–326, 420–50, 562–97; Bell, *The End of Ideology*, esp. pp. 265–375; Max Lerner, *America as a Civilization: Life and Thought in the United States Today* (New York, 1957).

11. Quoted in "The Showdown Fight over Inflation," *Time*, 16 August 1971, p. 68.

12. Ben J. Wattenberg, *The Real America: A Surprising Examination of the State of the Union* (New York, 1974), pp. 124–51; Nathan Glazer, ed., *Cities in Trouble* (Chicago, 1970); Glazer, "Limits of Social Policy," *Commentary*, September 1971, pp. 51–58.

13. Bayard Hooper, "Can We Believe What the Young Tell Us?" *Social Education*, March 1972, p. 270. See also the Harris Survey, "Record Lows in Public Confidence," mimeographed (6 October 1975), pp. 1–2; American Jewish Committee, *Group Life in America: A Task Force Report* (New York, 1972), pp. 2–3.

14. Jean-François Revel, *Without Marx or Jesus: The New American Revolution Has Begun* (New York, 1970).

15. Ralph Waldo Emerson, "Historic Notes of Life and Letters in New England," in *The Complete Works of Ralph Waldo Emerson*, with a biographical introduction and notes by Edward Waldo Emerson, 12 vols. (Boston, 1903–4), 10: 325; Lionel Trilling, *Beyond Culture: Essays on Literature and Learning* (New York, 1965), pp. ix–xviii and passim; Theodore H. White, *The Making of the President 1968* (New York, 1969), pp. 226–30; Norman Podhoretz, "Adversaries or Critics?" *Commentary*, March 1971, pp. 6–7; Daniel P. Moynihan, "The Presidency & the Press," ibid., pp. 41–52.

16. Norman Podhoretz, "What the Voters Sensed," *Commentary*, January 1973, p. 6.

17. Andrew M. Greeley, *Building Coalitions: American Politics in the 1970s* (New York, 1974), p. 13.

18. Quoted ibid., p. 32.

19. Ben J. Wattenberg quoted in White, *The Making of the President 1972*, p. 161.

20. Seymour Martin Lipset and Earl Raab, "The Election and the National Mood," *Commentary*, January 1973, p. 43.

21. See Theodore H. White's splendidly written and insightful *Breach of Faith: The Fall of Richard Nixon* (New York, 1975).

22. Quoted in Chicago *Tribune*, 28 June 1976.

23. U.S., Congress, House, Committee on Education and Labor, *Ethnic Heritage Studies Centers, Hearings before the General Subcommittee on Education of the Committee on Education and Labor* (HR 14910), 91st Cong., 2d sess., 1970, p. 262.

24. Quoted in Bryce Nelson, "White Ethnic Groups Look for Recognition," Los Angeles *Times*, 24 November 1969. See also Sheila Wolfe, "Ethnicity," *Illinois Journal of Education*, April 1970, pp. 30-32.

25. Quoted in *U.S. News & World Report*, 19 April 1971, p. 93.

## Chapter 2

1. Peter Binzen, *Whitetown, U.S.A.* (New York, 1970), pp. 6-7, 33.

2. Daniel P. Moynihan, "The Crisis in Welfare," *Public Interest* 10 (1968): 25.

3. "News from the Ford Foundation," Press Release, 15 January 1971.

4. Education Amendments Act, 86 Stat. 346 (1972).

5. *Wall Street Journal*, 24 April 1969.

6. Kevin P. Phillips, *The Emerging Republican Majority* (New Rochelle, N.Y., 1969).

7. For an illuminating account of the kinds of snobbisms to which some liberals were disposed, see Michael Lerner, "Respectable Bigotry," *American Scholar* 38 (1969): 606-17.

8. Bertram H. Gold, "Reducing Group Tension: A Strategy for Ethnic Whites," a project proposal submitted to the Stern Family Fund by the American Jewish Committee, May 1969, p. 4.

9. Irving M. Levine quoted in *Wall Street Journal*, 24 April 1969.

10. American Jewish Committee, "National Project on Ethnic America: A Depolarization Program of the American Jewish Committee" (New York, n.d.), leaflet.

11. Irving M. Levine and Judith M. Herman, "The Ethnic Factor in Blue Collar Life" (unpublished manuscript, 1971), p. 4.

12. Quoted in American Jewish Committee, *The Reacting Americans: An Interim Look at the White Ethnic Lower Middle Class* (New York, 1969), p. 8.

13. Quoted in Binzen, *Whitetown, U.S.A.*, pp. 28-29.

14. Gold, "Reducing Group Tension," p. 6.

15. Quoted in *Wall Street Journal*, 24 April 1969.

16. *Steel Labor*, September 1970, p. 8.

17. Quoted in New York *Times*, 17 June 1970. Also see Geno C. Baroni, ed., "Report on Urban Ethnic Affairs" (mimeo., 10 November 1970).

18. U.S. Catholic Conference, "1969 Labor Day Statement," *Catholic Mind* 67 (September 1969): 1.

19. Geno C. Baroni, "I'm a Pig Too," reprint, *Washingtonian Magazine*, July 1970, unpaginated.

20. Chapman to Arthur Mann, 27 August 1970.

21. See the illuminating essay by Thaddeus Radzialowski, "The View from a Polish Ghetto: Some Observations on the First One Hundred Years in Detroit," *Ethnicity* 1 (July 1974): 125–50.

22. Baroni, "I'm a Pig Too."

23. Andrew M. Greeley, *Why Can't They Be Like Us?: Facts and Fallacies about Ethnic Differences and Group Conflicts in America* (New York, 1969), pp. 20, 75.

24. M. L. Hansen, "The Problem of the Third Generation Immigrant," Augustana Historical Society Publications, Reports (Rock Island, Ill., 1938), pp. 9–13.

25. Cf. Barbara Miller Solomon, *Ancestors and Immigrants: A Changing New England Tradition* (Cambridge, 1956); John Higham, *Strangers in the Land: Patterns of American Nativism 1860–1925* (New Brunswick, N.J., 1955).

26. Baroni, "I'm a Pig Too."

27. Quoted in Chicago *Sun Times*, 12 June 1971.

28. U.S., Congress, House, Committee on Education and Labor, *Ethnic Heritage Studies Centers, Hearings before the General Subcommittee on Education of the Committee on Education and Labor* (HR 14910), 91st Cong., 2d sess., 1970, pp. 4, 129, 144.

29. Gunnar Myrdal, "The Case against Romantic Ethnicity," *Center Magazine* 7 (July–August 1974): 28.

30. John M. Cammett, ed., *The Italian American Novel*, Proceedings of the Second Annual Conference of the American Italian Historical Association, 25 October 1969.

31. U.S., Congress, *Ethnic Heritage Studies Centers Hearings*, pp. 153–67.

32. Andrew M. Greeley, *That Most Distressful Nation: The Taming of the American Irish* (Chicago, 1972), pp. 3–4, 262–64; Greeley, *Why Can't They Be Like Us?* p. 57.

33. John Hope Franklin, Thomas F. Pettigrew, and Raymond W. Mack, *Ethnicity in American Life* (New York: Anti-Defamation League of B'nai B'rith, 1971), p. 34.

34. U.S., Congress, *Ethnic Heritage Studies Centers Hearings*, p. 2.

35. Quoted in Robert Coles, "The White Northerner," *Atlantic Monthly*, June 1966, p. 55.

36. Michael Novak, "Black and White in Catholic Eyes," *A New America*, January 1976, pp. 2–6. For a penetrating criticism of Novak, see Andrew M. Greeley, "Column for Universal Press Syndicate—Catholic," January 1976.

37. See, for example, Michael Novak, *The Rise of the Unmeltable Ethnics* (New York, 1971); Peter Schrag, *The Decline of the WASP* (New York, 1971); Murray Friedman, ed., *Overcoming Middle Class Rage* (Philadelphia, 1971); Thomas C. Wheeler, ed., *The Immigrant Experience: The Anguish of Becoming American* (New York, 1971);

Michael Wenk, S. M. Tomasi, Geno Baroni, eds., *Pieces of a Dream: The Ethnic Worker's Crisis* (New York, 1972).

38. In the chronological order of publication, see Franklin, Pettigrew, Mack, *Ethnicity in American Life*, pp. 7 ff.; Arthur Mann, Neil Harris, and Sam Bass Warner, Jr., *History and the Role of the City in American Life* (Indianapolis, 1972), pp. 3–23; Harold R. Isaacs, "The New Pluralists," *Commentary*, March 1972, pp. 75–78; Norman Podhoretz, "The Idea of a Common Culture," ibid., June 1972, pp. 4–6; Robert Alter, "A Fever of Ethnicity," ibid., pp. 68–73; Oscar Handlin, *The Uprooted*, 2d ed. enl. (Boston, 1973), pp. 322, 330; John Higham, "Integration vs. Pluralism: Another American Dilemma," *Center Magazine* 7 (July–August 1974): 67–73; Nathan Glazer, "Ethnicity and the Schools," *Commentary*, September 1974, pp. 55–59; Daniel P. Moynihan, "The American Experiment," *Public Interest*, Fall 1975, p. 7.

39. Greeley has often been criticized for his popular books and articles, but his critics have failed to take notice of his scholarly work. See, for example, Greeley's "The Ethnic 'Revival' " (unpublished paper, Center for the Study of American Pluralism, University of Chicago, September 1974); "A Model for Ethnic Political Socialization," *American Journal of Political Science* 19 (May 1975): 187–206; *Ethnicity in the United States: A Preliminary Reconaissance* (New York, 1976); *The American Catholic: A Social Portrait* (New York, 1977); and, with William C. McCready, "The Transmission of Cultural Heritages: The Case of Irish and Italians," in *Ethnicity: Theory and Experience*, ed. Nathan Glazer and Daniel P. Moynihan (Cambridge, Mass., 1975), pp. 209–35.

## Chapter 3

1. Alexis de Tocqueville, *Democracy in America*, ed. Phillips Bradley, trans. Henry Reeve and Francis Bowen, 2 vols. (New York, 1945), 1:241–44.

2. James Bryce, *Modern Democracies*, 2 vols. (New York, 1921), 1:496; Gunnar Myrdal, *An American Dilemma: The Negro Problem and Modern Democracy* (New York, 1944), pp. 3, 5 ff.

3. Quoted in Daniel J. Boorstin, *The Lost World of Thomas Jefferson* (New York, 1948), p. 228.

4. Ibid.

5. Cf. Hans Kohn, *American Nationalism: An Interpretive Essay* (New York, 1957), pp. 3–8.

6. Tocqueville to Ernest de Chabrol [1831], quoted in Antoine Redier, *Comme disait M. de Tocqueville . . .* , 2d ed. (Paris, 1925), p. 97. My translation.

7. The best estimate—and it is only an estimate—of the ethnic composition of the American population at the end of the eighteenth century is the American Council of Learned Societies, "Report of Committee on Linguistic and National Stocks in the Population of the

United States," in *Annual Report of the American Historical Association for the Year 1931*, 3 vols. (Washington, D.C., 1932), 1:103–441. If one considers only the whites in the population, the proportion of English goes up (to 60 percent), but so does that of the non-English whites (to 40 percent). See 1:124.

8. Richard Hofstadter, *America at 1750: A Social Portrait* (New York, 1971), p. 31.

9. Winthrop S. Hudson, *American Protestantism*, Chicago History of American Civilization series (Chicago, 1961), p. 4.

10. Alexander Hamilton, James Madison, and John Jay, *The Federalist*, ed. Benjamin Fletcher Wright (Cambridge, Mass., 1961), p. 94.

11. Franklin to Peter Collinson, 9 May 1753, in *The Papers of Benjamin Franklin*, ed. Leonard W. Labaree, vols. 1–14; ed. William B. Willcox, vols. 15– (New Haven, 1959–), 4:483, 485; Charles Lee to James Monroe, [Summer 1780], *The Lee Papers* in *Collections of the New-York Historical Society of the Year 1781 [–1874]*, 4 vols. (New York, 1872–75), 3:431.

12. Thomas Paine, *Common Sense*, in *The Complete Writings of Thomas Paine*, ed. Philip S. Foner, 2 vols. (New York, 1945), 1:19; J. Hector St. John de Crèvecoeur, *Letters from an American Farmer* (London, 1782; reprint ed., New York, 1904), p. 54.

13. David Ramsay, *The History of South-Carolina from Its First Settlement In 1670, to The Year 1808*, 2 vols. (Charleston, 1809), 1:23; David Ramsay, *The History of the American Revolution*, 2 vols. (Philadelphia, 1789), 1:28; 2:311–12. For the quotation about Ramsay by Rush, see Page Smith, *The Historian and History* (New York, 1964), p. 166. Ramsay was not unique among native-born leaders of the Revolutionary generation in thinking that America was special because it had been peopled by more than one stock. For comparable views of John Adams, Benjamin Franklin, and Thomas Jefferson, who were appointed by the Continental Congress on 4 July 1776 to devise a seal for the United States of America, see *Journals of the Continental Congress 1774–1789*, ed. Worthington C. Ford et al., 34 vols. (Washington, 1904–37), 5:517–18, 689–90.

14. Herman Melville, *Redburn: His First Voyage* (New York, 1849), p. 214.

15. Tocqueville to Ernest de Chabrol, [1831], quoted in Jacob P. Mayer, *Alexis de Tocqueville: A Biographical Essay in Political Science*, trans. M. M. Bozman and C. Hahn (New York, 1940), pp. 37–38.

16. Crèvecoeur, *Letters*, p. 54.

17. Adams to Jefferson, 24 August 1815, *The Adams-Jefferson Letters: The Complete Correspondence Between Thomas Jefferson and Abigail and John Adams*, ed. Lester J. Cappon, 2 vols. (Chapel Hill, 1959), 2:455.

18. Thomas Paine, *Letter to the Abbé Raynal, on the Affairs of North America: in which the Mistakes of the Abbé's Account of the Revolution of America are Corrected and Cleared up*, in *Complete Writings*, 2:244.

19. Bernard Bailyn, *The Ideological Origins of the American Revolution* (Cambridge, Mass., 1967); Gordon S. Wood, *The Creation of the American Republic, 1776–1787* (Chapel Hill, 1969).

20. Quoted in Max Farrand, *The Framing of the Constitution of the United States* (New Haven, 1913), p. 62.

21. Cf. Daniel J. Boorstin, *America and the Image of Europe* (New York, 1960), pp. 19–20.

22. David Ramsay, "A Dissertation on the Manner of Acquiring the Character and Privileges of a Citizen of the United States" (1789), p. 1. Cf. Oscar and Mary Handlin, *The Dimensions of Liberty* (Cambridge, Mass., 1961), pp. 26–33; Yehoshua Arieli, *Individualism and Nationalism in American Ideology* (Cambridge, Mass., 1964), pp. 22–25; James H. Kettner, "The Development of American Citizenship in the Revolutionary Era: The Idea of Volitional Allegiance," *American Journal of Legal History* 18 (1974): 208–42.

23. For the Edwards, Adams, and Jefferson quotations, see, respectively, Hans Kohn, *The Idea of Nationalism: A Study in Its Origins and Background* (New York, 1944), p. 270; *Diary and Autobiography of John Adams*, ed. L. H. Butterfield, 4 vols. (Cambridge, Mass., 1961), 1:257; Boorstin, *Lost World of Jefferson*, p. 228.

24. Edmund Burke quoted in Halvdan Koht, *The American Spirit in Europe: A Survey of Transatlantic Influences* (Philadelphia, 1949), p. 7.

25. For the adulation of Washington, and Adams's objection, see Marcus Cunliffe, *George Washington: Man and Monument* (Boston, 1958), pp. 6, 16, 197, 198. The quotation by Webster can be found in Harry R. Warfel, *Noah Webster: Schoolmaster to America* (New York, 1936), p. 90.

26. Merle Curti, *The Roots of American Loyalty* (New York, 1946), p. 140.

27. See, for exampe, Lloyd Lewis, *Myths after Lincoln* (New York, 1929), pp. 106–17 passim.

28. Henry R. Esterbrook quoted in Ralph Henry Gabriel, *The Course of American Democratic Thought: An Intellectual History since 1815* (New York, 1940), p. 402. The Cleveland quotation is in ibid., p. 399. Also see Albert Bushnell Hart, *National Ideas Historically Traced, 1607–1907*, American Nation: A History, vol. 26 (New York, 1907), p. 353.

29. Charles A. Beard, *The Republic: Conversations on Fundamentals* (New York, 1943), p. 13.

30. The comparison of American history to the histories of other countries, a method that foreign travelers and foreign scholars have long taken for granted, is still in its infancy in the United States. For three hopeful beginnings see Seymour Martin Lipset, *The First New Nation: The United States in Historical and Comparative Perspective* (New York, 1963); Louis Hartz et al., *The Founding of New Societies: Studies in the Hitsory of the United States, Latin America, South Africa, Canada and Australia* (New York, 1964); and C. Vann

Woodward, ed., *The Comparative Approach to American History* (New York, 1968).

31. George Nadel, *Australia's Colonial Culture: Ideas, Men and Institutions in Mid-Nineteenth Century Eastern Australia* (Melbourne, 1957), p. 30.

32. Russel B. Ward, *The Australian Legend* (Melbourne, 1958).

33. For similar views to the ones I have just expressed about the strong transatlantic connections but weak transcolonial ties, see the remarks of Jack P. Greene and Bernard Bailyn in John A. Garraty, *Interpreting American History: Conversations with Historians*, 2 vols. (New York, 1970), 1:57–58, 82.

34. Quoted in Kohn, *Idea of Nationalism*, pp. 286–87.

35. Quoted in Kohn, *American Nationalism*, p. 13.

36. Ibid., pp. 9, 13. Cf. Henry Steele Commager's aptly titled *The Empire of Reason: How Europe Imagined and America Realized the Enlightenment* (Garden City, N.Y., 1977).

37. Abigail Adams to John Adams, 7 May, 1776, *Adams Family Correspondence*, ed. L. H. Butterfield, 4 vols. to date (Cambridge, Mass., 1963– ), 1:402.

38. George Santayana, *Character and Opinion in the United States: With Reminiscences of William James and Josiah Royce and Academic Life in America* (New York, 1920), p. 168; Woodrow Wilson, *War and Peace: Presidential Messages, Addresses, and Public Papers (1917–1924)*, in *The Public Papers of Woodrow Wilson*, ed. Ray Stannard Baker and William Dodd, 6 vols. (New York, 1925–27), 6:52.

39. Ebony, *Martin Luther King, Jr., 1929–1968* (Chicago: Johnson Publishing Co., 1968), p. 43.

## Chapter 4

1. Oscar Handlin, *The Uprooted: The Epic Story of the Great Migrations That Made the American People* (Boston, 1951), p. 3.

2. Quoted in John F. Kennedy, *A Nation of Immigrants* (New York, 1964), p. 18.

3. For an illuminating account of "The Transformation of the Statue of Liberty," see John Higham, *Send These to Me: Jews and Other Immigrants in Urban America* (New York, 1975), pp. 78–87.

4. Thomas Paine, *Common Sense*, in *The Complete Writings of Thomas Paine*, ed. Philip S. Foner, 2 vols. (New York, 1945), 1:30–31; George Washington, *The Writings of George Washington*, ed. John C. Fitzpatrick, 39 vols. (Washington, 1938), 27:252.

5. See, for exampe, Frank George Franklin, *The Legislative History of Naturalization in the United States: From the Revolutionary War to 1861* (Chicago, 1906), pp. 33 ff.

6. Thomas Jefferson, *Notes on the State of Virginia*, ed. William Peden (Chapel Hill, 1955), pp. 83–85.

7. Maurice R. Davie, *World Immigration, with Special Reference to the United States* (New York, 1936), pp. 11–12.

8. U.S., Bureau of the Census, *Eighth Census, 1860: Population* (Washington, D.C., 1864), pp. xxxi–xxxii; U.S., Bureau of the Census, *Eleventh Census of the United States, 1890: Population*, 2 vols. (Washington, D.C., 1895), 1:clxii; U.S., Bureau of the Census, *Statistical Abstract of the United States: 1973* (Washington, D.C., 1973), p. 94.

9. U.S., Bureau of the Census, *Eleventh Census, 1890: Population*, 1:clv, clxii–clxiii; U.S., Bureau of the Census, *Fourteenth Census of the United States, 1920: Population*, 4 vols. (Washington, D.C., 1922), 2:33.

10. Davie, *World Immigration*, p. 15.

11. Emilio Willems, "Brazil," in *The Positive Contribution by Immigrants*, ed. Oscar Handlin and Brinley Thomas (Paris, 1955), p. 120.

12. Herman Melville, *Redburn: His First Voyage* (New York, 1849), p. 214; Robert C. Park, *The Immigrant Press and Its Control* (New York, 1922), p. 318; Higham, *Send These to Me*, pp. 14, 16; Imre Ferenczi and Walter F. Willcox, *International Migrations*, 2 vols. (New York, 1929), 2:135, 153, 164.

13. U.S., Bureau of the Census, *Statistical Abstract of the United States: 1972* (Washington, D.C., 1972), p. 92.

14. Quoted in Franklin, *Legislative History of Naturalization*, p. 97.

15. Naturalization Act, 2 Stat. 153 (1802).

16. See, for example, Sir Alex Cockburn, *Nationality; or the Law Relating to Subjects and Aliens, Considered with a View to Future Legislation* (London, 1869), pp. 27–36, 38–41. For the relevant documents, there is a handy compendium in Sir Francis Piggott, *Nationality Including Naturalization and English Law on the High Seas and Beyond the Realm*, two parts (London, 1907), part I.

17. Alexis de Tocqueville, *Democracy in America*, ed. Phillips Bradley, trans. Henry Reeve and Francis Bowen, 2 vols. (New York, 1945), 1:394.

18. Quoted in John Bassett Moore, *A Digest of International Law*, 8 vols. (Washington, D.C., 1906), 3:587.

19. Act Concerning Right of Expatriation, 15 Stat. 223 (1868); Moore, *Digest of Internationl Law*, pp. 552 ff.; Cockburn, *Nationality*, pp. 70–135; United Nations, General Assembly, *Universal Declaration of Human Rights* (1949), art. 15.

20. Frances Wright quoted in Frank Thistlethwaite, *America and the Atlantic Community: Anglo-American Aspects, 1790–1850* (New York, 1963), p. 72.

21. Quoted in U.S., Immigration and Naturalization Service, *Gateway to Citizenship*, ed. Edwina Austin Avery (Washington, D.C., 1948), p. 185.

22. Cf. John Higham, *Strangers in the Land: Patterns Of American Nativism, 1860–1925* (New Brunswick, N.J., 1955), pp. 4, 6, 8.

23. Lincoln to Joshua Speed, 24 August 1855, *The Collected Works of Abraham Lincoln*, ed. Roy P. Basler, 9 vols. (New Brunswick, N.J., 1953), 2:323.

24. For the connection between the Revolution and antislavery, see J. Franklin Jameson's pioneering work, *The American Revolution*

*Considered as a Social Movement* (Princeton, 1926), pp. 30–39. Cf. John Hope Franklin, *From Slavery to Freedom: A History of Negro Americans*, 3d ed. (New York, 1967), pp. 126–44; David Brion Davis, *The Problem of Slavery in the Age of Revolution, 1770–1823* (Ithaca, N.Y., 1975), pp. 255 ff. Arthur Zilversmit's *The First Emancipation: The Abolition of Slavery in the North* (Chicago, 1967) is the best account of that subject.

25. *Edinburgh Review* quoted in Merle Curti, *The Growth of American Thought*, 2d ed. (New York, 1951), p. 246; Lincoln, "Speech at Peoria, Illinois, October 16, 1854," *Collected Works*, 2:255.

26. See, for example, Winthrop D. Jordan, *White over Black: American Attitudes toward the Negro, 1550–1812* (Chapel Hill, N.C., 1968), pp. 3–98; David Brion Davis, *The Problem of Slavery in Western Culture* (Ithaca, N.Y., 1966), pp. 50–53, 223–90, and passim; Carl N. Degler, *Out of Our Past: The Forces That Shaped Modern America* (New York, 1959), pp. 26–39; Oscar Handlin, *Race and Nationality in American Life* (Boston, 1957), pp. 3–28.

27. Cherokee Nation v. Georgia, 30 U.S. 1 (1831).

28. John L. Thomas, *The Liberator: William Lloyd Garrison* (Boston, 1963), pp. 93–100, 143–54; John Hope Franklin, *The Emancipation Proclamation* (New York, 1963), pp. 19, 21–22, 33–34, 50; Leon F. Litwack, *North of Slavery: The Negro in the Free States, 1790–1860* (Chicago, 1951), pp. 63–112, 153–86; Franklin, *From Slavery to Freedom*, p. 220.

29. Quoted in Frederick Van Dyne, *A Treatise on the Law of Naturalization of the United States* (Washington, D.C., 1907), p. 40.

30. Paul Rundquist, "A Uniform Rule: The Congress and the Courts in American Naturalization, 1865–1952," Ph.D. diss., University of Chicago, 1975, pp. 44–54.

31. For a brilliant analysis of the legal difficulties in the "white person" phrase, see John H. Wigmore, "American Naturalization and the Japanese," *American Law Review* 28 (1894):818–27.

32. See for example, Frederick Van Dyne, *Citizenship of the United States* (Rochester, N.Y., 1904), pp. 53–248; Luella Gettys, *The Law of Citizenship in the United States* (Chicago, 1934), pp. 142–59.

33. For the Dawes Act and the Elk, Camille, and Rodriguez cases, see Rundquist, "A Uniform Rule," pp. 59–67, 81–83, 101–6; Van Dyne, *Citizenship of the United States*, pp. 59–61, 151–59.

34. On the Chinese, see Rundquist, "A Uniform Rule," pp. 72–75, 89–95; Van Dyne, *Law of Naturalization*, pp. 42–43.

35. Van Dyne, *Citizenship of the United States*, pp. 58–59, 234–35.

36. For an analysis of the two Supreme Court decisions on the ineligibility of Japanese and Hindus, Ozawa v. United States and United States v. Thind, see Milton R. Konvitz, *The Alien and the Asiatic in American Law* (Ithaca, N.Y., 1946), pp. 81–95; Gettys, *The Law of Citizenship*, pp. 63–65.

37. Quoted in Rundquist, "A Uniform Rule," p. 327.

38. Immigration and Naturalization Act, 66 Stat. 239 (1952).

39. Carl N. Degler, *Neither Black nor White: Slavery and Race Relations in Brazil and the United States* (New York, 1971).

40. Horace Mann, *Twelfth Annual Report of the Board of Education, together with the Twelfth Annual Report of the Secretary of the Board* (Boston, 1849), p. 78.

41. E. Porter Belden, *New-York: Past, Present, and Future; Comprising a History of the City of New-York, a Description of Its Present Condition, and an Estimate of Its Future Increase* (New York, 1850), p. 44.

## Chapter 5

1. Eric Hoffer, *First Things, Last Things* (New York, 1971), p. 102. See also Eric Hoffer, *The Temper of Our Time* (New York, 1967).

2. Roosevelt to Zangwill, 15 October 1908, Theodore Roosevelt, *Letters of Theodore Roosevelt*, ed. Elting E. Morison, 8 vols. (Cambridge, Mass., 1951–54), 6:1289. Also see Joseph Leftwich, *Israel Zangwill* (New York, 1957), p. 252.

Mrs. Zangwill of course liked Roosevelt's praise, but she thought very poorly of his taste in general. His reaction to *The Melting-Pot* "is encouraging from a box office standpoint," she wrote to a friend, "because I always feel that Roosevelt is a glorified man in the street, a . . . commonplace person raised to the n*th* power and what would appeal to him would also be likely to appeal to the masses. Among other things Roosevelt said to me," she went on to say, " 'I'm not a Bernard Shaw man or Ibsen man, Mrs. Zangwill. No, *this* is the stuff.' Poor Israel. I had to repeat it to him to keep him humble. Not that the Shaw contrast matters but I thought everyone recognized Ibsen as a great genius." Edith Zangwill to Mrs. Yorke, 7 October 1908, Annie Russell Papers, New York Public Library.

3. There is an enormous amount of material about Zangwill's play, consisting of reviews, advertisements, and playbills, in the Robinson Locke Collection of Dramatic Scrapbooks and the Walker Whiteside Collection, Theater Collection, New York Public Library. Also see Walter Rigdon, ed., *The Biographical Encyclopedia and Who's Who of the American Theater* (New York, 1966), p. 31. For sales figures of *The Melting-Pot*, see enclosure in Zangwill to Brett, 16 June 1921, Macmillan Company Records, New York Public Library. The quotation from the Connecticut teacher is in Israel Zangwill, *The War for the World* (New York, 1916), p. 37.

4. Israel Zangwill, *The War God* (New York, 1912), p. 47.

5. Quoted in Maurice Wohlgelernter, *Israel Zangwill: A Study* (New York, 1964), p. 195.

6. For biographical details, I have relied on Leftwich's *Zangwill* and Wohlgelernter's *Zangwill*, both full of useful information and insight.

7. New York *Herald*, 6 November 1904.

8. Israel Zangwill, *The Next Religion* (New York, 1912); Wohlgelernter, *Zangwill*, p. 25.

9. Israel Zangwill, *Dreamers of the Ghetto* (New York and London, 1898), pp. 289–429. The preceding quotations are to be found in Wohlgelernter, *Zangwill*, p. v; Barnet Litvinoff, "Zangwill's Ghetto Is No More," *Commentary* 10 (October 1950):363.

10. Israel Zangwill, "The East Africa Offer," in Maurice Simon, ed., *Speeches, Articles, and Letters of Israel Zangwill* (London, 1937), pp. 226–27. For Zangwill's activities in the Zionist movement, see Wohlgelernter, *Zangwill*, pp. 38–40.

11. For a superb analysis of the Dillingham Commission, see Oscar Handlin, "Concerning the Background of the National-Origin Quota System," in President's Commission on Immigration and Naturalization, *Hearings before the President's Commission on Immigration and Naturalization* (Washington, 1952), pp. 1839–63.

12. Henry James, *The American Scene*, ed. Leon Edel (London, 1907; reprint ed., Bloomington, Ind., 1968), pp. 84–87, 118–20, 125, 132, 139, 195, 199, 206, 245, 265, 454–55.

13. H. G. Wells, *The Future in America: A Search after Realities* (New York, 1906), pp. 71–77, 119–20, 133–51, and passim.

14. James, *American Scene*, p. 64.

15. "Zangwill," *Literary Digest* 90 (21 August 1926):33.

16. Cf. Philip Gleason, "The Melting Pot: Symbol of Fusion or Confusion?" *American Quarterly* 16 (Spring 1964):20–46.

17. For the quarrel between Zangwill and his English critics, see John Palmer, "The Melting-Pot," *Saturday Review* 117 (16 May 1914):628; Zangwill, *War for the World*, p. 33; Israel Zangwill, Afterword to *The Melting-Pot* (New York, 1914), pp. 198–99.

18. The quotations, in the order of their appearance, are in: Burns Mantle, Chicago *Tribune*, 20 October 1908; "Mr. Zangwill's New Dramatic Gospel," *Current Literature* 45 (December 1908):671, 673; *English Review* 17 (April 1914):132; *Athenaeum*, no. 4501 (31 January 1914), p. 171.

19. New York *Daily Tribune*, 8 December 1909.

20. Holbrook Jackson, "Israel Zangwill," *Living Age* 282 (26 September 1914):795; Zangwill, Afterword, p. 208; *Athenaeum*, no. 4501, p. 171.

21. *American Magazine* 69 (January 1910):411.

22. *Independent* 67 (21 October 1909):931–32.

23. Roosevelt wrote a good deal about the subject of immigration over a long period of time, without changing his mind about the dangers of "hyphenated Americanism." See, for example, *The Works of Theodore Roosevelt*, ed. Hermann Hagedorn, 20 vols. (New York, 1926), 13:13–26; 14:192–207; 18:278–94, 371–76, 388–405. On Jane Addams's attitudes toward pluralist Chicago, see Steven J. Diner's insightful essay, "Chicago Social Workers and Blacks in the Progressive Era," *Social Service Review* 44 (December 1970):393–410. For the relationship between Addams's domestic pluralism and her internationalism, see John C. Farrell, *Beloved Lady: A History of Jane Addams' Ideas on Reform and Peace* (Baltimore, 1967).

24. Clayton Hamilton, "The Melting-Pot," *Forum* 42 (November 1909):434–35.

25. Quoted in "Mr. Zangwill's New Dramatic Gospel," p. 672. Even Reform rabbis, who, since the Pittsburgh Platform of the mid-1880s, had taken the position that Jews were not a people but a religious denomination, officially disapproved (in 1908 and 1909) of intermarriage as "contrary . . . to the Jewish religion." See David Philipson, "The Central Conference of American Rabbis, 1889–1939," *American Jewish Year Book 1940–41* (Philadelphia, 1940), pp. 205–6. For the dismissal of Reform rabbis who, among other things, preached intermarriage, see Arthur Mann, ed., *Growth and Achievement: Temple Israel, 1854–1954* (Cambridge, Mass., 1954), pp. 45–83.

26. Zangwill, Afterword, p. 208.

27. Ibid., p. 207; Zangwill, *War for the World*, p. 39.

28. Zangwill, Afterword, pp. 210, 213.

29. "Zangwill," p. 33. New York *Times*, 2 August 1926; Edward Price Bell, "Creed of the Klansmen, Interviews with H. W. Evans, Israel Zangwill . . . ," *Chicago Daily News Reprints* (1924), p. 11; Zangwill, "A Few Reflections, Is America Forsaking the Ideals of Her Founders?" Simon, ed., *Speeches* . . . , pp. 106–12.

30. New York *Times*, 3 August 1926.

31. Quoted in "Zangwill," p. 33.

32. J. Hector St. John de Crèvecoeur, *Letters from an American Farmer* (London, 1782; reprint ed., New York, 1904), pp. 54–55.

33. Ralph Waldo Emerson, *Journals of Ralph Waldo Emerson*, ed. Edward Waldo Emerson and Waldo Emerson Forbes, 10 vols. (Boston, 1909–14), 7:115–16.

34. Frederick Jackson Turner, *The Frontier in American History* (New York, 1920), pp. 22–23.

35. Theodore Roosevelt, *The Winning of the West*, 4 vols. (New York, 1889–96), 1:20; Theodore Roosevelt, *The Foes of Our Own Household* (New York, 1917), p. 58.

36. Winthrop D. Jordan, *White over Black: American Attitudes toward the Negro, 1550–1812* (Chapel Hill, 1968), p. 337. Cf. Carl Bridenbaugh, *Myths and Realities: Societies of the Colonial South* (Baton Rouge, 1952), p. 134: "We surely err," Professor Bridenbaugh writes, ". . . if we apply the concept of the *melting pot* to the Back Settlements, which, to choose a Biblical metaphor all its inhabitants would have readily understood, much more accurately resembled the Tower of Babel. Fate designated the Back Settlements as the scene of cultural conflict for many decades." For Crèvecoeur's own writings on unmelted ethnic communities, see his *Letters from an American Farmer*, p. 51, and his *Journey into Northern Pennsylvania and the State of New York*, trans. Clarissa S. Bostelman (Paris, 1801; reprint ed., Ann Arbor, 1964), pp. 31–41, 90–100, 253, 323–24, 344–59, 427–42, 458–60, 502, 527, 563. The latter view, namely, on the persistence of ethnicity, is corroborated by William Winterbotham, *An Historical, Geographical, Commercial and Philosophical View of the*

*United States, and the European Settlements in America and the West Indies*, 4 vols. (London, 1795), 2:437–40; Timothy Dwight, *Travels in New England and New York*, ed. Barbara Miller Solomon, 4 vols. (New Haven, 1821–22; Belknap Press ed., Cambridge, Mass., 1969), 1:xxxiv–xxxix, 365; 3:322, 329; 4:327; and David Ramsay, *The History of South-Carolina from Its First Settlement in 1670, to the Year 1808*, 2 vols. (Charleston, 1809), 1:1–25. For an earlier view of multiethnic New York than Crèvecoeur's but much the same as Dwight's later view, see Peter Kalm, *Travels into North America* (London, 1771–72); I have used the most recent American edition, *Peter Kalm's Travels in North America*, ed. Adolph B. Benson, 2 vols. (New York, 1937), 1:115–43.

37. Oscar Handlin, *Boston's Immigrants, 1790–1865: A Study in Acculturation* (Cambridge, Mass., 1941), pp. 182–83.

38. Merle Curti, *The Making of an American Community: A Case Study of Democracy in a Frontier County* (Stanford, 1959), pp. 99–105, 444.

39. For Turner's ancestry, see Ray Allen Billington, *Frederick Jackson Turner: Historian, Scholar, Teacher* (New York, 1973), pp. 3–5. The quotation about Portage, Wisconsin, can be found in Edward N. Saveth, *American Historians and European Immigrants, 1875–1925* (New York, 1948), p. 123.

40. There is now a considerable but nevertheless inconclusive and sometimes contradictory literature about the rates, variables, and patterns of intermarriage in the United States for this century. See, for example, the best and most recent compendium of its sort, Milton L. Barron, ed., *The Blending American: Patterns of Intermarriage* (Chicago, 1972). Compare it to the pioneering work of Julius Drachsler, *Intermarriage in New York City: A Statistical Study of the Amalgamation of European Peoples* (New York, 1921). Advocates of the "triple melting-pot" theory include: Ruby Jo Reeves Kennedy, "Single or Triple Melting-Pot? Intermarriage Trends in New Haven, 1870–1940," *American Journal of Sociology* 49 (January 1944):331–39; Kennedy, "Single or Triple Melting-Pot? Intermarriage Trends in New Haven, 1870–1950," ibid. 58 (July 1952): 56–59; Milton L. Barron, *People Who Intermarry: Intermarriage in a New England Industrial Community* (Syracuse, 1946), pp. 342–44 and passim; Will Herberg, *Catholic-Protestant-Jew: An Essay in American Religious Sociology* (New York, 1955), pp. 18–58. Comparative rates of religious intermarriage for the 1950s can be gleaned from U.S., Bureau of the Census, "Religion Reported by the Civilian Population of the United States: March, 1957," *Current Population Reports*, series P-20, no. 79, 2 February 1958, p. 8. For the rising rates of intermarriage between Jews and non-Jews, and the concern of Jewish leaders over that phenomenon, see Erich Rosenthal, "Studies of Jewish Intermarriage in the United States," *American Jewish Year Book 1963* (Philadelphia, 1963), pp. 3–53; Rosenthal, "Jewish Intermarriage in Indiana," *American Jewish Year Book 1967* (Philadelphia, 1967), pp. 243–64; Werner

J. Cahnman, ed., *Intermarriage and Jewish Life: A Symposium* (New York, 1963); Albert I. Gordon, *Intermarriage: Interfaith, Interracial, Interethnic* (Boston, 1964); Louis A. Berman, *Jews and Intermarriage: A Study in Personality and Culture* (New York, 1968); Fred Massarik and Alvin Chenkin, "United States National Jewish Population Study," *American Jewish Year Book 1973* (Philadelphia, 1973), pp. 292–306.

41. Francis G. Blair, "American Melting Pot," *Proceedings of the National Education Association of the United States*, 65 (1927):34; Arthur S. Link, *The Growth of American Democracy* (Boston, 1968), p. 414.

42. For the melting pot as a symbol of diversity and welcome, see Oscar Handlin, *The American People in the Twentieth Century* (Cambridge, Mass., 1954), p. 161; Arthur Mann, *La Guardia: A Fighter against His Times, 1882–1933* (Philadelphia, 1959); John R. Alden, *Rise of the American Republic* (New York, 1963), pp. 507–8; Neil Larry Shumsky, "Zangwill's *The Melting Pot*: Ethnic Tensions on Stage," *American Quarterly* 27 (March 1975):29–41; "Code for the Melting Pot," *Time* 59 (2 June 1952):16; "No More Melting Pot," *New Republic* 127 (7 July 1952):8; Meg Greenfield, "Melting Pot of Francis E. Walter," *Reporter* 25 (26 October 1961):24–28; "New Mix for America's Melting Pot," *U.S. News and World Report* 59 (11 October 1965):55–57.

## Chapter 6

1. Henry Pratt Fairchild, *The Melting-Pot Mistake* (Boston, 1926), p. 261.

2. Quoted in Albert K. Weinberg, *Manifest Destiny: A Study of Nationalist Expansionism in American History* (Baltimore, 1935), p. 361.

3. Hans Kohn, *The Idea of Nationalism: A Study in Its Origins and Background* (New York, 1944), pp. 329 ff.

4. Cf. Oscar Handlin, "Concerning the Background of the National-Origin System," in President's Commission on Immigration and Naturalization, *Hearings before the President's Commission on Immigration and Naturalization* (Washington, D.C., 1952), pp. 1839–63; John Higham, *Strangers in the Land: Patterns of American Nativism, 1860–1925* (New Brunswick, N.J., 1955); Barbara Miller Solomon, *Ancestors and Immigrants: A Changing New England Tradition* (Cambridge, Mass., 1956); Mark H. Haller, *Eugenics: Hereditarian Attitudes in American Thought* (New Brunswick, N.J., 1963).

5. Freeman quoted in Thomas F. Gossett, *Race: The History of an Idea in America* (Dallas, Tex., 1964), p. 109; Adams to Elizabeth Cameron, 15 September 1893, *Letters of Henry Adams*, ed. Worthington Chauncey Ford, 2 vols. (Boston, 1930–38), 2:33.

6. Quoted in Isaac B. Berkson, *Theories of Americanization: A Critical Study, with Special Reference to the Jewish Group* (New York, 1920), p. 59.

7. Richmond Mayo-Smith, *Emigration and Immigration: A Study in Social Science* (New York, 1890), pp. 53–78.

8. Ellwood P. Cubberley, *Changing Conceptions of Education* (Boston, 1909), p. 15.

9. See, for example, Edward G. Hartmann, *The Movement to Americanize the Immigrant* (New York, 1948); Joseph P. O'Grady, ed., *The Immigrant's Influence on Wilson's Peace Policies* (Lexington, Ky., 1967).

10. Walter Lippmann, *Men of Destiny* (New York, 1927), pp. 2, 9. Cf. Edmund A. Moore, *A Catholic Runs for President: The Campaign of 1928* (New York, 1956).

11. U.S., Congress, Senate, *Congressional Record*, 68th Cong., 1st sess., 1924, 65, pt. 6: 5961.

12. U.S., Congress, House, *Congressional Record*, 68th Cong., 1st sess., 1924, 65, pt. 6: 5887.

13. See, for example, *Whom We Shall Welcome: Report of the President's Commission on Immigration and Naturalization* (Washington, D.C., 1953); Arthur Mann, "Attitudes and Policies on Immigration: An Opportunity for Revision," *Publication of the American Jewish Historical Society* 46 (1957):289–305.

14. *Weekly Compilation of Presidential Documents,* I, no. 11 (Monday, 11 October 1965), p. 365. On Kennedy's role as a senator in the repeal movement, see John F. Kennedy, *A Nation of Immigrants* (New York, 1958), particularly pp. 33–37. Later published in the 1960s by Harper and Row, this work was originally commissioned and published by the Anti-Defamation League of B'nai B'rith, a Jewish defense organization prominent in the repeal movement.

15. Herman Melville, *Redburn: His First Voyage* (New York, 1849), p. 214; Philip Schaff, *America: A Sketch of Its Political, Social, and Religious Character*, ed. Perry Miller (New York, 1855; Belknap Press ed., Cambridge, Mass., 1961), p. 45; Carl Schurz, "German Day," in *Speeches, Correspondence and Political Papers of Carl Schurz*, ed. Frederic Bancroft, 6 vols. (New York, 1913), 5:190.

16. Horace M. Kallen, Interviewed by Milton R. Konvitz and Dorothy Oko (William E. Wiener Oral History Library of the American Jewish Committee, 1964), tape 4, p. 48. For Kallen's linking Zionism to cultural pluralism, see his untitled address in Intercollegiate Menorah Association, *The Menorah Movement for the Study and Advancement of Jewish Culture and Ideals: History, Purposes, Activities* (Ann Arbor, Mich., 1914), pp. 85–86. The distinction he made between Hebraists and Judaists can be found in "The Third Annual Convention of the Menorah Societies," *Menorah Journal* 1 (1915): 130–32. He acknowledged Ahad Ha'am's importance in Horace M. Kallen, "In the Hope of the New Zion," *International Journal of Ethics* 29 (1918–19):452–53. The Brandeis quotation comes from Louis D. Brandeis, "A Call to the Educated Jew," *Menorah Journal* 1 (1915):18. For an overview of Kallen's long concern with things Jewish, see his *Judaism at Bay: Essays toward the Adjustment of Judaism to Modernity* (New

York, 1932) and *"Of Them Which Say They Are Jews" and Other Essays on the Jewish Struggle for Survival* (New York, 1954). There are useful biographical details in Sidney Ratner, ed., *Vision and Action: Essays in Honor of Horace M. Kallen on His 70th Birthday* (New Brunswick, N.J., 1953), pp. v–xi; Kallen, *Individualism: An American Way of Life* (New York, 1933), pp. 5–14; Kallen, "The Promise of the Menorah Idea," *Menorah Journal* 49 (1962):9–16; Kallen, *What I Believe and Why—Maybe*, ed. Alfred J. Marrow (New York, 1971), pp. 9–12.

17. Quoted in Emily Greene Balch, *Our Slavic Fellow Citizens* (New York, 1910), pp. 398–99.

18. For the foregoing quotations, see Horace M. Kallen, *Culture and Democracy in the United States: Studies in the Group Psychology of the American Peoples* (New York, 1924), pp. 116, 122.

19. Bertrand Russell, "Americanization," *Dial* 77 (1924):158–60; Nicholas Roosevelt, "Professor Kallen Proposes to Balkanize America," *New York Times Book Review*, 20 April 1924, p. 3; Brander Matthews, "Making America a Racial Crazy-Quilt," *Literary Digest International Book Review*, 1924, pp. 641–42, 644.

20. Berkson, *Theories of Americanization*, pp. 79–93; Alexander M. Dushkin, *Jewish Education in New York City* (New York, 1918), pp. 17–27. Berkson was supervisor of schools and extension activities of the Bureau of Jewish Education, and Dushkin was head of that Bureau's Department of Research. Cf. Julius Drachsler, *Democracy and Assimilation: The Blending of Immigrant Heritages in America* (New York, 1920), pp. 75–84.

21. See, for example, Louis D. Brandeis, *Brandeis on Zionism: A Collection of Addresses and Statements* (Washington, D.C., 1942); Randolph S. Bourne, "The Jew and Trans-National America," *Menorah Journal* 2 (1916):277–84; Norman Hapgood, "The Jews and American Democracy," ibid. 2 (1916):201–5.

22. Oscar Handlin, "Historical Perspectives on the American Ethnic Group," *Daedalus*, Spring 1961, p. 232. The two educators previously cited were William E. Vickery and Stewart G. Cole, *Intercultural Education in American Schools: Proposed Objectives and Methods* (New York, 1943), p. 35. For the history of cultural pluralism's reception, see James Henry Powell's splendidly detailed "Concept of Cultural Pluralism in American Social Thought, 1915–1965," Ph.D. diss., University of Notre Dame, 1971. I have also profited from the insights of John Higham, *Send These to Me: Jews and Other Immigrants in Urban America* (New York, 1975), pp. 196–230; and Milton M. Gordon, *Assimilation in American Life: The Role of Race, Religion, and National Origins* (New York, 1964), pp. 156–59.

23. W. Lloyd Warner and Leo Srole, *The Social Systems of American Ethnic Groups* (New Haven, 1945), pp. 295–96. Compare their prediction of the ethnic group's demise with the earlier Chicago prediction of Robert E. Park and Robert A. Miller, *Old World Traits Transplanted* (New York, 1925), particularly pp. 296–308. For the

theory of disappearance through neighborhood dispersion, see, in addition to Warner and Srole's *Social Systems,* pp. 33–52, the following: Ernest Burgess, "Residential Segregation in American Cities," *Annals of the American Academy of Political and Social Science* 140 (1928):105–15; Paul F. Cressey, "Population Succession in Chicago, 1898–1930," *American Journal of Sociology* 44 (1938):59–69; Richard G. Ford, "Population Succession in Chicago," *American Journal of Sociology* 56 (1950):156–60; Otis D. Duncan and Stanley Lieberson, "Ethnic Segregation and Assimilation," *American Journal of Sociology* 64 (1959):364–74. For a convincing rebuttal of the theory of disappearance through dispersion, see Nathan Kantrowitz, *Ethnic and Racial Segregation in the New York Metropolis: Residential Patterns among White Ethnic Groups, Blacks and Puerto Ricans* (New York, 1972).

24. New York *Times,* 10 December 1972.

25. There is a superb but curiously neglected history of the New York failure by Arthur A. Goren, *New York Jews and the Quest for Community: The Kehillah Experiment, 1908–1922* (New York, 1970). For the full details of Jewish pluralism, see Moses Rischin's painstakingly researched *The Promised City: New York's Jews, 1870–1914* (Cambridge, Mass., 1962).

26. Horace M. Kallen, Interviewed by Alfred J. Marrow (William E. Wiener Oral History Library of the American Jewish Committee, 1973), tape 1, pp. 17–22.

27. For a contrary argument, see Milton R. Konvitz, "Horace Meyer Kallen, Philosopher of the Hebraic-American Idea," *American Jewish Year Book 1974–1975* (Philadelphia, 1975), pp. 55–80.

28. James quoted in Solomon, *Ancestors and Immigrants,* p. 185.

29. Charles William Eliot, *American Contributions to Civilization and Other Essays and Addresses* (New York, 1897), pp. 30–32; Eliot, "What Is an American?" *Collier's* 57 (12 August 1916):20.

30. Balch, *Our Slavic Fellow Citizens,* pp. 378–425; Randolph S. Bourne, "Trans-National America," *Atlantic Monthly* 118 (1916): 86–97.

## Chapter 7

1. In this and subsequent comparisons, I am indebted to S. N. Eisenstadt, *The Absorption of Immigrants: A Comparative Study Based Mainly on the Jewish Community in Palestine and the State of Israel* (Glencoe, Ill., 1955); Eisenstadt and Stein Rokkan, eds., *Building States and Nations,* 2 vols. (Beverly Hills, Calif., 1973); Nathan Glazer and Daniel P. Moynihan, eds., *Ethnicity: Theory and Experience* (Cambridge, Mass., 1975).

2. See, for example, the unpaginated maps in City of Chicago, Department of Development and Planning, *Historic City: The Settlement of Chicago* (Chicago, 1976).

3. Marcus L. Hansen, *The Immigrant in American History* (Cambridge, Mass., 1940), p. 132.

4. Richard J. Jensen, *The Winning of the Midwest: Social and Political Conflict, 1888–1896* (Chicago, 1971), pp. 123–40, 145–46, 148, 159–60, 219–21.

5. Quoted in Harold R. Isaacs, *Idols of the Tribe: Group Identity and Political Change* (New York, 1975), p. 211.

6. Antonio Mangano, "The Associated Life of the Italians in New York City," *Charities* 12 (1904):476–82; Robert E. Park and Herbert A. Miller, *Old World Traits Transplanted* (New York, 1921), pp. 146–47, 242; John Horace Mariano, *The Second Generation of Italians in New York City* (Boston, 1921); Oscar Handlin, *The American People in the Twentieth Century* (Cambridge, Mass., 1954), pp. 57–61; Joseph Lopreato, *Italian Americans* (New York, 1970), pp. 101–6; Humbert S. Nelli, *The Italians in Chicago, 1880–1930: A Study in Ethnic Mobility* (New York, 1970), pp. xiii, 6, 22–54, 156–200; Humbert S. Nelli, "Italians in Urban America," in Silvano M. Tomasi and Madeline H. Engel, eds., *The Italian Experience in the United States* (New York, 1970), pp. 77–102.

7. Arthur Mann, *La Guardia: A Fighter against His Times, 1882–1933* (Philadelphia, 1959) and *La Guardia Comes to Power: 1933* (Philadelphia, 1965). Cf. Robert A. Varbero, "The Politics of Ethnicity: Philadelphia's Italians in the 1920's," in Francesco Cordasco, ed., *Studies in Italian American Social History: Essays in Honor of Leonard Covello* (Totowa, N.J., 1975), pp. 164–81.

8. Olha della Cava, "Italian American Studies: A Progress Report," in S. M. Tomasi, ed., *Perspectives in Italian Imimgration and Ethnicity: Proceeding of the Symposium Held at Casa Italiana* (New York, 1977), pp. 165–72.

9. For a brilliant analysis in detail of the process from small to larger identities, see Handlin, *American People*, pp. 47–85.

10. Rowland T. Berthoff, *British Immigrants in Industrial America, 1790–1950* (Cambridge, Mass., 1953), pp. 125–280.

11. For the details that lie behind the generalizations I have made about the Jewish experience in America, see Oscar Handlin, *Adventure in Freedom: Three Hundred Years of Jewish Life in America* (New York, 1954); Arthur Mann, ed., *Growth and Achievement: Temple Israel, 1854–1954* (Cambridge, Mass., 1954); Will Herberg, *Protestant-Catholic-Jew: An Essay in American Religious Sociology* (New York, 1955); Nathan Glazer, *American Judaism*, Chicago History of American Civilization (Chicago, 1957); Moses Rischin, *The Promised City: New York's Jews, 1870–1914* (Cambridge, Mass., 1962); Irving Howe, *World of Our Fathers* (New York, 1976).

12. E. Clifford Nelson, ed., *The Lutherans in North America* (Philadelphia, 1975), pp. 3–77.

13. For details of the leaching, transmutation, and containment process, see Abdel R. Wentz, *Pioneer in Christian Unity: Samuel Simon Shmucker* (Philadelphia, 1967); Vergilius Ferm, *The Crisis in American Lutheran Theology: A Study of the Issue between American*

*Lutheranism and Old Lutheranism* (New York, 1927); Carl Mauelshagen, *American Lutheranism Surrenders to Forces of Conservatism* (Athens, Ga., 1936); Walter O. Forster, *Zion on the Mississippi: The Settlement of the Saxon Lutherans in Missouri, 1839–1841* (St. Louis, 1953).

14. Abdel R. Wentz, *A Basic History of Lutheranism in America* (Philadelphia, rev. ed., 1955), pp. 376–82; E. Clifford Nelson, *Lutheranism in North America, 1914–1970* (Minneapolis, 1972), pp. 156–96.

15. For Missouri's leaching down through World War II, see Dean A. Kohlhoff, "Missouri Synod Lutherans and the Image of Germany, 1914–1945," Ph.D. diss., University of Chicago, 1973.

16. I am indebted to Martin E. Marty, a participant-observer of the recent controversy in the Missouri synod, for sharing his experiences and views with me.

## Chapter 8

1. John Higham, *Send These to Me: Jews and Other Immigrants in Urban America* (New York, 1975), p. 9.

2. Donald E. Pienkos, "Foreign Affairs Perceptions of Ethnics: The Polish-Americans of Milwaukee," *Ethnicity* 1 (October 1974):227–28.

3. Andrew M. Greeley to Arthur Mann, 5 June 1978.

4. Conor Cruise O'Brien, "On the Rights of Minorities," *Commentary*, June 1973, p. 48.

5. Andrew M. Greeley, "Intellectuals as an 'Ethnic Group,'" New *York Times*, 12 July 1970.

6. Cf. James Q. Wilson, "The Young People of North Long Beach," *Harper's*, December 1969, pp. 83–90.

7. Harold R. Isaacs, *The New World of Negro Americans* (New York, 1963), pp. 62–71.

8. W. E. Burghardt Du Bois, "Strivings of the Negro People," *Atlantic Monthly* 80 (August 1897):194; New York *Times*, 29 August 1963.

9. Alain Locke, ed., *The New Negro: An Interpretation* (New York, 1925), pp. ix–xi, 153.

10. Orlando Patterson, *Ethnic Chauvinism: The Reactionary Impulse* (New York, 1977), p. 185. The best starting point for understanding the impact of recent improvements on higher expectations is William Julius Wilson's scholarly study, *The Declining Significance of Race: Blacks and Changing American Institutions* (Chicago, 1978). For an earlier, abbreviated emphasis on the need to distinguish among blacks according to culture, status, and opportunities, see Arthur Mann, "A Historical Overview: The *Lumpenproletariat*, Education, and Compensatory Action," in Charles U. Daly, ed., *The Quality of Inequality: Urban and Suburban Public Schools* (Chicago, 1968), pp. 25–26.

# Index